ENDO

Many have not realized that there has been an unfortunate division of labor between the academy (the university or seminary) and the church; the former emphasizing the "head" or doctrine, and the latter the "heart" or devotion. Most books, unfortunately, are born and raised in one of these two worlds, with little experience of the other. John Crocker's *Divine Rendezvous* is a rare book that bears the marks and qualities of both worlds, written with a depth that is grounded in robust exegesis and theology, and yet accessible to the average Christian reader. Like a very full meal, Crocker prepares for his reader a robust encounter with the Lord's Prayer, supported and explained out of the fullness of the biblical story and its subject matter. At the same time, this meal is made edible and savory by a bountiful collection of stories of people, places, and ministry all told from the insightful perspective of a seasoned pastor, written in a manner that is engaging, delightful, and potent.

With reasonably-sized chapters that conclude with discussion or application questions, this book is user-friendly for both personal and group study. As both a pastor and professor, I see this book functioning well in both classrooms and Bible studies. Crocker compares the one who prays this "great prayer" to a little child who finds confidence and clarity while holding the hand of their father. In this book Crocker serves like such a mentor, whose guiding presence and discerning experience helps the reader partake in the Lord's Prayer, and therefore the Christian life.

Edward W. Klink III, Ph.D., Senior Pastor
Hope Evangelical Free Church, Roscoe, IL,
Author of several books, including *Zondervan Exegetical Commentary on the New Testament: John* (2016)

DIVINE RENDEZVOUS

Prayer for the Perilous Journey
to Our Heavenly Home

John Crocker

First edition June 2018
Second edition July 2019

Published by John D. Crocker

© John D. Crocker

Cover designed by Chuck Jarrell
Edited by Sally Rushmore

ISBN-13 978-0-692-13783-3
ISBN-10 0692137831

Printed by Kindle Direct Publishing, an Amazon.com
company

To our twin grandchildren

Lucy Elizabeth and Wrigley Michael Crocker.

May you walk the dangerous path of life

holding tightly to the hand of your heavenly Father.

Table of Contents

PREFACE

There are some minor changes and one important addition in this new edition of Divine Rendezvous. I have added an appendix to include Scripture references.

In my graduate studies in seminary my biblical research benefited greatly from a listing of Scripture references in the volume I was reading. It became my research practice to consult the biblical reference section at the end of the book, if there was one. In this way I was able to identify the location in the book of every occurrence of the biblical text I was studying.

This proved to be immensely helpful to me. I hope you will likewise benefit from the listing of the biblical references at the end of Divine Rendezvous.

ACKNOWLEDGMENTS

This study of the Lord's Prayer has been in process for more than a decade. God's Spirit gave me many of the insights while I was kneeling to pray the Lord's Prayer.

The perceptions of a few biblical commentators on the Lord's Prayer were helpful for comparison with my study. Doubtlessly it would have been beneficial to read or to listen to sermons on the Lord's Prayer, but I was reluctant to subject to any potential interference what I had gained from God's Spirit. The lone exception was the series of sermons on the Lord's Prayer by the German Lutheran pastor Helmut Thielicke in Stuttgart during the worst of the Allied bombing raids in World War II. His series was compiled and published in 1953 as *Das Gebet das die Welt umspannt.* It was translated and published in English in Great Britain as *The Prayer that Spans the World* (James Clarke & Co. Ltd., Cambridge. 1965).

The general theme of my work bears a slight resemblance to John Bunyan's blessed allegory of the pilgrim's journey to the celestial city. For almost four hundred years *The Pilgrim's Progress* has held a position of unparalleled significance in English literature and in Christian devotional study. Aside from the general theme, there is no allusion to Bunyan's *The Pilgrim's Progress* in *Divine Rendezvous: Prayer for the Perilous Journey to Our Heavenly Home.*

Kudos to Liz, my dear wife of forty-three years. We have often discussed various parts of the manuscript. She has provided many insightful suggestions, which I have included in the document. Her encouragement to continue and to complete this work has been invaluable.

During meetings for prayer in the 1980s and 1990s, my dear friend Frank Currie called prayer "a holy tryst" with our Father. His expression profoundly affected my concept of prayer. On a number of occasions Pastor Tom Macy, unbeknownst to him, stimulated my thinking on various aspects of this great theme.

I am especially grateful to my dear friend Dr. Edward (Mickey) Klink III, pastor and New Testament scholar, for his review of my work and for urging me to pursue publication. I am convinced that Sally Rushmore's thorough editing has made this a better book. Chuck Jarrell's cover design and other illustrative contributions have made the book appealing to the eye.

Thanks also to my loving family and many dear friends for their encouragement to complete this work. They include John and Ellen Borseth, Kim Cone, Al and Dee Dee Cooper, Denise Dash, Jim and Merryl DeWeerd, Bob and Gwen Eriks, Don Fields, Ruth Ann Gigax, Larry and Susan Graf, Sue Jensen, Charlie and Loraine Kelley, Jami Koester, Linda Lambert, Dean Leonard, Tom and Linda Macy, Matthew C. Mitchell, Scott Nyquist, Bill Patterson, Orv and Mary Qualsett, Les and Dee Reid, Roy and Marg Rowe, Zoltan and Nancy Rozsa, Fred Schmitt, Jon Sweet, Betty Tansey, Sheila Tiemens, Rodrigo Merino, Robert Wall, Tim Wall, and Howard Westlund.

THE LORD'S PRAYER

Our Father in heaven,
hallowed be your name,
your kingdom come,
your will be done
on earth as it is in heaven.
Give us today our daily bread.
And forgive us our debts,
as we also have forgiven our debtors.
And lead us not into temptation,
but deliver us from the evil one.
(Matthew 6:9–13)

Father,
hallowed be your name,
your kingdom come.
Give us each day our daily bread.
Forgive us our sins,
for we also forgive everyone who sins against us.
And lead us not into temptation.
(Luke 11:2–4)

1. THE PRIORITY OF PRAYER

There is nothing that tells the truth about us
as Christian people so much as our prayer life.
Everything we do in the Christian life is easier than prayer.

D. Martyn Lloyd-Jones[1]

You can do more than pray
After you have prayed;
But you cannot do more than pray
Until you have prayed.
Pray often, for prayer is
a shield to the soul,
a sacrifice to God, and
a scourge to Satan.

John Bunyan[2]

The Nature of Prayer

What is prayer? According to John Stott, "A Christian's priorities are always indicated in his prayers."[3] Prayer is essentially reaching out in spirit and talking to our Father in heaven.

Talking to God ranks higher than talking about God. We do well to speak of God's goodness, his grace, his holiness, his majesty, and more. Through Moses God told his people Israel to talk about him and about his mighty deeds on their behalf (Deuteronomy 6:20–25). Our heavenly Father wants us to review his mighty and merciful deeds. But our words to others *about* God pale alongside our words *to* God. In the prophet Jeremiah's complaint to the Lord about the faithless he said, "You are always on their lips but far from their hearts" (Jeremiah 12:2).

Talking about others is a common practice. People are social beings; we talk to people and we talk about people.

We often say things about them that we would not say to them. When talking directly to people we may be hesitant to say what is on our minds. Our passions have to be provoked before we blurt out any critical opinions face-to-face. Conversely, we utter our most intimate words when we gaze intently into a lover's eyes.

When we address someone face-to-face, we make a personal connection. Prayer says something to God's face. God himself instructed his people to "seek his face" (2 Chronicles 7:14). Sincere prayer is spiritual eye contact with our heavenly Father as we address him directly. Through prayer we make an intimate connection with our Father in heaven. If we bear this in mind, our words are more likely to be reverent rather than disrespectful grumblings.

We may be adept at speaking about God, yet fall short in speaking to God. Nothing in the life of a child of the Father in heaven supersedes speaking directly to God in prayer.

It has been my daily practice to pray the Lord's Prayer on my knees in a semi-prostrate posture. I frequently wept in humility because the prayer granted me entrance to the throne room of the Lord God Almighty, our Father in heaven. My insights into the manifold implications of this great prayer from the Lord Jesus Christ overwhelmed me. I kept a notebook nearby to record the lessons the Holy Spirit taught me.

Each year I read through the entire Bible. I included in my notebook various Scripture references that elaborated on the components of the Lord's Prayer. I also engaged in exegetical study of the prayer's two texts in Matthew's and Luke's gospels.

During this process I became convinced that these observations were not for me alone. I began to organize all my notes into a manuscript. At the end of each chapter of this book I include suggested discussion questions. I hope these will prove useful for those who use this book in small group Bible studies or in their daily devotions.

What is Unique About This Book

Jesus gave this prayer to his disciples. His words "this day" and "daily" reveal that he intended this for their daily use. He did not tell them to pray, "Give us this week our weekly bread."

The essence of my thesis in this book is as follows:

- Christ's followers are pilgrims on this earth;
- God their Father is in heaven;
- Jesus Christ has provided them an eternal dwelling with the Father (John 14:2);   *view from train*
- For God's children earthly life is a transit through a corrupt, dangerous world (1 John 5:19)
- Christ gave this prayer as the principal part of a Christian's daily rendezvous with God on the journey to his or her heavenly home.

Christ did not intend this prayer to be a model prayer for our occasional use. He gave it to have an indispensable role for our daily use. There are many ways to express sincere prayer to our God, but the prayer Christ gave stands apart as unique.

How This Book can Make a Powerful Impact on Your Life

what would I talk with R daily?

Praying to God Almighty is an incomparable privilege. God the Son, Jesus Christ, instructed God's children to pray this prayer specifically. We therefore have ample reason to conclude that God, our heavenly Father, will give heed to all who pray it sincerely.

When you pray this prayer you have an audience with God concerning matters of the highest import in the universe. You address God's ineffable majesty and glory.

15

Your soul longs for God's reign and his purposes to have full expression in this fallen world.

It is impossible for anyone who prays this prayer slowly and contemplatively to be unaffected by the sheer force of it. The prayer Jesus taught his disciples is the best-known and most beloved prayer in Christendom. For centuries millions have recited the "Our Father," or the Latin "Paternoster," as a religious ritual. Everyone with a Christian affiliation is familiar with this prayer. When a new pope is introduced to the waiting throng in St. Peter's Square in the Vatican, the Lord's Prayer is one of the first parts of the ritual. From the balcony the new Pope recites the Lord's Prayer with the faithful gathered before him. The "Our Father" is also one of the prayers specified in the rosary of the Catholic Church.

The familiarity of the Lord's Prayer may, unfortunately, degrade it to an empty ritual. Many people who never crack open a Bible are to some degree acquainted with this prayer. It may comprise the sum of their knowledge of the Christian religion. Some merely know that an important prayer called the Lord's Prayer exists.

Harry and Jack were two of the four brothers behind the founding of Warner Brothers Studio. According to legend, Harry once bet that his brother Jack could not recite the words of the Lord's Prayer. Jack accepted the wager and began, "Now I lay me down to sleep . . ." Harry glowered and shoved the money across the table. "That's enough," he said, "I didn't think you knew it."

From my earliest years, the Lord's Prayer was like a satellite orbiting my spiritual consciousness. It was a daily ritual that had little effect on me. We prayed the Lord's Prayer before classes began each day in primary school in South Africa. A ritual can become so dry that, in the words of one of my mentors, Dr. Lloyd M. Perry, it will "dehydrate the dew of heaven from your soul."

We face a challenge in our efforts to make the Lord's Prayer come alive. Familiarity makes our focus susceptible

16

to myriad distractions. Often while reciting this sublime prayer our thoughts may stray shamelessly to mundane matters. As a little English schoolboy I had to memorize A. A. Milne's *Christopher Robin* in my elocution lessons. The poem offers an example of intrusive diversions into our prayers:

> Little Boy kneels at the foot of the bed,
> Droops on the little hands little gold head.
> Hush! Hush! Whisper who dares!
> Christopher Robin is saying his prayers:
> "God bless Mummy. I know that's right.
> Wasn't it fun in the bath tonight?
> The cold's so cold, and the hot's so hot.
> Oh! God bless Daddy – I quite forgot.
> If I open my fingers a little bit more,
> I can see nanny's dressing-gown on the door.
> It's a beautiful blue, but it hasn't a hood.
> Oh! God bless Nanny and make her good.
> Mine has a hood, and I lie in bed
> And pull the hood right over my head,
> And I shut my eyes, and I curl up small
> And nobody knows that I'm there at all.
> Oh! Thank you, God, for a lovely day.
> And what was the other I had to say?
> I said "Bless Daddy," so what can it be?
> Oh! Now I remember it. God bless Me."
> Little Boy kneels at the foot of the bed.
> Droops on the little hands little gold head.
> Hush! Hush! Whisper who dares!
> Christopher Robin is saying his prayers.[4]

When praying the Lord's Prayer we must be alert to trespassing thoughts. Like Christopher Robin, we too must back up to re-engage with the prayer where our minds drift away from it. Is there any surefire way to keep the recitation of this prayer from becoming mindless prattle? How do we safeguard the Lord's Prayer as an intimate daily rendezvous with our heavenly Father? I trust that this study will prove helpful.

Pilgrims Journeying Through Dangerous Territory

Among my fondest memories are special Saturdays with my father. He took me along on the train to Johannesburg, about 25 miles from our home. I stayed close as he conducted whatever business he went to do. The highlight of the day was lunch on the balcony at Woolworth's. Johannesburg was a bustling place compared to our hometown. Being just a little tike, I clung to my dad's hand as we made our way down Eloff Street or Rissik Avenue. I was afraid that if I let go and became separated from my father in the bustle of pedestrians, I would suffer unimaginable terrors. But with my hand in his to guide and protect, I knew I was safe. Praying the Lord's Prayer should be as sincere as a little boy reaching out to hold his father's hand for protection and guidance on a dangerous path.

This image underscores these essential truths:

- We are strangers here (1 Peter 1:17).
- We do not belong to this world. We are members of God's household (Ephesians 2:19).
- Our citizenship is in heaven (Philippians 3:20).

Jesus Christ gave this prayer to his followers for their safe spiritual passage through a dark world under the control of the evil one.

The Lord's Prayer is supposed to be a daily—sometimes desperate—reaching out of children to their heavenly Father. This helps us maintain a godly equilibrium. The Prayer is not a cheap trinket that Jesus tossed to God's children, but a gem more precious than the religious baubles that can clutter our sparkling intimacy with our heavenly Father. There is a huge void in our souls that only the Lord's

Prayer can fill. So the Lord's Prayer deserves a prominent place in the life of every child of our heavenly Father.

Jesus Christ gave this prayer to teach his followers how to pray. The Lord's Prayer includes themes that God's children must address every day. The prayer itself holds the indisputable evidence that it is a daily prayer ("give us this day our daily bread"). Many years ago I began the practice of putting the Lord's Prayer first in my daily devotional exercise, before my meditation on God's holy word.

The Lord's Prayer can regulate life for God's children on their earthly pilgrimage. Our reflection on the six themes of the Lord's Prayer serves as a spiritual gyroscope to keep us upright as we face the fury of our spiritual enemy's onslaughts.

Jesus' followers are a counterculture devoted to their heavenly Father during their sojourn in this corrupt world. The Lord's prayer has the power to fashion within us a worldview that clashes with the ethos of a secular culture.

Elements of the Lord's Prayer

In the Lord's Prayer we ask our Father in heaven to do whatever it takes for the whole earth to acknowledge and celebrate his perfection, his might, and his glory. Accordingly, the elements of the Lord's Prayer are:

- A plea that God's holiness be extolled among all people;
- A petition that God's kingdom, or his righteous rule, may come;
- A longing that his will be done on this fallen planet as it is done in heaven;
- A request that God's children will depend utterly upon our heavenly Father;
- An earnest supplication that God will forgive our sins as we likewise are diligent to forgive others; and

19

- An entreaty that our Father will protect his children from the evil one during our earthly sojourn.

The Lord's Prayer is like the clothing the children of the heavenly Father wear while in transit through this hostile world.

Godly parents are delighted when their children lovingly honor them and ask for their advice. They are heartbroken if their children become snared by the devious solicitations of the evil one. We may infer from the Lord's Prayer that God the Father is pleased when his children turn to him instead of the allurement of mundane distractions.

Our Father in heaven is merciful and mighty. Nevertheless, we complain about him. We fault him for not doing for us what we expect our Father should do for his children. We accuse our Father of inconsistency and insensitivity. He permits hardships that upset the structures we put in place to make life manageable and comfortable. Sometimes we express our complaint to others; sometimes we hold it in and let it fester in our souls.

The Lord's Prayer in Religious Tradition

Jesus instructed his disciples to utter this prayer. They were to consider themselves children of the heavenly Father. The Lord's Prayer has thus become a vital part of the liturgies in Catholic, Orthodox, and many Protestant churches. Liturgies include key doctrinal formularies of the church. Each Sunday congregants recite the familiar lines of the Lord's Prayer together. Jesus Christ gave the Lord's Prayer to be enshrined at the epicenter of the faith of God's children. I have had the delight of praying with worshipers who recited the Lord's Prayer with a warm-hearted devotion to their Father in heaven.

During every era of Christendom people have held firmly to their religious traditions. Prayers recited in religious liturgies are ostensibly spoken to God; but for some congregants they become only formularies about God. Like the Pharisees and teachers of the Law with whom Jesus was often at odds, some staunch religionists give no evidence of a personal connection to God. In a *Time* magazine essay Lance Morrow asked the poignant question, "Do prayers performed by imposters have any spiritual voltage?"[5] I have heard rapid-fire recitations of the Lord's Prayer that seemed at best half-hearted or absent-minded. In his lead-in to this prayer, Jesus warned his followers: "And when you pray, do not keep on babbling like pagans, for they think they will be heard because of their many words" (Matthew 6:7; cf. Hebrews 9:14 ["cf" means "see also"]).

Likewise, John Bunyan urged, "When thou prayest, rather let thy heart be without words, than thy words without heart"[6] The widespread familiarity of the Lord's Prayer can reduce it to empty phrases on the lips of people whose minds and hearts are elsewhere. Such people have no sense of being in the presence of the heavenly Father. Like an item of furniture that has for years been in the corner of a room, the Lord's Prayer draws their attention only if it is removed. George MacDonald wrote, "nothing is so deadening to the divine as a habitual dealing with the outsides of holy things."[7] It is no small challenge to convince all God's children that the Lord's Prayer should occupy a prominent place in the daily exercise of their faith.

A Prayer of Desperation

The Lord's Prayer is the default prayer for many who have a marginal connection to the Christian faith—the prayer they keep within reach for desperate occasions. They do not know how to pray sincerely, but they file the Lord's Prayer away in a handy corner of their brain where they can retrieve it if a crisis so warrants.

Late one night during adolescence I was driving with two friends on Highway 10 in Ontario, Canada. The road seemed deserted when we came upon the detritus of a car

21

wreck scattered across the highway. It seemed strange that no vehicle was on the scene, so we backed up and found a wrecked car in a gulley beside the road. It reeked of alcohol. We found the other car in a gulley on the opposite side. One of my friends left in search of a farmhouse to call the sheriff (cell phones weren't in anyone's imagination in those days). In one of the cars we found the lone occupant hanging on to life. Oblivious to our presence and writhing in pain, in a faint voice the driver kept repeating the Lord's Prayer. I do not know if the man had only a faint familiarity with the Christian religion, or if he was a delinquent child of God our Father. The tragic incident underscored the far-flung attachment to the Lord's Prayer.

Posture for Prayer

From my viewpoint there is a widespread tendency toward a casual mishandling of the Lord's Prayer. This moved me to adopt a posture that demonstrated my obeisance to my Father in heaven. I knelt on the floor with my elbows and head to the ground. Kneeling helps me to condition my attitude for focused prayer and worship of our Father in heaven.

Does Scripture prescribe an approved posture for prayer? In Scripture, bowing or lying prostrate is sometimes associated with the act of praying. We read the following report of the public reading of the Law of God to the returned Jewish exiles:

> Ezra opened the book. All the people could see him because he was standing above them; and as he opened it, the people all stood up. Ezra praised the Lord, the great God; and all the people lifted their hands and responded, "Amen! Amen!" Then they bowed down and worshiped the Lord with their faces to the ground (Nehemiah 8:5, 6. cf. 2 Chronicles 6:13; 7:3).

Similarly, the Psalmist invited the people to bow: "Come, let us bow down in worship, let us kneel before the Lord our Maker; for he is our God and we are the people of his pasture, the flock under his care" (Psalm 95:6–7). The women at Jesus' empty tomb reacted in a similar manner to the sudden appearance of two men in clothes that gleamed like lightning: "In their fright the women bowed down with their faces to the ground . . ." (Luke 24:5). Their reaction was a spontaneous posture of reverence. The presence of something beyond their comprehension overwhelmed them. If they bowed to the presence of angels, should such humble posture not be immeasurably more fitting in an audience with our heavenly Father?

But the effectiveness of prayer should not be tied to a particular physical position. Your posture might be restricted by your circumstances. My wife and I share lengthy and blessed times in prayer while driving in our car. Both necessity and the law demand a secure seated posture. Some folks take "prayer walks." Physical impairment may also limit some to praying while lying in a bed or seated in a wheelchair.

When I adopted this way of praying the Lord's Prayer, it magnified the prayer's effect on me. I compare its impact to an experience many years ago as a seminary student when I was the speaker at a youth camp in Banff National Park in the Canadian Rocky Mountains. When my host and I arrived at the camp, it was pitch-dark. Since it was very late, I retired to my cabin. The next morning when I stepped from the cabin, before me, soaring to its peak seemingly from just a few feet in front of my doorstep, stood Mt. Rundle in all its majesty. My spine tingled and my knees felt weak. Few times have I experienced so powerful a sensation. A huge mountain had been fired at me point-blank. Its glory overwhelmed me.

Kneeling each day to pray the Lord's Prayer, the wonder of God's majesty has not faded. The immensity of the prayer still overwhelms me. From this perspective I invite you to catch the wonder of this awesome gift Christ gave to his followers. I urge you to make it a vital part of your daily rendezvous with God.

Questions for Discussion and Personal Application

1. What is your earliest recollection of the Lord's Prayer?
2. Do you struggle with distracting thoughts when you pray? How do you deal with them?
3. How does your relationship with God give you a sense of security?
4. John Stott said, "A Christian's priorities are always indicated in his prayers."[8] What are the priorities of most of God's children? What should they be?
5. Does the concept of prayer as speaking face-to-face with God help your understanding of prayer? In what way?
6. Which do you do more: speak to God, or talk about God?
7. What are some of the benefits and some of the dangers in religious rituals?
8. To what extent do you include the Lord's Prayer in the practice of your faith? Are you satisfied with your practice?
9. To what extent is your physical posture a consideration when you pray?
10. Tell of a prayer experience when you felt overwhelmed by having an audience with God.

25

2. THE CHALLENGE OF THE LORD'S PRAYER

I think you will agree with St. Augustine and Martin Luther and many other saints who have said that there is nothing more wonderful in the entire Bible than the Lord's Prayer.

D. Martyn Lloyd-Jones[9]

The Lord's Prayer is probably the most familiar prayer among all the world religions. The Lord Jesus Christ gave it to his followers to teach them how to pray. For this reason it is called the Lord's Prayer. In Matthew's Gospel Jesus contrasts this prayer with insincere and worthless prayer. He taught the disciples to address the Lord God as "Our Father in heaven." He told them to pray for their heavenly Father's glorious majesty to be celebrated on earth.

As children of our heavenly Father, we are aliens on a pilgrimage through an inhospitable world to our heavenly home. As sojourners in enemy territory, this prayer fixes our attention on our heavenly Father.

Effective Prayer

The Lord's Prayer addresses the Lord God Almighty, not "the Man Upstairs." But the prayer is not our channeling of positive energy toward an impersonal force in the great beyond. For example, when television star Robert Urich battled cancer many people sent cards telling him they were praying for him. He expressed his gratitude, saying he was impressed by "all that positive energy."[10] People who do not know God as their heavenly Father may view prayer as a mystical projection of positive energy. But Jesus taught his disciples to pray with words as direct and personal as when addressing someone face-to-face.

Does God in heaven hear his children on earth when they pray? The author Arthur Koestler, who committed suicide along with his wife in 1983, had mused, "God seems to have left the receiver off the hook and time is running out."[11] Each day countless people express the same sentiment. Can we only sigh with uncertainty, "I shot a prayer into the air; it reached to heaven, or who knows where"?[12] We read in Scripture about some whose prayers were futile, like King Saul (1 Samuel 28:5) or the Pharisee in the temple (Luke 18:10–14). But David said, "O you who hear prayer, to you all men will come" (Psalm 65:2). On the occasion of King Hezekiah's restoration of the Passover observance in Israel, "The priests and the Levites stood to bless the people, and God heard them, for their prayer reached heaven, his holy dwelling place" (2 Chronicles 30:27). The blessing and the prayer on that sacred occasion followed the obedience of the priests and Levites.

When we obey God's will, our prayers reach heaven, God's holy dwelling place. God our Father pays attention to our prayers. We ought, therefore, to give careful attention to praying because prayer is not a last extremity but a first necessity.

The Occasion of the Lord's Prayer

Luke's account of the context of the Lord's Prayer includes elements absent from Matthew's record. Luke adds valuable insights into the reason Jesus gave this prayer to his followers. On one occasion when Jesus had finished praying, a disciple requested, "Lord, teach us to pray, just as John taught his disciples" (Luke 11:1). Jesus responded by teaching them this prayer.

Some of Jesus' disciples had been disciples of John the Baptist. John's mentoring evidently included lessons on prayer. Would Jesus do the same for his followers? How would Jesus teach his disciples to pray? They assumed Jesus would not do exactly what John had done. Jesus did not respond, "Just go ahead and pray the same prayer John taught you. It is a good prayer." Jesus gave them a unique prayer intended exclusively for the children of God. The One who taught the Lord's Prayer to his followers shared a oneness with their Father in heaven (John 17:22).

If you were invited to an audience with a king, who could best prepare you to know the proper etiquette for approaching a king? It would be the one who knows that king best, someone like the king's son. The one who knows God the Father best is God the Son. There is no finer prayer to offer to our heavenly Father than the prayer taught by God the Son, the Lord Jesus Christ.

In Matthew's account of the Lord's Prayer, Jesus had just warned his followers about prayer that is like pagan babbling (Matthew 6:7). Prayer is not religious prattling.

More Than a Model Prayer

Is the Lord's Prayer a model to guide us when we pray? It is, but the Lord's Prayer is more than an example for us. Most of our prayers do not include the words of the Lord's Prayer. The prayers we offer to our heavenly Father usually comprise more than the fifty-two words of the Lord's Prayer.

I infer from Jesus' teaching that not a day should go by without God's children offering the essential elements of this prayer to our Father. The daily prayers of a child of God are incomplete if the Lord's Prayer is absent. The particulars that comprise the Lord's Prayer are components of our daily supplication to our heavenly Father.

John Stott called this prayer a model given by Jesus Christ of what genuine prayer is like. He added, "we can both use the prayer as it stands and also model our own praying upon it."[13] D. Martyn Lloyd-Jones commented: "There is a sense in which you can never add to the Lord's Prayer; nothing is left out. That does not mean, of course, that when we pray we are simply to repeat the Lord's Prayer and stop at that."[14] He continued: "To say that this prayer is all-inclusive, and is a perfect summary, simply means, therefore, that it really does contain all the principles. We might say that what we have in the Lord's Prayer is a kind of skeleton."[15] We give careful attention to this prayer because it came directly from the lips of our Lord.

Did Jesus expect his followers to devote themselves to this prayer, to the exclusion of other prayers? Certainly not! Scripture is replete with instructions on prayer for the faithful, along with examples of prayer that bear little resemblance to The Lord's Prayer. A few examples are Solomon's prayer at the dedication of the temple (1 Kings 8:22–53), Christ's prayer for his disciples in John 17, and the apostle Paul's description of how he prayed for the church at Ephesus (Ephesians 1:15ff, 3:14ff ["ff" means "and following verses"]). Paul also wrote this to the Ephesian Church: "And pray in the Spirit on all occasions with all kinds of prayers and requests" (Ephesians 6:18). The Lord's Prayer in no way restricts our prayer practices, but it includes specific components that Jesus instructed his followers to include in their daily prayer routine. It is appropriate to extrapolate from the six themes of the Lord's Prayer and to include other related petitions, along with thanksgiving.

Qualified to Pray the Lord's Prayer

Who has the right to pray this daily prayer—all people everywhere, or only a certain category of people? The Lord's Prayer is for all who may rightfully address God as their Father in heaven. Many people call God their heavenly Father. Their behavior is exemplary as they may paint an attractive portrait of a child of God, but the external picture may not match the internal reality. Jesus denounced the Jewish religious leaders for pretending to be righteous. He said,

> "Woe to you, teachers of the law and Pharisees, you hypocrites! You are like whitewashed tombs, which look beautiful on the outside but on the inside are full of the dead men's bones and everything unclean. In the same way, on the outside you appear to people as righteous but on the inside you are full of hypocrisy and wickedness" (Matthew 23:27–28).

Appearances are often deceiving. I was aboard the Pendennis Castle ocean liner on a voyage from Cape Town, South Africa to Southampton, England. One day I noticed some birds flying alongside the ship's keel. I asked one of the crew what kind of bird they were, since we were hundreds of miles from shore. He told me they were not birds but fish—flying fish. They live in the water, but occasionally they use their fins as wings to propel themselves into the air for brief excursions.

Some people are a bit like those flying fish. They call themselves children of God, but that is not their true character. They may make a brief excursion each week into the fellowship of God's children, but the rest of the time they are immersed in the dark world that is under the control of the evil one.

The Lord's Prayer is not a magical mantra for desperate times. It is a daily prayer for the children of the heavenly Father. Jesus gave this prayer to his followers who have received him and believed in him. He said they have the right to be called children of God (John 1:12). Some who pray the Lord's Prayer exult in the fresh glow of being born anew into God's family by faith in Jesus Christ. God has rescued them from the dark domain of the evil one (Colossians 1:13). In their dire predicament they had all but given up hope. They used to live in fear of God's disapproval and judgment. Now they pray "Our Father" with a passion they never thought possible.

Some pray this prayer through pain. They are struggling to gain traction in their faith. The letter of James explains, "We all stumble in many ways" (James 3:2). Lee Eclov wrote, "Some offices, of course, are filthier than sewers. Some schools are darker than underground tunnels. Some families are toxic. A lot of Christians spend their week trying to keep the gunk off their hearts, trying to keep their hearts from smelling like a cesspool."[16] Some who cry from the heart "Our Father in heaven," are crippled by guilt and regret. They feel humiliated by the disdain of proud religionists. Church members who look down on these sincere strugglers have hearts darkened to the truths of God's mercy and forgiveness. Out of loneliness and rejection battered believers cry out to their Father in heaven whom they are just beginning to know as the God of all comfort.

Most churches are fraught with myriad challenges, some excruciating. In fact, churches should be messy. A healthy church has a steady influx of people rescued by God's grace from the septic tank of a decadent society. The residue of that muck still encrusts their souls.

But some churches are messy because of rottenness in members whose lives offer no evidence of godly graces. Leaders in some churches do not meet biblical qualifications for leadership (1 Timothy 3:1–13; Titus 1:6–9; 1 Peter 5:1–3). Having attained positions of power they wreak dreadful damage to the body of Christ. A godly pastor who attempts to lead such a church inevitably faces heartbreaking challenges. It is nearly impossible to be an effective leader of God's people if a pastor's biblically-based counsel is spurned. In more than forty years as a pastor I have encountered hellish wickedness in some church leaders. I have learned that the nicest people in the world and the nastiest people may both be found in churches. This adds credence to the remark, "Many people who love God cannot stand his ground crew."[17]

The Church and God's Kingdom

How does the Church relate to the Kingdom of God? If you are a citizen of the Kingdom of God, you are a member of a spiritual community. In the present age this spiritual community is a living spiritual organism called the Church—the "body of Christ." The church is one way in which God's kingdom is manifested in this world that is held in the grip of evil. The church in its local expressions is a real but imperfect representation of God's kingdom in this world.

A Costly Prayer

Praying is an exacting exercise. E. M. Bounds wrote, "Praying, true praying, costs an outlay of serious attention and of time, which flesh and blood do not relish."[18] The Lord's Prayer is not easy, but it has become an anchor for my soul. As a pastor I usually began the day in my office praying the Lord's Prayer in a bowed posture. On Sundays I knelt in prayer several hours before the start of the first worship service. Were it not for a box of tissues beside me, I'm sure my tears would have permanently stained the carpet.

The Lord's Prayer addresses the holiness of our Father in heaven. Pondering the absolutes of God's nature stretches our comprehension to the extreme. The plea for God's kingdom to come and his will to be done on the earth likewise taxes our understanding. We are born to this earth. Our experiences as we grow from infancy into adulthood are our "normal," even though we groan at the perversity of mankind. The petitions in the Lord's Prayer are in conflict with the ordinary, the familiar. To pray this prayer as Christ intends his followers to pray it demands a recalibration of our worldview and values.

Each part of the Lord's Prayer reflects wholehearted devotion to God. This prayer could have been a fitting addendum to God's commands to the homeless hordes of Israel as they entered the land he had promised them. Moses said, "Love the Lord your God with all your heart and with all your soul and with all your strength" (Deuteronomy 6:4). It corresponds with David's counsel to his son Solomon who would succeed him as king:

> "And you, my son Solomon, acknowledge the God of your father, and serve him with wholehearted devotion and with a willing mind, for the Lord searches every heart and understands every motive behind the thought" (1 Chronicles 28:9).

Uttering this prayer with all the seriousness Christ intends is a colossal undertaking. Jesus' demands upon his followers are costly. For example, the implications of "your will be done" are no less demanding than Jesus' mandate to go into the world and make disciples of all nations. That is one aspect of God's revealed will to his children. Only after Pentecost, with the impetus of the indwelling Holy Spirit, could Jesus Christ's followers undertake his commission with the determination he intended. Jesus expected his followers to leave houses or brothers or sisters or father or mother or children or fields for his sake, promising that they would receive a hundred times as much and inherit eternal life (Matthew 19:29). He did not hide from them the great cost involved in following him (Mark 8:34–38). The Lord's Prayer exposes the heavenly Father's children to unfamiliar, challenging realities. The Lord's Prayer recalibrates our priorities. The Lord's Prayer can transform us.

A Bold Petition for Today

A pivotal question is whether the Lord's Prayer is for us today. Did Jesus perhaps intend it solely for his disciples at that stage of their training?

Do not overlook the fact that Scripture claims to be useful for succeeding generations. The apostle Paul wrote, "For everything that was written in the past was written to teach us, so that through endurance and the encouragement of the Scriptures we might have hope" (Romans 15:4). This justifies the conviction that the Lord's Prayer is also for succeeding generations of his followers. That includes us today. The apostle Paul was crystal clear in his instructions to Timothy:

> All Scripture is God-breathed and is useful for teaching, rebuking, correcting and training in righteousness, so that the man of God may be thoroughly equipped for every good work (2 Timothy 3:16–17, cf. 1 Corinthians 10:6, 11; Deuteronomy 29:29).

The petitions "give," "forgive," and "lead us not . . . but deliver us" are bold. This may seem impolite and presumptuous to some people. In polite social relationships a person making a large request usually presents a demeanor of meekness. But Jesus' instructions were forthright: "Give . . . Forgive . . . Lead us not . . . deliver us . . . ." He directed his followers to ask with confidence, expecting the requests to be granted.

When we were children and we asked our parents for something large and desirable, the answer was often "no," or "I'll think about it." So we adopted a pattern of broaching such a matter delicately, beating around the bush, and waiting for the right time to bring it up. If we were to say to our earthly parent "give," we could expect a sharp rebuke, "You cheeky little blighter! Don't you be telling me what I must give you!" We are unaccustomed to what we find in the Lord's Prayer. It is crucial to understand that petitions to our Father in heaven by his children here on earth differ vastly from children's petitions to their earthly parents.

Focus on Our Father in Heaven

Our modern proclivity to outline and analyze literature was not a practice of the ancients. If the biblical writers could see our commentaries and outlines of the texts they wrote, they would undoubtedly be intrigued. They might be amazed and amused by some things that are attributed to them. How fascinating to see their narratives, prophecies, gospels, and letters divided into thematic sections! They might exclaim, "Amazing! I had no idea that I did that." Nevertheless, some parts of the inspired Scripture fall into natural outlines, as does this prayer given by our Lord Jesus Christ.

There are six petitions in the prayer. The first three petitions focus on our Father in heaven. The first part of the prayer addresses our Father's glory, his rule, and his will. This prayer does not begin and end with us. The last three requests relate to the Father's children on earth. We may assume that Christ deliberately established the sequence of the petitions in the prayer. In his *Summa Theologica* Thomas Aquinas wrote concerning this prayer: "In it we ask, not only for all the things we can rightly desire, but also in the sequence that they should be desired."[19]

What prompts people to pray to the Father in heaven? Some honest soul might answer, "my fears, my needs, my desires." But the prayer our Lord gave his followers is not even remotely for such purposes. He is the focus of the prayer. When the sequence of themes moves from the Father to us—from "your" to "our"—even our requests for our daily needs express our perpetual dependency on our Father. We do not, however, regard our Father in heaven as a repository of goods available for our gratification.

Aspects and Attributes of the Divine

Theologian Charles Hodge wrote:

> Prayer is the converse of the soul with God. Therein we manifest or express to Him our reverence, and love for His divine perfection, our gratitude for all His mercies, our penitence for our sins, our hope in His forgiving love, our submission to His authority, our confidence in His care, our desires for His favor, and for the providential and spiritual blessings needed for ourselves and others.[20]

The Lord's Prayer addresses our Father in heaven who is the Almighty God. It engages the following aspects of his deity:

1. **He is our father.** We call on God our heavenly Father. Our principal and ultimate relationship of dependence is with our eternal heavenly Father.
2. **He is holy.** He is the triune God—Father, Son, and Holy Spirit. He is the unique and consummate definition of deity. He is the self-existent one, the eternal *I am*. In all aspects of his being and all his attributes he is incomparable. He is wholly other, in contrast with the earthly idols and with the spiritual forces of evil who must bow before him, as they did repeatedly before God the Son during his earthly ministry.
3. **He is the king.** We long for his reign and rule to be fully realized on the earth as in heaven.
4. **He is the universal and sovereign ruler** whose will is done in heaven.
5. **He is our provider.** We look to him for our daily needs—physical, emotional, and spiritual. Without his provision we would be destitute.
6. **He is our judge.** He is the one to whom we appeal for forgiveness of sins.
7. **He is our guide** who keeps us from severe trials that would test us beyond our abilities.
8. **He is our protector.** He delivers us from the destructive power of the evil one who is the "god of this world."

The Context of the Lord's Prayer

The Lord's Prayer is the anchor of Jesus Christ's instruction about prayer to his followers. Being Christ's disciple encompasses all aspects of life. Those who belong to Christ do not fashion their conduct according to the standards of the secular culture. Jesus said, "Be careful not to do your 'acts of righteousness' before men to be seen by them. If you do, you will have no reward from your Father in heaven" (Matthew 6:1). He warned them not to be deceived by the hypocrites who pray in order to be seen and heard by others. Nor should they be like the pagans who babble words that God does not hear (Matthew 6:5–8). Instead, Jesus gave his followers a prayer with precise petitions rather than verbose ramblings.

Our authentic self is who we are in attitude and conduct when no one except our Father in heaven can see us. Being sinful by nature, we follow the pattern of Adam and Eve in the garden. We try to hide our real selves. We wear facades to conceal the truth. Deception has been woven into the fabric of fallen human nature. But there is no place for deception in this prayer our Lord taught his disciples to pray. Disingenuousness as we utter the Lord's Prayer renders it just a waste of time and energy.

This prayer has value only if it comes from an honest soul, offered with faith that the Father hears it. The writer of the letter to the Hebrews said, "And without faith it is impossible to please God, because anyone who comes to him must believe that he exists and that he rewards those who earnestly seek him" (Hebrews 11:6). Jesus Christ gave his followers this prayer for their earnest approach to their heavenly Father.

The Supernatural Realm

To pray effectively, we must believe in the existence of the supernatural realm. We live within the orbit of the supernatural. If we are children of God, he has rescued us from the dominion of the evil one and has brought us into the kingdom of his Son (Colossians 1:13). The heavenly Father's children belong to God's kingdom. The apostle Paul wrote to God's children in Thessalonica, "You are all sons of the light and sons of the day. We do not belong to the night or to the darkness" (1 Thessalonians 5:5). Jesus said his kingdom is not of this world (John 18:36). When we placed our faith in Jesus Christ as our Savior we experienced the dynamics of the supernatural.

God's children live in one realm while belonging to another. While they are upon this earth God's children live where two kingdoms intersect—the kingdom of this world and the kingdom of God. Picture two circles, with one partially overlaying the other. The children of God live in that "overlay" where the two circles intersect. It may be likened to a rugby/football-shaped sphere, a prolate spheroid.

Figure 1: Prolate Spheroid

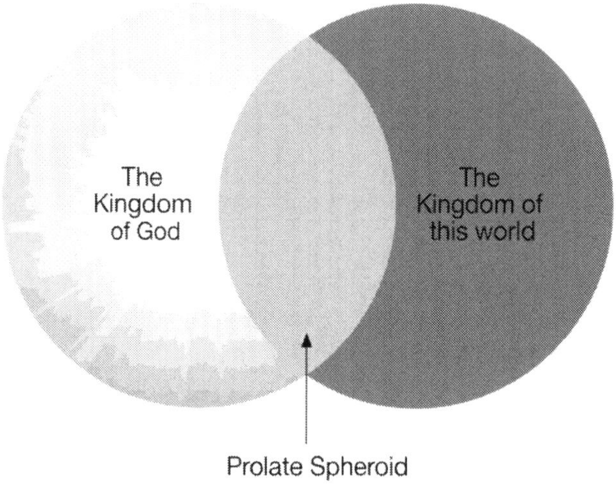

The
Kingdom
of God

The
Kingdom of
this world

Prolate Spheroid

We live in the kingdom of this world, which is a dark dominion. We are surrounded by evil and unspeakable decadence, but we are not held bondage in it. God has rescued us from the dominion of darkness. We belong to God's kingdom, which is characterized by light. We live where the light of God's kingdom has penetrated the darkness of this world.

This explains the apparent contradiction between biblical statements about the dominion of Satan and the kingdom of God in this world. The apostle John wrote to the churches, "We know that we are children of God and that the whole world is under the control of the evil one—or, of evil" (1 John 5:19). Jehoshaphat, king of Judah, prayed, "O Lord, God of our fathers, are you not the God who is in heaven? You rule over all the kingdoms of the nations. Power and might are in your hand, and no one can withstand you" (2 Chronicles 20:6).

The Lord God is the ultimate ruler over all. But Jesus instructed his disciples to pray for God's kingdom to come, presumably to this fallen world. We pray, "your kingdom come" because the evil one, the devil, usurped dominion over part of God's universal realm through the temptation and fall of mankind in the garden. With the coming of God the Son Jesus Christ into this world, the kingdom of God came to earth. The kingdom of God intersects the kingdom of this world, as the example of the prolate spheroid explains. When Christ returns as Lord, his kingdom will extend to the whole world and he will hand over the kingdom to God the Father.

Jesus said, "I am the light of the world. Whoever follows me will never walk in darkness, but will have the light of life" (John 8:12). The apostle Paul addressed this in his letter to the Philippian Christians:

> Do everything without complaining or arguing, so that you may become blameless and pure, children of God without fault in a crooked and depraved generation, in which you shine like stars in the

universe as you hold out the word of life (Philippians 2:14–16).

To the Ephesian Church he wrote, "For you were once darkness, but now you are light in the Lord. Live as children of light" (Ephesian 5:8).

Supernatural Beings

These are the beings whose habitat is the spiritual, or supernatural realm:

- God—the holy Trinity
- Angels—messengers of God; ministering spirits
- Satan—also known as the devil, the "serpent," tempter, deceiver, liar
- Fallen angels—Demons

This is the spiritual context in which we pray the Lord's Prayer. We are keenly aware of the existence of supernatural forces, both angelic and demonic. To what extent do God's children demonstrate an awareness of the supernatural realm when they pray together? It seems that relatively few of God's children know how to pray. In prayer meetings we endure periods of awkward silence until some dear soul relents and prays aloud. If we are conscious of the supernatural, we should be eager to pray without hesitation. In my experience, most prayer meetings address first and foremost issues of physical health or financial need. Spiritual matters are secondary—like a prayer for the salvation of a family member or friend. We acknowledge that God our heavenly Father cares about our illnesses and our physical welfare (Matthew 10:28–30; Luke 12:6–7). But our heavenly Father is surely not pleased when temporal matters perpetually eclipse issues of spiritual consequence.

Questions for Discussion and Personal Application

1. Have you ever identified with Arthur Koestler in his remark, "God seems to have left the receiver off the hook." What were you experiencing at the time?

2. Why were the prayers of King Saul and the Pharisee (1 Samuel 28:5; Luke 18:10–14) ineffective? Cite some additional reasons why God does not hear prayers.

3. Jesus taught his disciples to pray. How did you learn to pray?

4. Do you include the Lord's Prayer in your daily prayers? If you were to add the Lord's Prayer, how would you fit it in?

5. How can we distinguish people who only pretend to be children of the heavenly Father from those who are truly his children, albeit very imperfect? *32*

6. Why is praying the Lord's Prayer so costly?

7. How does your normal way of asking for something differ from your prayer requests?

8. What can we do to shift our focus from ourselves to God when we pray?

9. Review the aspects of our heavenly Father's deity that are brought out in the Lord's Prayer. What impact should they have on you when you pray this prayer?

10. How do you explain that our heavenly Father is Sovereign over all, but that this world is in bondage to evil?

11. If someone asks you to pray about something on his or her behalf, what kind of "something" is it most likely to be?

3. THE DIVINE RENDEZVOUS

Dear friends, I urge you, as aliens and strangers
in the world, to abstain from sinful desires,
which war against your soul. Live such good lives
among the pagans that, though they accuse you
of doing wrong, they may see your good deeds
and glorify God on the day he visits us.

(1 Peter 2:11–12)

In the opening clause of the Lord's Prayer we have an implied but nevertheless clear contrast between heaven and earth. Our Father is in heaven; we are on earth. The Lord's Prayer is intended for sojourners—for pilgrims away from home. Our Father's children are the church in this world. They are called members of God's household (Ephesians 2:19; 1 Timothy 3:15). Our Father's abode is not here on the earth he created. Jesus told his disciples that he was going to his Father's house to prepare a place for them (John 14:2–3).

Living in a Hostile World

Robert Orben quipped, "Life is the detour you follow while looking for the main road."[21] The children of the heavenly Father are taking a bumpy trek on a narrow, winding detour through an inhospitable wilderness riddled with obstacles. Sin's debut rendered this world a hazardous habitation for mankind.

How Did This Happen?

God created humankind and placed the first couple in a pristine, perfect setting known as the Garden of Eden (Genesis 2:8, 15). In that idyllic habitat Adam and Eve enjoyed intimate communion with God. But God's archenemy, a powerful fallen angel known as Satan or the devil, trespassed on God's earthly creation. By subterfuge in the form of a serpent he succeeded in deceiving the innocent couple. He declared that God's rule for their conduct in the garden was not in their best interest. Adam and Eve fell for his lie and chose to believe Satan and to disobey God the Creator.

By their fateful choice Adam and Eve validated Satan's right to residency on Planet Earth (for an elaboration of this, see Chap. 10, Forgive us our Sins as we . . Subtitle: *The Entrance of Sin*). Little did they know that their choice enabled Satan to seize control of the whole world, as the apostle John wrote, "We know that we are children of God, and that the whole world is under the control of the evil one" (1 John 5:19).

As the antithesis of our holy God, Satan corrupted the world, especially the beings created in God's image and likeness—people. That devastating corruption is known as sin. This is the state of the world in which God's children are pilgrims journeying through this life to their eternal home.

We are in great peril. Hence, the paramount importance of our daily rendezvous with God our Father.

Our Desperate Plight

In the Lord's Prayer Jesus addressed his disciples' need of protection. We should, therefore, disabuse ourselves of the notion that Christ's followers will be comfortable here. The world's depraved culture is not a friendly environment for the children of God. The idea that the Father's children will enjoy easy living is a fantasy. Bad things happen to us, because the effects of sin on the human race have impacted all of us. Some of God's children are stricken with illness. They suffer and die. Some become unemployed. In his kindness God may choose to intervene to mitigate the impact of evil in certain of his children's lives. Others continue to suffer. The apostle Paul assured the Father's children in Rome: "I consider that our present sufferings are not worth comparing with the glory that will be revealed in us" (Romans 8:18).

Every good thing God has for his children cannot be measured by anything in this mortal life. This is an important lesson, but some have not learned it. Many who claim to be the children of God are constantly whining about how hard life is and that everything goes wrong for them. They view minor setbacks as major trials. They have not grasped what it means to be a sojourner in hostile territory.

Jesus Christ gave the Lord's Prayer to the heavenly Father's children who cannot thrive in this fallen world. The prevalent state of this world is evil. Crime, violence, deception, hatred, and terrorism dominate the media. Many of God's children have grown accustomed to the grim signs of the secular culture rotting at its core. Sports, business, technology, politics, or entertainment have won their affections. But this fallen world is not a fit home to those God has rescued from the dark dominion of Satan (Colossians 1:13). I appreciate Randall Balmer's perspective on earthly life for God's children:

> I have come to see the Christian life no longer as a steep and steady ascent toward holiness but as a tortuous journey full of twists and turns and switchbacks and perhaps a rockslide or two along the way.[22]

A Realistic Outlook on Life

Life is more than the sum of our experiences between physical birth and death. Life does not make sense within the orbit of our earthly experiences. Solomon soliloquized,

> In this meaningless life of mine I have seen both of these: a righteous man perishing in his righteousness, and a wicked man living long in his wickedness (Ecclesiastes 7:15).

All of Solomon's attempts to find purpose in life yielded only empty disappointment. Nor does a righteous life yield lasting benefits in this world. The validation of righteousness lies beyond this mundane existence. Only in God's kingdom do we discover life's meaning. Therefore we pray, "Your kingdom come, your will be done." By making this petition to our heavenly Father, we ask for an otherworldly intervention into our languid sojourn on earth.

We should disabuse ourselves of the notion that our daily prayer to God profits him in some way. Our heavenly Father has no needs or desires that we might satisfy. In the account of mankind's creation, God gave his assessment: "It is not good for man to be alone" (Genesis 2:8). God did not say, "It is not good for God to be alone, let us make man in our image in order to fulfill us." God constituted human beings to find their fulfillment in him alone. The manner in which Jesus phrased this prayer for his followers leaves no doubt about this.

Our Lord God Almighty has absolute authority and power throughout his universe. But during this age he does not demonstrate control over all things earthly. The apostle John provides this poignant insight into the present state of God's children: "The one who is born of God keeps him safe and the evil one does not touch him. We know that we are children of God and that the whole world is under the control of the evil one" (1 John 5:18–19). Jesus came into this corrupt world as God the Son, Emmanuel, to deal with the curse of sin. In anticipation of the successful completion of his earthly mission, Jesus prayed to God the Father for his disciples:

> I have given them your word and the world has hated them, for they are not of the world any more than I am of the world. My prayer is not that you take them out of the world but that you protect them from the evil one (John 17:14–15).

Later, when the apostle Paul addressed Governor Festus and King Agrippa, he explained how Jesus Christ had apprehended him. Jesus said:

> "I am sending you to them [the Gentiles] to open their eyes and turn them from darkness to light, and from the power of Satan to God, so that they may receive forgiveness of sins and a place among those who are sanctified by faith in me" (Acts 26:17–18).

All who have been rescued from Satan's dark domain join with the children of God on the pilgrimage to the Father's home. It is the will of God Incarnate, Jesus Christ, and of God the Father that his children sojourn as aliens in this dark world. Jesus Christ did not ask to have his followers removed from it. But we pray for divine protection while we live as aliens here.

The apostle Peter referred to the heavenly Father's children as "God's elect, strangers in the world, scattered throughout Pontus, Galatia, Cappadocia, Asia and Bithynia, who have been chosen according to the foreknowledge of God the Father, through the sanctifying work of the Spirit, for obedience to Jesus Christ and sprinkling by his blood" (1 Peter 1:1–2). Further on in his letter Peter wrote,

Since you call on a Father who judges each man's work impartially, live your lives as strangers here in reverent fear. For you know that it was not with perishable things such as silver or gold that you were redeemed from the empty way of life handed down to you from your forefathers, but with the precious blood of Christ, a lamb without blemish or defect (1 Peter 1:17–19; cf. Philippians 3:18–21).

God's guidance through his Holy Word is a navigational system for his children passing through this perilous world. The Psalmist prayed, "I am a stranger on earth; do not hide your commands from me" (Psalm 119:19). David made his appeal to the Father: "Show me the way I should go, for to you I lift up my soul" (Psalm 143:8). Without our Father's hand on the helm of our lives we would suffer shipwreck.

In 1963 I was aboard the ocean liner Empress of England traveling from Liverpool, England to Canada. Just before dawn, as we approached Quebec City on the St. Lawrence Seaway, I went up on deck to see the lights. I saw a motor launch come from shore to deliver someone to our ship through a door down near the water line. Who was this mysterious figure sneaking aboard under cover of the pre-dawn darkness? I asked a member of the ship's crew nearby who that might be. "Young man," he said, "that is the pilot of the Port of Quebec City. He has to be on the bridge from this point to guide our ship to its berth at the pier." He explained that the pilot knew where any dangerous shoals or reefs were. He knew things the captain couldn't see.

It occurred to me later that God our Father is like a ship's pilot. He knows the dangers his children cannot see on their pilgrimage through this dangerous world. The refrain of the *I Don't Belong (Sojourner's Song)* by Buddy Greene and Gloria Gaither is a striking statement about the Father's children being strangers in this world:

> I don't belong
> And I'm going some day
> Home to my own native land
> I don't belong
> And it seems like I hear
> The sound of a "welcome home" band
> I don't belong
> I'm a foreigner here
> Singing a sojourner's song
> I've always known
> This place ain't home
> And I don't belong[23]

Why are God's children strangers in this world? The Scriptures explain the reason. The first human couple disobeyed God's declared will, and sinned. God's judgment came upon Adam and Eve and upon all creatures, as well as the ground that produced plants (Genesis 3:14–19). Sin entered God's pristine creation and caused everything in mankind's earthly environment to be cursed and to become corrupted.

God's children have been cleansed from their sins through faith in Jesus Christ who suffered the penalty of the curse on their behalf by his death on the cross. The apostle Paul told the Galatian churches,

> But the Scripture declares that the whole world is a prisoner of sin, so that what was promised, being given through faith in Jesus Christ, might be given to those who believe (Galatians 3:22).

God's children are wayfarers who do not belong to this sin-cursed world. Pilgrims passing through do not allow themselves to become entangled in the surrounding culture. As sojourners our influence on the secular society is limited. Nor can we accomplish by our efforts the agenda stated in the Lord's Prayer. Prayer alone is effective for getting God's will done in this world. From beginning to end the Lord's Prayer is our appeal to our Father to act primarily for his own glory.

A Common Attitude Toward God

At present God's rule is not acknowledged by all mankind on earth. Relatively few honor God in their thoughts or behavior. The inclinations of people's depraved natures govern them. The apostle John wrote this about the natural human condition:

> This is the verdict: Light has come into the world, but men loved darkness instead of light because their deeds were evil. Everyone who does evil hates the light, and will not come into the light for fear that his deeds will be exposed (John 3:19–20).

In their natural sinful condition people are so corrupted that they prefer the familiarity of evil to the good. The Psalmist David made this observation:

> God looks down from heaven on the sons of men to see if there are any who understand, any who seek God. Everyone has turned away, they have together become corrupt; there is no one who does good, not even one. Will the evildoers never learn—those

who devour my people as men eat bread and who do not call on God? (Psalm 53:2–4)

At heart the people of this world are like the crowd that wanted to kill Jesus. He said to them, "You belong to your father, the devil, and you want to carry out your father's desire" (John 8:44).

Light in the Darkness

As aliens passing through a world hostile to God, his children need his constant protection. The prophet Isaiah observed, "See, darkness covers the earth and thick darkness is over the peoples, but the Lord rises upon you and his glory appears over you" (Isaiah 60:2). God our heavenly Father pierces the darkness through the light reflected by his children. The apostle Paul encouraged the Philippian church,

Do everything without complaining or arguing, so that you may become blameless and pure, children of God without fault in a crooked and depraved generation, in which you shine like stars in the universe as you hold out the word of life (Philippians 2:14–16).

Helmut Thielicke preached a series of sermons on the Lord's Prayer to congregations in Stuttgart during the horrors of World War II. His congregants faced the nightly ordeals of Allied air raids, not knowing whether they would survive the next onslaught. They felt the fury of living in a hostile world. They had firsthand experience in the blackness of evil that permeates the world's societies. Cardinal Bergoglio (Pope Francis) wrote, "Man's life on earth is warfare."[24] Jesus said his followers would face hostility until they realize the consummation of their redemption.

When some of Jesus' disciples admired the beauty of the Jerusalem temple he said to them,

> "There will be great earthquakes, famines and pestilences in various places, and fearful events and great signs from heaven. But before all this, they will lay their hands on you and will persecute you. They will deliver you to the synagogues and prisons, and you will be brought before kings and governors, and all on account of my name . . . All men will hate you because of me" (Luke 21:11, 12, 17).

The control exercised by the evil one—also called the devil and Satan in Scripture—is pervasive, but not absolute. He has awesome power over the forces of nature and over nations. Job chapters 1 and 2 report calamities caused by Satan. But the devil does not have authority to control the lives or the destiny of the children of the heavenly Father. Job's godly devotion was commendable (Job 1), but it did not exempt Job from suffering intense persecution from the evil one.

The Lord's Prayer clarifies an accurate worldview for God's children as they wend their way through perilous territory to their heavenly Father's home. Before he departed with his disciples for the olive grove, Jesus prayed to the Father:

> "I will remain in the world no longer, but they are still in the world, and I am coming to you. Holy Father, protect them by the power of your name— the name that you gave me—so that they may be one as we are one. While I was with them, I

protected them and kept them safe by that name you gave me" (John 17:11–12).

The Lord's Prayer is for all who are not at home in this broken-down world. But there are those who say we should find our happiness here. It is God's will, they claim, that his children enjoy the best health and the world's finest luxuries. But such a self-centered perspective is contrary to what God has said in his Word. God's children live in an environment inhospitable to righteousness. The curse of sin has ravaged God's creation. God grants his children many good things, but life in this fallen world is hard. The apostle Paul made this eminently clear:

> For the creation was subjected to frustration, not by its own choice, but by the will of the one who subjected it, in hope that the creation itself will be liberated from its bondage to decay and brought into the glorious freedom of the children of God (Romans 8:20–21).

Misfits in This Corrupt World

God's children are "misfits" in a world that lies in evil. The apostle Paul explained to the Corinthian Christians that the wisdom of this age has no room for our message. The wisdom of God was hidden from people prior to the revelation of Jesus Christ, the Lord of glory (1 Corinthians 2:7–9). The principles and values that regulate God's children are poles apart from the ways of the secular culture. The distinctive life of God's children is foreign to people imbedded in this fallen world.

I grew up on a small farm in South Africa. My father kept an assortment of farm critters from bantam chickens to Jersey cattle. I recall the time when he placed some duck eggs in a nest under a brooding hen. In due course the hen hatched the ducks along with her own chicks. The little ducklings followed the hen as if they were a natural part of her brood. The hen seemed none the wiser. Then the inevitable happened. The happy little brood found the pond. The ducklings immediately took to the water. I remember it well, because I made it happen. The mystified mother hen clucked and strutted back and forth along the bank of the pond. She watched her ducklings, as if to say, "What in tarnation are you doing in there? That is not where you belong!" I saw the invisible inner nature of "duckdom" expressing itself, but it made no sense to the hen. So it is with the secular world that does not understand the inner spiritual nature of the children of God. We live beside people of the secular culture, but we are radically different. We belong to another realm, the kingdom of our Father in heaven.

The apostle Peter cited Lot as "a righteous man, who was distressed by the filthy lives of lawless men (for that righteous man living among them day after day, was tormented in his righteous soul by the lawless deeds he saw and heard)" (2 Peter 2:7–8). Lot had made his home in the degenerate culture of Sodom. Admittedly, Lot made a foolish choice that exacerbated his struggle with the wickedness around him. But the point is made repeatedly that he was a righteous man. That is why his soul was tormented. The souls of our heavenly Father's children sojourning in a decadent society should likewise feel similar torment today. It is a great pity when God's children feel comfortable in the vile culture of a depraved society. Alas, we indulge much of society's vices without even batting an eye.

The people of the age are marked by spiritual blindness. "The god of this age," Paul reminds God's children, "has blinded the minds of unbelievers, so that they cannot see the light of the gospel of the glory of Christ, who is the image of God" (2 Corinthians 4:4). But mankind is without excuse, because "God's invisible qualities—his eternal power and divine nature—have been clearly seen, being understood from what has been made" (Romans 1:20).

Flourishing in a Fallen Culture

As the heavenly Father's children, we belong to his eternal kingdom. But we are also native to this planet that God created. How do we conduct ourselves in a world fouled by evil? Even though we are on a trek through this world, we are not to keep to ourselves, intent only on making it through without contamination. God has not exempted us from the responsibility to live productive lives here.

When the Israelites were taken into exile in Babylon, God made it clear that their captivity was not to be a bitter endurance for them. As the people of God they were to involve themselves in the Babylonian society. The prophet Jeremiah said to them:

> This is what the Lord Almighty, the God of Israel, says to all those I carried into exile from Jerusalem to Babylon: "Build houses and settle down; plant gardens and eat what they produce. Marry and have sons and daughters; find wives for your sons and give your daughters in marriage, so that they too may have sons and daughters. Increase in number there; do not decrease. Also, seek the peace and prosperity of the city to which I have carried you into exile. Pray to the Lord for it, because if it prospers, you too will prosper" (Jeremiah 29:4–7).

As a Jewish exile, Daniel's uncompromising devotion to the Lord God while at the same time winning the favor of the highest authority in the land is exemplary. He served with distinction in the secular arena, and all the people were blessed because of him. Similarly, as Luke reports, the first church in Jerusalem enjoyed the favor of all the people (Acts 2:47).

Our heavenly Father has a crucial role for his children in a hostile environment. Jesus Christ's mandate to the apostles and to others who placed their faith in him was to go into the world with the good news of God's grace. We are to reach out to all people with a message of hope, urging them to confess their sins to God and to believe in our Savior and Lord, Jesus Christ.

Jesus told his followers they were the salt of the earth and the light of the world (Matthew 5:13–16). He did not want them to hide from the world, but to retard the rottenness of society by their influence, and to broadcast the truth that can rescue people from bondage in darkness. The apostle Paul also urged God's children to become compassionately engaged with the world:

> I urge, then, first of all, that requests, prayers, intercession and thanksgiving be made for everyone—for kings and all those in society [authority], that we may live peaceful and quiet lives in all godliness and holiness (1 Timothy 2:1–2).

As sojourners here and as pilgrims on our way to our heavenly home we must live godly lives in this corrupt world. A beloved hymn speaks to the challenge this is for God's children:

O to grace how great a debtor
daily I'm constrained to be!
Let thy goodness, like a fetter,
bind my wandering heart to Thee;
Prone to wander, Lord, I feel it,
prone to leave the God I love;
Here's my heart, O take and seal it;
seal it for thy courts above.[25]

This proclivity in God's children to stray from our Father's way calls for the utmost diligence. We are to guard against contamination, but we are not to practice isolation. Paul addressed this responsibility with the Galatian churches:

Let us not become weary in doing good, for at the proper time we will reap a harvest if we do not give up. Therefore, as we have opportunity, let us do good to all people, especially to those who belong to the family of believers (Galatians 6:9–10).

I have grimaced at the "holier-than-thou" attitude with which some church folk condemn those who do not profess faith in Christ. It is shameful when those who claim to be children of God make themselves odious to the secular world. The apostle Paul said to the Roman church, "If it is possible, as far as it depends on you, live at peace with everyone" (Romans 12:18; cf. Hebrews 12:14). The heavenly Father's children should excel in doing good in this world through their godly influence in local, state, and federal leadership roles. Let us heed the guidance of the apostle Peter:

Dear friends, I urge you, as aliens and strangers in the world, to abstain from evil desires, which war against your soul. Live such good lives among the pagans that, though they accuse you of doing wrong, they may see your good deeds and glorify God on the day he visits us. Submit yourselves for the Lord's sake to every authority instituted among men: whether to the king, as the supreme authority, or to governors, who are sent by him to punish those who do wrong and to commend those who do right (1 Peter 2:11–14).

As children of our heavenly Father we are called to be holy. But we do not spend our sojourn here whining and complaining because we are offended by the decadence in the world. God's children have a blessed hope. God has guaranteed an inheritance in heaven for his children (Colossians 1:12; 1 Peter 1:4). During their earthly sojourn they face the fury of the devil, the temporary ruler of this realm. God's children will not be spared trials. The writer of the letter to the Hebrews lauds history's heroes of faith who admitted that they were aliens and strangers on earth. They suffered abuse, torture and death. He wrote, "the world was not worthy of them" (Hebrews 11:38).

Today a glut of advertising clutters our television programs. Commercials that tout pharmaceutical products are particularly annoying. After extolling the benefits of a particular product, a string of disclaimers follows. They warn that the medicine might cause nausea, diarrhea, high or low blood pressure, skin rash, depression, stroke, heart attack, or even death. The rapid-fire manner in which the disclaimers are given often renders them incomprehensible. The law requires that the warnings be stated, but the marketers do their utmost to blur the truth. In contrast, God wants everyone to hear the good news of his grace in Jesus Christ. No disclaimers are hidden. Those who believe in Jesus Christ have eternal life, but those who do not believe do not have eternal life (1 John 5:11–12). Christ Jesus is the only way to God.

The Preacher (Solomon) tells us in Ecclesiastes of his thorough investigation into the nature of life's hardships. King Solomon was the most qualified person ever to engage in such research. At the beginning of his reign God offered Solomon anything he desired. He asked for a discerning heart. The Lord granted his request: "I will do what you have asked. I will give you a wise and discerning heart, so that there will never have been anyone like you, nor will there ever be" (1 Kings 3:12).

Solomon recounted his fruitless search to find the meaning of life. He wrote, "I wanted to see what was worthwhile for men to do under heaven during the few days of their lives" (Ecclesiastes 2:3). His somber assessment was, ". . . the day of death [is] better than the day of birth" (Ecclesiastes 7:1). He gave an apt summary of life in a hopeless world:

> Again I looked and saw all the oppression that was taking place under the sun: I saw the tears of the oppressed—and they have no comforter; power was on the side of their oppressors—and they have no comforter (Ecclesiastes 4:1).

Solomon learned that trials, unfairness, and frustrations are our lot. For most people life has more negatives than positives. Our experiences may not be as extensive as Solomon's, but our conclusions are the same. He rendered his verdict that a life disconnected from God is meaningless. "Meaningless! Meaningless!" says the Teacher, "Everything is meaningless" (Ecclesiastes 12:8). God alone adds value to our sojourn on earth. Solomon summarized his observations: "I know that there is nothing better for men than to be happy and do good while they live. That everyone may eat and drink, and find satisfaction in all his toil—this is the gift of God" (Ecclesiastes 3:12–13). Then, in conclusion, he gave the *coup de grace:* "Now everything has been heard; here is the conclusion of the matter. Fear God and keep his commandments, for this is the whole [duty] of man" (Ecclesiastes 12:13). If we exclude God from the equation, life on this earth will not make sense.

Suffering and Judgment

Billions of people suffer extreme hardships, like the poor emaciated woman who said life for her would be best when it is over. Many have swallowed dose after dose of the culture's toxins and long to find a remedy. Terrorists lay down their lives as suicide bombers because they believe the false promise of a better life hereafter. Lost souls who have no hope of a home with the Father crave deliverance from their excruciations here.

Most people do not grasp their catastrophic plight. This is a cursed, corrupt world under the control of the evil one. They have no orientation toward God. They are blind, misguided, and deceived. They are spiritually enslaved.

Job's saga is a vivid example of the world under the control of the evil one. But Satan did not initiate Job's trials. God set Job up to be afflicted (Job 2:3, 10). Job's companions assessed his calamity according to their worldview. They told Job he was suffering divine recompense for his evil deeds. Their perspective exemplifies a common notion that suffering is divine judgment.

Job experienced more catastrophes than any of us are likely to encounter. But he determined that he would not jettison his devotion to God. He guarded his godly orientation as an alien suffering in hostile territory. The apostle Paul also maintained his spiritual equilibrium during his trials. He said, "I consider that our present sufferings are not worth comparing with the glory that will be revealed in us" (Romans 8:18).

But as God's children we belong to his household. Our citizenship is in heaven. The apostle Peter wrote to Asian Christians, "Since you call on a Father who judges each man's work impartially, live your lives as strangers here in reverent fear" (1 Peter 1:17). If we attempt to find the meaning of life in terms of our earthly experience, we will be confused and disappointed. Life makes sense only in relation to God. I appreciate Charles Wesley's words of hope for God's wayfaring children:

> A stranger in the world below,
> I calmly sojourn here;
> Nor can its happiness or woe
> Provoke my hope or fear;
> Its evils in a moment end,
> Its joys as soon are past!
> But O! the bliss to which I tend
> Eternally shall last.[26]

All God's children take this earthly journey. But our destiny is not here, because our home is not here. "For a little while," we suffer trials and hardships. These are "trials" to prove our faith. The apostle Peter explained the place of God's children in this world vis-à-vis their place in heaven. He wrote,

> Praise be to the God and Father of our Lord Jesus
> Christ! In his great mercy he has given us new birth

into a living hope through the resurrection of Jesus Christ from the dead, and into an inheritance that can never perish, spoil or fade—kept in heaven for you, who through faith are shielded by God's power until the coming of the salvation that is ready to be revealed in the last time. In this you greatly rejoice, though now for a little while you may have had to suffer grief in all kinds of trials. These have come so that your faith—of greater worth than gold which perishes even though refined by fire—may be proved genuine and may result in praise, glory and honor when Jesus Christ is revealed (1 Peter 1:3–7).

The apostle Paul encouraged the Corinthian church:

Therefore we do not lose heart. Though outwardly we are wasting away, yet inwardly we are being renewed day by day. For our light and momentary troubles are achieving for us an eternal glory that far outweighs them all. So we fix our eyes not on what is seen, but on what is unseen. For what is seen is temporary, but what is unseen is eternal (2 Corinthians 4:16–18).

When we ask to be spared temptations or trials, are they the trials of which Peter spoke in 1 Peter 1:3–7? We may ask our Father to ameliorate our sufferings, but we should not expect exemption from them. They have a worthy purpose. The apostle Paul wrote, "we also rejoice in our sufferings because we know that suffering produces perseverance; perseverance, character; and character, hope" (Romans 5:3).

As pilgrims in a world disposed toward evil, we have a joy that cannot be quashed. We cannot be stealthy, hoping to escape the evil one's notice. The devil knows where the heavenly Father's children are. We cannot hide from Satan, but we walk confidently under the watchful eye of our Father. In some lands today God's children are persecuted for their faith. To meet for worship they must hide from hostile authorities. The evil one knows where they are, but he cannot rob them of their joy. They are vigilant, but they do not despair.

Homesick for Heaven

South Africa used to be known as a land of twelve tribes; ten black, two white. Among the white population, the majority was Afrikaans and the minority was English (comprising British and Europeans). Our family was of the minority group. My mother and father were born in England. Their families moved to South Africa just after the turn of the twentieth century for employment with the DeBeers Diamond Corporation.

As far back as I can recall, I felt a deep visceral discontentment with the land where I lived. My discomfort was doubtlessly abetted by groups of Afrikaner hooligans who took delight in bullying a lone English boy whenever they happened upon one. I longed to be elsewhere; some place where I belonged. At the age of 18 I left South Africa to move to Canada. My sister Margaret and I took advantage of an opportunity to move to our new homeland ahead of our parents and our older married sisters. During the interval of separation from family I experienced occasional homesickness. I had a longing in my heart—not for a place, but for the rest of my family. Home was where they were.

When we are homesick we struggle with a visceral sense of being out of place. It aggravates the ache in our souls. This world is not home for the children of our Father in heaven. It is hostile territory. God's children are homesick for heaven, where our Father awaits us. Jim Reeves expressed this longing in song:

> This world is not my home, I'm just a-passing through
> My treasures are laid up somewhere beyond the blue
> The angels beckon me from heaven's open door
> And I can't feel at home in this world anymore.[27]

Healthy Homesickness

During forty-plus years as a pastor I have observed that few of God's children display signs of homesickness to be with their heavenly Father. Nevertheless, I have had the exquisite joy of looking into the dim eyes of a saint who is not long for this world. I sensed a yearning to go home to the Father in his heavenly abode. If we love our heavenly Father with all our heart and soul and mind and strength, we too will know that longing. In Christ's intercessory prayer for his disciples he said,

> I have given them your word and the world has hated them, for they are not of the world any more than I am of the world. My prayer is not that you take them out of the world, but that you protect them from the evil one. They are not of the world, even as I am not of it. Sanctify them by the truth. Your word is truth (John 17:14–17).

God is the Father of all who have been born anew into his holy family through faith in Christ. The apostle Paul told the Philippian church that God's children do not blend in with the crooked and depraved generation where they live. Instead, they stand out like stars shining in the universe (Philippians 2:15–16). Even though God's children in this world may be splattered with the muck of a decadent culture, they are not part of it.

Our Common Attachment to Earthly Dwellings

Most people feel a strong attachment to their house. Many cherish the old family homestead because of the memories it holds. Others are fixated on the house they have at last been able to afford after moving up from a "starter home." They take pride in their abode, frequently redecorating and refurnishing it. It may cost a small fortune to transform the house into a dream home. Like Lot in Sodom, they have made a comfortable home for themselves in a debauched society.

I too admire the charm of some houses. But I take issue with God's children who are enamored with earthly habitations. We are not surprised to find such an attitude in people who have no hope beyond their earthly dwelling. They want to hold on to their worldly stuff, and they fear having to let go some day. We are, however, saddened if we see our heavenly Father's children captivated by a piece of earthly real estate.

God's Household

The apostle Paul explained to the Ephesian Christians, "Consequently you are no longer foreigners and aliens, but fellow citizens with God's people, and members of God's household" (Ephesians 2:19). Speaking at a Bible camp, Vance Havner said: "The Christian moves through the kingdom of this world as a citizen of the kingdom of God. He is not a citizen of earth trying to get to heaven, but a citizen of heaven making his way through the world."[28] The Lord's Prayer as a daily exercise helps us maintain our equilibrium in the vicissitudes of this mortal life.

On their way to the Promised Land the Israelites were sojourners in the wilderness for forty years. Even though they were the children of the Lord God, their conduct was deplorable. They turned aside from the way that the Lord God had prepared for them (Deuteronomy 9:16). They became idolatrous, rebellious, faithless, and stubborn. The Lord God became angry with his people and threatened to destroy them. After Moses interceded with God on their behalf, he said to them:

> "And now, O Israel, what does the Lord your God ask of you but to fear the Lord your God, to walk in all his ways, to love him, to serve the Lord your God with all your heart and with all your soul, and to observe the Lord's commands and decrees that I am giving you today for your own good?" (Deuteronomy 10:12–13).

King David gave a similar charge to his son Solomon: "observe what the Lord your God requires: Walk in his ways, and keep his decrees and commands, . . ." (1 Kings 2:3) The apostle Paul admonished the churches of Galatia, "So I say, live by the Spirit, and you will not gratify the desires of the sinful nature" (Galatians 5:16).

"Walk" is a biblical idiom for "live." Walking in the Spirit is a fitting metaphor for our heavenly Father's children on their pilgrimage to their heavenly home. Our earthly sojourn is our walk through this hostile, fallen world on our way to the place prepared for us in our heavenly Father's household. If we turn aside from God's way, either to the right or to the left, we become trapped in a spiritual quagmire and we fall prey to the evil one.

God With Us

Many people speak of finding God in the wonders of the beauty of nature. But God is not enmeshed in the natural world, magnificent and amazing though it may be. The wonders and delights found in nature are God's handiwork. They bear witness to the existence and activity of a divine being of intelligence, might, and beneficence that we cannot comprehend with our puny intellects. In a George MacDonald pastoral novel the question is posed, "Have you ever seen God, Marion?" Marion paused for a moment and then answered, "No, but I have seen things just after He did them."[29] God our Father created the wonders of the natural world, but they do not define him. Our Father in heaven is with his children through the Spirit of Christ who is in us and with us. Apart from Jesus Christ and the indwelling Spirit of Christ, we would be "without hope and without God in the world" (Ephesians 2:12).

God in heaven is Father to all who have received Jesus Christ and believed in his name (John 1:12). By his Spirit he is present with us during our earthly pilgrimage. Therefore we pray, "Lead us not into temptation; deliver us from evil." Because our Father is with us, these are not empty requests.

> The apostle Philip asked Jesus, "Lord, show us the Father and that will be enough for us." Jesus answered, Don't you know me, Philip, even after I have been among you such a long time? Anyone who has seen me has seen the Father. How can you say, 'Show us the Father'? Don't you believe that I am in the Father, and that the Father is in me? The words I say to you are not just my own. Rather, it is the Father, living in me, who is doing his work" (John 14:8–10).

Learning to Let Go

How should we conduct ourselves as children of the Father in heaven while we live as aliens and strangers in a fallen world? Life for us here is hard and often disappointing. One day my wife Liz and I were talking about the hardships of life in this corrupt world. She said, "Lately I have realized that for the child of God, one of the chief purposes of life is learning to let go." That insight resonated in my soul. On our trek homeward we learn to let go of the temporal allurements and to live with open hands.

Clutching earthly possessions is antithetical to the values of God's children. We are pilgrims on the way to the place Jesus Christ went to prepare for us. We must not overload ourselves with stuff that weighs us down and can cause us to stall.

We do not allow mundane matters to fashion our values. We thank our Father for the good things he created for mankind in this world. But we know that our enjoyment of earthly goods is temporary. We hold this world's goods loosely because we can take none of them with us. A line from an anonymous Puritan prayer fits well here: "Teach me the happy art of attending to things temporal with a mind intent on things eternal."[30] Admittedly, this perspective is difficult to sustain while surrounded by earthly enchantments. But easy or not, these truths regulate our hope.

Jesus asked, "What good will it be for a man if he gains the whole world, yet forfeits his soul?" (Matthew 16:26). The apostle Peter urged the scattered Christians as aliens and strangers in the world to abstain from sinful desires which war against the soul (1 Peter 2:11–12). James warned,

> You adulterous people, don't you know that friendship with the world is hatred toward God?

Anyone who chooses to be a friend of the world becomes an enemy of God (James 4:4).

When someone's earthly sojourn ends, family members sort through the deceased's earthly possessions. They handle items the departed person valued. The sobering truth is that all the things God's children value during their earthly stay will be left behind for others. Film mogul Louis B. Mayer was invited to make a sizeable donation to a charity. The miserly Louis was reluctant to part with any of his wealth. He said, "They say you can't take it with you when you go. Well, if I can't take it with me, I won't go."[31] But Louis did go and the wealth stayed behind.

My father once took me to a gold mine in South Africa to see the smelted gold poured into large bullion ingots. A supervisor invited me to try to pick up one of the ingots. He said if I could pick it up I could keep it. What an offer! That single brick was worth more money than a young boy could imagine. I tried, but my fingers kept slipping off it. I could not even move it slightly. Then we watched as the gold bricks were taken to an armored truck for transportation to a vault. Two men placed a single gold ingot on another man's shoulder. He carried the heavy treasure to the truck where others lifted it off his shoulder. I watched a line of men carrying the precious bars, surrounded by armed guards. When it was over, I went home and the gold went elsewhere. I didn't recognize it at the time, but that is a lesson about life for the child of God. We see and touch worldly treasures, but they slip from our grasp. They stay behind in this world's vault, and we go on. Whether you are a child of God or not, stuff stays and you go. Our passage through this world is brief. We are sojourners.

Many of God's children hug this world system tightly, as if the ultimate goal of life lies somewhere in this world.

My wife Liz said, "What makes us feel secure this side of heaven is the familiar. But it is a false sense of security." We are well aware of this world's allurements and perversions. But if we become immersed in them, we are as secure as someone living in a rickety house on a seismically active fault line. The next temblor may jounce our earthly castle down to a pile of rubble.

Most of God's children suffer some degree of anxiety about temporal and material matters. Our most common prayer requests seem to be for physical health, employment, finances, and sundry temporal matters. Our heavenly Father certainly cares about these things. But relatively few of our prayers focus on God's grace. Should we not implore the Spirit of God to grant us opportunities to demonstrate his love to our neighbors? How often do we ask our heavenly Father to develop in us patience and kindness in dealing with people who are mean-spirited, dishonest, abusive, and selfish?

Much as we feel like strangers in our world, the Jewish exiles felt out of place in Babylon. Their struggle as strangers in the land moved them to tears.

> By the rivers of Babylon we sat and wept when we remembered Zion. There on the poplars we hung our harps, for there our captors asked us for songs, our tormentors demanded songs of joy; they said, "Sing us one of the songs of Zion!" How can we sing the songs of the Lord while in a foreign land? (Psalm 137:1–4).

The Effects of Captivity to the World

We should not feel comfortable in a society that dishonors our heavenly Father. But those who belong to the secular culture want God's children to entertain them, and not indict them. Christian gospel music has become popular in the secular music world. A dearly loved song of God's children is *Amazing Grace* which starts, "Amazing grace, how sweet the sound, that saved a wretch like me."[32] I cringe when popular musicians use it only to show off their vocal prowess, and their lifestyles give no hint of God's amazing grace. They have hijacked some of the grandest truths of God's love for their own entertainment.

As God's children who do not belong to this world, how should we recalibrate our values and our desires? Do our prayers reflect an awareness that we do not belong to this world? Have we become preoccupied with securing a comfortable life here? The writer of the letter to the Hebrews speaks of God's children who endured great hardship because of their faith, "You sympathized with those in prison and joyfully accepted the confiscation of your property, because you knew that you yourselves had better and lasting possessions" (Hebrews 10:34). King David helped God's people gain the right perspective. After gathering the necessary materials for building the temple in Jerusalem he prayed, "We are aliens and strangers in your sight, as were all our forefathers. Our days on earth are like a shadow, without hope" (1 Chronicles 29:15).

Even though the creation is corrupted, it belongs to God. In the instructions concerning the Year of Jubilee, the Lord declared to his people, "The land must not be sold permanently, because the land is mine and you are but aliens and my tenants" (Leviticus 25:23). This world is presently under the control of the evil one, but God remains sovereign over all. As aliens we pray for the consummation of our Father's reign in this earthly realm. The apostle John gives an urgent warning to the heavenly Father's children:

Do not love the world or anything in the world. If anyone loves the world, the love of the Father is not in him. For everything in the world—the cravings of sinful man, the lust of his eyes and the boasting of what he has and does—come not from the Father but from the world. The world and its desires pass away, but the man who does the will of God lives forever (1 John 2:15–17).

As citizens of heaven we must focus our affections and longings on our heavenly Father. The foremost commandment that Moses gave to God's people Israel as they prepared to occupy the Promised Land was, "Love the Lord your God with all your heart and with all your soul and with all your strength" (Deuteronomy 6:5). The apostle Peter appealed to God's children, "Beloved, I urge you as aliens and strangers in the world to abstain from fleshly lusts, which wage war against the soul" (1 Peter 2:11).

The solicitations of innumerable temptations make this world a perilous place. Our physical and emotional natures are susceptible to many seductions. Temptations are doorways into the world's corrupt system. Many have stepped beyond the threshold of godly standards and succumbed to a lifestyle they had all their life eschewed. God's children must acknowledge the futility of struggling in their own strength to reject the allurements of a world that is not their home.

Earthly Conduct of the Heavenly Father's Children

Even though this world is not our home, we have no right as God's children to withdraw from worldly affairs. We who have the hope of eternal life must do good to all people. C. S. Lewis explained,

If you read history, you will find that the Christians who did the most for the present world were those who thought most of the next. It is since Christians have largely ceased to think of the other world that they have become ineffective in this. Aim at heaven and you get earth thrown in. Aim at earth and you get neither.[33]

God's children can be a voice for good and for God in local, state, and national arenas. But if they become embroiled in political power struggles, earthly dreams will snag their deepest longings. The apostle Paul warned God's children in Rome,

And do not be conformed to this world, but be transformed by the renewing of your mind, that you may prove what the will of God is, that which is good and acceptable and perfect (Romans 12:2 in New American Standard Bible).

The Impact of Evil's Contamination

In the Garden of Eden mankind rejected the will of God. The Garden of Eden became the garden of evil. Through the sin of our forebears evil invaded the earth and infected the human race. This corrupt world that is the home of unrighteousness will be destroyed, but God's people look forward to a new heaven and new earth that will be the "home of righteousness" (2 Peter 3:13). The apostle John wrote, "The world and its desires pass away, but the man who does the will of God lives forever" (1 John 2:17). For this reason God's children must be discriminating about where we direct our affections.

We take care of our physical bodies, but our bodies are destined for destruction. The apostle Paul wrote, "Now we know that if the earthly tent we live in is destroyed, we have a building from God, an eternal house in heaven, not built by human hands" (2 Corinthians 5:1). Paul tried to redirect our affections: "Since, then, you have been raised with Christ, set your hearts on things above, where Christ is seated at the right hand of God. Set your minds on things above, not on earthly things" (Colossians 3:1–2).

A popular beer slogan in the 1960s said, "You only go around once in life, so you've got to grab for all the gusto you can." Many people still hold to that philosophy of life. This life is their only certainty, so they want to enjoy all it offers for as long as they can. Why should they set their minds and hearts on the uncertainties of the hereafter? But for the children of the heavenly Father the hereafter is not uncertain; it is home. Our earthly life is fraught with hostility and danger. If God's children focus their strongest affections on earth-bound things, they contradict their hope of a heavenly destiny.

A soldier deployed to the war theater on foreign soil does not set his affections on that war-torn land. He doesn't belong there. His heart is back home with his family. He may enjoy good experiences with his army comrades, but he is an alien, sojourning in a land that is not his home. No sane person would say to that soldier, "Why have you set your heart on going home? What you have here is best, so grab for all the gusto you can get here." That would be ludicrous. It is also ridiculous for God's children to tie their hopes and affections to this hostile world where they do not belong.

Does this mean God's children must resign themselves to a wretched pilgrimage to their heavenly home? No, this physical world is not entirely vile. God's blessings for his children are all around us. The corruption caused by sin has not robbed God's children of all his blessings. The grandeur displayed in God's physical creation should evoke our wonder at his power and majesty (see Psalm 8). In these things we still delight. God's word declares that he created good things for our enjoyment (1 Timothy 4:4). Let us not call evil what God created as good. The 19th century Scottish evangelist Henry Drummond wrote,

> For Christianity not only encourages whatsoever things are lovely, but wars against the whole theory of life which would exclude them. It prescribes aestheticism [good taste, refinement]; it proscribes [condemns] asceticism [self-denial, stoicism].[34]

We live in an enchanting world filled with breathtaking beauty. We delight in loving relationships. The thrill of love, adventure, and achievement are God's gifts to us. The heavenly Father's children discover ample reasons each day to laugh, to sing, to dance, and to discover. God's children are not in an endurance contest, hoping to escape the pitfalls and moral sewage until we reach our heavenly home. Isaac Watts's hymn celebrates the felicity of God's children upon this earth:

> I sing the Almighty power of God, that made the mountains rise
> That spread the flowing seas abroad, and built the lofty skies.
> I sing the wisdom that ordained the sun to rule the day;
> The moon shines full at his command, and all the stars obey.
> I sing the goodness of the Lord, who filled the earth with food,
> Who formed the creatures through the Word,
> and then pronounced them good.

Lord, how Thy wonders are displayed, where're I turn
my eye,
If I survey the ground I tread, or gaze upon the sky.[35]

The physical world itself is not a threat to us. Yes, God
cursed the ground because of Adam's sin. It would
henceforth require hard work to make the ground produce
food for mankind's sustenance. But the magnificence of
God's creation would not be forfeited to the curse of sin. The
breadth of wickedness has made this world an uncomfortable
home for us. Nevertheless, our Father's children can thrive
because we have within us a spiritual force that is more than
sufficient to repel the assaults from the surrounding
degenerate culture.

After I concluded fifteen years as the senior pastor of a
local church, Liz and I entered a different kind of pastoral
service with Interim Pastor Ministries. We sold our home
and placed most of our possessions in storage. In the
succeeding years we moved from church to church during
crucial intervals between the departure of one pastor and the
calling of the next. We became accustomed to living in
temporary dwellings. Like most women Liz enjoys the
familiar comforts of her own "nest." This concept of God's
children being wayfarers without a lasting home on earth
became more meaningful and precious to her. She has never
craved luxury or coveted possessions, but she understands as
never before what it means to delight in varied experiences
and to live with open hands before God.

The Genesis account of creation says God gave
mankind the responsibility of managing his creation and the
privilege of enjoying its benefits. The Lord's Prayer
repudiates a theology that promotes material prosperity as
the distinctive mark of divine blessing. We depend on our
heavenly Father for our daily provision. (See Chapter 9

under the subtitle of "Our Greater Needs" for a discussion of the scope of "daily bread.") God's children are fulfilled in this world by extolling the Father's glory, looking for his kingdom, and pledging to do his will. An authentic Christian life is full and joyful; it is also morally discriminating in its interaction with all things worldly.

Jesus instructed his disciples to pray for daily bread from our Father. God's children cannot experience life's fullness apart from daily dependence on our heavenly Father. All the stuff we accumulate, even if a blessing from God, cannot sustain us. In many lands some of God's children struggle to make ends meet or to survive a serious illness, while others flourish. A crucial truth we all must learn is that nothing caught in the gravity of this planet can supply what we need in order to stand firm in a degenerate society. Only our intimate relationship with our heavenly Father can keep us from withering as persons.

The Tragedy of Distorted Values

Some of God's children spend obscene sums of money pampering their cats and dogs. They lavish more on their pets than most of the world's people have to feed and clothe their entire family. This is shameful testimony to mankind's diminishing respect for the worth of human beings.

Let me be clear on this matter, pets are lovely gifts from God. They provide companionship to the lonely, therapy of devotion to many who have emotional struggles, fun playmates for children, and protection for those who may be in danger.

It is imperative to recognize that, precious though our pets may be to us, they are animals. That is their God-designed identity and status. Tragically, some of God's people actually refer to their pets as their babies or brothers or sisters, and state unabashedly that they love them more than they love people.[36]

Some people will question whether these remarks about pets belong in a study of the Lord's Prayer. They consider the matter so trivial that its inclusion is unwarranted. Not so. The place Christ has prepared in heaven is for those who have become children of God because they have believed in and received Jesus Christ (John 1:12). The place was not prepared for other creatures. It is for those who bear the image and likeness of God, who have the right to call God their Father, and who have eternity in their hearts.

When people seek assurance that their beloved pets will be with them in heaven, they cheapen the biblical truth about heaven. They shift their longing from being with our heavenly Father to being forever with their dog or cat.

While Scripture does not specifically exclude animals from heaven, it is clear that the focus of everyone in heaven is on the Almighty God on the throne and on the Lamb slain to redeem mankind from sin. Therefore, I contend that it is spiritually harmful to permit any concern for a pet to eclipse the rightful glory that belongs only to our heavenly Father.

A pastor or preacher that attempts to comfort parishioners with promises of an eternal state of bliss for their pets, argues from Scripture's silence. There is no biblical basis for giving the comfort they crave. Such a preacher is peddling in false confidence. To many people such a claim may sound true, but it is not sound truth. (For further discussion see Endnote 36.)

Divine Strength for the Pilgrimage

Much in this world is pleasant, but it is not our playground. It is a battlefield on which our enemy, the devil, does his utmost to get God's children mired in the muck of his machinations. We pray daily to our Father to deliver us from the entanglements that trap us. The writer of the letter to the Hebrews addressed this:

> Therefore, since we are surrounded by such a great cloud of witnesses, let us throw off everything that hinders and the sin that so easily entangles, and let us run with perseverance the race marked out for us. Let us fix our eyes on Jesus, the author and perfecter of our faith, who for the joy set before him endured the cross, scorning its shame, and sat down at the right hand of the throne of God. Consider him who endured such opposition from sinful men, so that you will not grow weary and lose heart (Hebrews 12:1–4; cf. 13:14; 2 Corinthians 5:4, 5).

As God's children, we have the Holy Spirit with us on our pilgrimage to our heavenly home. Jesus Christ framed the Lord's Prayer to enable us to flourish on the journey. We delight in the wonders of creation that our omnipotent heavenly Father safeguards from being mucked up in earth's moral rot. An experience I had as a young boy illustrates this truth. I was walking in a field of wild grass and weeds on the back acreage of our little farm. Close to the neighbor's fence I came upon a large bright orange flower that stood out among the weeds. It was a pumpkin flower. I followed its stalk to the other side of the fence. It was rooted in the well-tilled garden of our neighbor, and it was flourishing in the midst of weeds yards away. I thought of Paul's words to the Colossian Christians, "So then, just as you received Christ Jesus as Lord, continue to live in him, rooted and built up in him, strengthened in the faith as you were taught, and overflowing with thankfulness" (Colossians 2:6–7). As God's children we live in a hostile world under the control of the evil one. But we have life in Christ, and for that reason we are able to bloom and flourish among the weeds of a fallen world.

In this world we are always "out of our element" as the children of God's household. If we assume that we are able to travel safely through this corrupt temporal world by depending on our own strength instead of daily seeking what only God can provide, we are utterly deluded, conceited, and foolish.

Picture a little child learning to ride a bicycle. Her father runs behind holding the seat to keep the little tike from losing balance and falling. After a while the child is able to pedal a short distance alone. After she gains confidence she calls out, "You can let go now, Daddy. I can do it on my own." As children of our heavenly Father we never reach the stage when we can call out, "You can let go now, *Abba*, I can do it on my own." We cannot "do life" on our own. We always need the steady hand of our Father to keep us from falling. I know a mother who planned to get a tiny child's bicycle to put in her daughter's dorm room during her first year away from home at university. It was to be a reminder to the daughter that she still needed her parents. The lesson is: never tell your earthly parents or your heavenly Father that they can let go of you now.

The Clear Focus of Prayer

Wayne Gretzky, arguably the greatest professional ice hockey player ever, explained his success, "I skate where the puck is going to be, not where it has been."[37] Many of God's children spend their energy focusing on mundane matters that they later realize have mostly yielded failure and regrets for them. Christ gave the Lord's Prayer to sojourners to be a daily habit of directing our attention to where we will be. The apostle Paul wrote to the Philippian church, "Forgetting what is behind and straining toward what is ahead, I press on toward the goal to win the prize for which God has called me heavenward in Christ Jesus" (Philippians 3:13–14).

We are pilgrims pressing on to the place Christ has prepared for God's children. We belong to God's household. Our citizenship is in heaven. We belong to the kingdom of God our Father. Jesus said, "I tell you the truth, anyone who will not receive the kingdom of God like a little child will never enter it" (Mark 10:15). In order to belong to the kingdom of God, we must be as humble and dependent as little children are upon their father. We long for the full realization of God's reign and for his will to be done here and everywhere. We rely on his daily provision and his mercy. We look to our heavenly Father to guide and protect us as we press on toward our eternal inheritance. These comprise the substance of the incomparable Lord's Prayer.

The Supremacy of the Prayer

The Lord's Prayer is the prime prayer for all God's people everywhere. It may seem pedestrian when juxtaposed with the weighty matters that accost God's children in their pilgrimage through a depraved society. But it is a fallacy to suppose that we may graduate to prayers of greater consequence. This prayer is essential both for the wobbly beginner on the pilgrimage and for the sure-footed trekker.

For all children of our heavenly Father, the Lord's Prayer is a daily exercise. It is not an optional accessory to our spiritual disciplines. In an episode of the television sitcom, *All in the Family,* Archie Bunker explained why he did not vote in a little local "meatball election." He said he saved his vote for the "biggies."[38] Prayers are not rationed. God's children do not set aside this rudimentary prayer and reserve their prayers for the heavy crises of life. We must never discard the Lord's Prayer as a religious relic to be replaced by more contemporary prayers of our invention.

The Lord's Prayer *is* the "biggie" for all children of the heavenly Father, both novices and veterans. It is preeminent.

E. M. Bounds seems to have considered the Lord's Prayer an elementary exercise for the immature. He wrote, "The 'Lord's Prayer' is a divine epitome for infant lips, . . ."[39] I contend that in all our praying we must not forsake this prayer, even for a day. Its divine origin compels us to plumb its implications. God does not give to his children anything that is trivial. More than all other prayers, whether spontaneous or liturgical, this prayer merits careful pondering. Let it never be uttered hastily, half-heartedly, or absent-mindedly.

One Prayer; Two Contexts

Matthew and Luke cite separate contexts from which the Lord's Prayer emerged. Though not identical, both iterations of the Prayer are essentially the same. In Matthew's Gospel Jesus was teaching a crowd on a mountain. In Luke's Gospel it followed Jesus' personal prayer time. One of the disciples asked him to teach them to pray. In two disparate situations Jesus trained his disciples by citing the same prayer with minor variations. Jesus taught his followers to give regular, careful attention to prayer.

In Matthew 6:9–13 Jesus taught his disciples: "This, then, is how you should pray." Luke writes, "One day Jesus was praying in a certain place. When he finished, one of his disciples said to him, "Lord, teach us to pray, just as John taught his disciples." He said to them, "when you pray, say: . . . ." (Luke 11:2–4). This prayer is for those who do not know how to pray. But all who have learned how to pray must never discard the Lord's Prayer as training wheels no longer needed. This is the prototypical prayer. If you truly want to pray, Jesus said to pray this way. This is a sufficient reason to call it "The Lord's Prayer."

A Daily Prayer of Desperation

There is no hint that the Lord's Prayer should be a prayer of convenience, or a prayer suitable for times of crisis only. There is nothing in this prayer that accommodates selfish desires. Even the clauses that address our own welfare ("give us . . , forgive us . . , lead us not . . .") are implicit confessions of our frailty, depravity, and vulnerability. We offer this prayer to our Father with a sense of urgency. All who sincerely utter this prayer admit readily their desperate need of their Father in heaven.

The Lord's Prayer does not spring spontaneously from our natural inclinations; it clashes with our innate tendencies. In this world corrupted by sin, our natural predisposition is to pursue our own will. We find the first instance of this impulse in the Genesis narrative, where it describes mankind's fall. Genesis chapter 3 relates the intrusion of Satan in the form of a serpent that deceived Adam and Eve. They rejected God's revealed will and yielded instead to a sensual enticement.

Rejection of Secular Vices

All who pray the Lord's Prayer sincerely must understand that they cannot be fulfilled by anything this corrupt world offers. The prayer is a manifest refusal to conform to the principles of a world culture under the control of Satan, the evil one. As children of the heavenly Father we pray that we might not embrace this world's values or become entangled in its vices. We ask that our aspirations become conformed to the will of our Father in heaven. We place God's honor before our own desires. Our plea is to be who we *should* be while living in a corrupt culture that is actively hostile to our Father and his children.

The sobering truth underlying this prayer is that God's reign does not encompass the world where his children live.

The apostle John said this world literally "lies in evil" (1 John 5:19). Upon commencing his public ministry, Jesus confronted an evil spirit and cast it out.

> "Be quiet!" said Jesus sternly. "Come out of him!" The evil spirit shook the man violently and came out of him with a shriek. The people were all so amazed that they asked each other, "What is this? A new teaching—and with authority! He even gives orders to evil spirits and they obey him" (Mark 1:25–28).

People recognized the activity of evil forces that could seize control of them. Jesus came to drive out the demons and to wrest people from their control. The Creator had come as Savior into the world that by mankind's disobedience had been opened to Satanic intrusion.

A Rebel's Prayer

Jesus taught his disciples to turn their attention to their heavenly Father, and to pray that his reign and his will would characterize this world as it does heaven. Each day we pray fervently to be radically different from those who are under the control of the evil one. This makes the Lord's Prayer indispensable for all God's children. If we neglect the great themes in this prayer we will inevitably become contaminated by the world's debauched culture. The heavenly Father's children do not capitulate to society's values as the *status quo.* Most appropriately, Professor David Wells defined prayer as "rebellion against the status quo":

> What, then, is the nature of petitionary prayer? It is, in essence, rebellion—rebellion against the world in

its fallenness, the absolute and undying refusal to accept as normal what is pervasively abnormal. It is, in this its negative aspect, the refusal of every agenda, every scheme, every interpretation that is at odds with the norm as originally established by God. As such, it is itself an expression of the unbridgeable chasm that separates Good from Evil, the declaration that Evil is not a variation on Good but its antithesis.[40]

The scope of The Lord's Prayer is enormous. Jesus Christ's prayer for his followers in John chapter 17 is conceptually connected to this prayer:

I have given them your word and the world has hated them, for they are not of the world any more than I am of the world. My prayer is not that you take them out of the world but that you protect them from the evil one. They are not of the world, even as I am not of the world. Sanctify them by the truth; your word is truth. As you sent me into the world, I have sent them into the world. For them I sanctify myself, that they too may be truly sanctified (John 17:14–18).

Let us now examine more closely the substance of this incomparable prayer from God the Son given to all the Father's children for their pilgrimage to their heavenly home.

Questions for Discussion and Personal Application

1. Choose one of the Bible texts referenced in the section "Living in a Hostile World" (p. 45) Explain how it helps you to understand your place in this world as a child of the heavenly Father.

2. How does the Lord's Prayer help you to cope with the evil in the world?

3. Explain how we should balance our responsibilities as God's children who belong to his kingdom but must also live as his people in a corrupt society.

4. How can you answer people who teach that God wants all his children to be healthy and wealthy in this world?

5. Throughout the Old Testament Book of Ecclesiastes Solomon explained that it is futile to pursue fulfillment in the things and experiences of this world. He said, "Meaningless! Meaningless" says the Teacher. "Everything is meaningless!" . . . "Now all has been heard; here is the conclusion of the matter: Fear God and keep his commandments, for this is the whole [duty] of man" (Ecclesiastes 12:8, 13). Do you share his conviction? If so, how did you arrive at this conviction?

6. In your opinion, why are many who consider themselves God's children confused and upset when they suffer hardship?

7. If you have ever felt homesick, were you mostly homesick for certain people or for a particular place? Have you ever known someone who was homesick for heaven?

8. How does the concept of journeying to our Father's heavenly home affect you as a Christian living in a corrupt society?

9. What comforts or surprises you about God's presence with his children on earth?
10. What advice can you give to help people hold the things of this world with open hands?
11. To what extent is the experience of God's children today similar to that of the Jewish exiles in Babylon (Psalm 137:1–4)?
12. What are some ways God's children can resist the allurement of temptations to compromise godly standards?
13. How can God's children redirect their pursuits from earthly to heavenly goals?
14. In light of the realities of a corrupt society, give some reasons you think people may choose a monastic or ascetic life?
15. How do you celebrate the magnificence of God's physical creation?
16. What is your attitude toward pets? In light of what God's Word says about the worth of human beings, do you need to adjust your viewpoint?
17. Give an example of how you learned that you never reach the point when you can let go of your heavenly Father's guiding and protecting grasp?
18. How might you incorporate the Lord's Prayer into your daily devotional exercises?
19. In light of Romans 12:1–2 and David Wells' remarks in his article "Rebellion Against the Status Quo" (p. 86), how can you use the Lord's Prayer to take your stand against society's corrupt value system?

4. OUR FATHER

("Father" in Luke's account)

According to legend,
A friend asked Mrs. Einstein,
"Do you know Albert's theory?"
She answered, "No, but I know Albert."
None of us can rightly claim to know the complexities of
God's awesome designs, but we should be able to say,
"I know God."

The Concept of God

Faith in an invisible almighty deity that provides no empirical proof of its existence is a tough proposition. If intelligent beings do not have sufficient evidence, the idea of God is just a fantasy. We say, "seeing is believing." Nevertheless, among all peoples, nations, tribes, and languages there is a belief in the existence of unseen transcendent spiritual entities. Throughout history both primitive and civilized people have claimed to interact with forces outside our natural perception. They pay homage to astral phenomena or to idols their hands have made as visible representations of their imagined deities. Human beings have a disposition toward divinity etched into their psyches. In the seventeenth century the French philosopher Blaise Pascal wrote,

> What does this craving, and this helplessness, of
> which all that now remains is the empty print and
> trace? . . . this infinite abyss can be filled only with

91

an infinite and immutable object; in other words by God himself.[41]

Molecular geneticist Dean Hamer offers his opinion on this human proclivity:

Most people, psychologists and theologians would argue, have some capacity for spirituality. It is among the most ubiquitous and powerful forces in human life. It has been evident throughout recorded history in every civilization and culture, in every nook and cranny of the globe. For many people, it is the main focus of their lives.[42]

Spirituality, Hamer claims, is distinct from the precepts of any particular religion, and this explains why a high percentage of people believe in God. Hamer calls this spiritual sensitivity a human instinct that is hardwired into our genes:

Why is spirituality such a powerful and universal force? Why do so many people believe in things they cannot see, smell, taste, hear, or touch? Why do people from all walks of life, around the globe, regardless of their religious backgrounds or the particular god they worship, value spirituality as much as, or more than, pleasure, power, or wealth? I argue that the answer is, at least in part, hardwired into our genes. Spirituality is one of our basic human inheritances. It is, in fact, an instinct.

Spirituality is an intensely personal activity. It involves private feelings, thoughts, and revelations. These are often difficult if not impossible to describe, much less to share. Yet only rarely does spirituality occur in a complete vacuum; even the most isolated ascetic must sometimes come in contact with other people. More often than not, spirituality is associated with a much more public domain of human life: religion.[43]

Hamer's insights may help to explain why children do not struggle with the concept of God watching over them, or why they delight in praying to Jesus. Perhaps the propensity in many little ones to have an imaginary friend whom they name and expect the rest of their family to recognize, stems from this same innate sense. Young children do not struggle as much as mature adults to accept the reality of invisible beings.

People who dispute the existence of supernatural forces and beings comprise a tiny minority. Some immerse themselves in a belief system based on empirical evidence alone. This quashes their natural predisposition to believe in the existence of supernatural entities.

Mankind's Incentive to Pray

Scripture states that God made mankind singularly in his image and likeness (Genesis 1:26). Our basic design inclines us toward God. This explains our incentive to pray. Human creatures of dust have been predisposed to identify with and to seek the approval of supernatural beings. People who accept all or part of the Judeo-Christian Scriptures as God's inspired revelation to mankind, turn their attention toward our Father in heaven. This inclination prompts the primal exercise of the human spirit. It inclines us to pray, "Our Father in heaven," and to believe that in doing so we do not indulge in fantasy.

Helmut Thielicke remarked that the world seems a dreadfully "unfatherly place."[44] On the other hand, Scripture assures us that heaven is the quintessential fatherly place. It is the abode of God our Father. The Lord's Prayer begins with the bold address: "Our Father in heaven." In his prayer for his disciples Jesus called on God as "Holy Father" (John 17:11). The Apostle John wrote that those who received the Word who became flesh, Jesus Christ, and believed in his name, had the right to become children of God (John 1:12). The children's home is with their Father. Jesus explained to his disciples, "In my Father's house are many rooms; if it were not so, I would have told you. I am going there to prepare a place for you" (John 14:2). Jesus declared himself to be the only way to God the Father: "I am the way and the truth and the life. No one comes to the Father except through me" (John 14:6). We can take our earthly pilgrimage to our dwelling place with our heavenly Father only because of our connection to Jesus Christ, the Way.

Jesus spoke of the unity with him that belongs to God's children: "On that day you will realize that I am in my Father, and you are in me, and I am in you" (John 14:20). Being "in Christ" is a common Scriptural expression for those who are united with Christ through faith in him. The only way to pass successfully through this hostile world to our destiny with our Father is in union with Jesus Christ through faith.

The Right Mindset for Prayer

The Lord's Prayer is a family prayer. In the New Testament Greek text, "Father" is the first word in both Matthew's and Luke's rendering of the prayer. It was a common practice in Jewish prayers to address God as Father. Jesus did not introduce a unique element into prayer when he taught his disciples to call God their Father in heaven. Each part of the Lord's Prayer stems from the rudimentary truth that we are the family of God.

A son who loves his father wants to please him. He aspires to be successful so that his father will approve of him. But he also wants to feel good about himself. The son's motives may be noble, but they are also mixed. Many of us have similar motives in striving to please God. We are conscientious about doing his will, but we also wish to be spared the nagging guilt of displeasing God. Many of God's children struggle with guilt feelings because they fear that God's acceptance of them depends on their performance. But none of us can perform well enough to earn God's approbation. Our heavenly Father takes delight in his children, not because of anything we have done, but because we belong to him.

The right way to pray "Our Father" is to rivet our attention on God as he has disclosed himself in his Holy Word. Avoiding feelings of guilt is an incidental benefit. When we pray each day to our Father in heaven, we care far more about our heavenly Father's honor than about our own sense of well being. This is the correct mindset for praying "Our Father."

My favorite flower is the wild California golden poppy. In the shade and at night its petals curl up into a tight spiral. But in the fullness of the sunlight the flower opens to display all its beauty. A hillside lush with golden poppies is a magnificent sight. The Lord's Prayer implies that this is what our heavenly Father wants to see. As God's love shines upon mankind he looks for the open, adoring response of his children to the warmth of his love.

Prayer to the Consummate Prodigal

In the parable of the Prodigal Son life had turned sour for the younger son (Luke 15:11–32). He had asked for his inheritance and then wasted it all on profligate living in a far land. He was destitute, living with pigs and living like a pig. When he came to his senses and returned to his father, he did not expect to be welcomed as a son. But his father would always receive him as his son.

Most people think the term "prodigal" means a skuzzy, rebellious, immoral loser. The term actually means "extravagantly wasteful" or "profuse in giving." Who do you think was more 'prodigal'—the younger son, or the father? The father was outrageously extravagant in extending lavish generosity to a rebellious, undeserving son. This is precisely the truth we must learn if we are the children of God. Our heavenly Father is kind, generous, and forgiving beyond all measure. He is our prodigal Father in heaven.

Moses called the Lord God the Father of a people named Israel, chosen out of all the nations of earth. The other nations did not have this privilege. He said:

> You are the children of the Lord your God. Do not cut yourselves or shave the front of your heads for the dead, for you are a people holy to the Lord your God. Out of all the peoples on the face of the earth, the Lord has chosen you to be his treasured possession (Deuteronomy 14:1–2).

Jesus told his detractors who were determined to kill him, "You belong to your father, the devil, and you want to carry out your father's desire" (John 8:44). He added, "He who belongs to God hears what God says. The reason you do not hear is that you do not belong to God" (John 8:47). There are no spiritual orphans. Nobody is without spiritual parentage. People are either children of the heavenly Father or children of the devil.

The Unseen Father

Our heavenly Father is invisible to our natural sight. This is both a challenge and a blessing. It is a challenge to conceive of a Father we cannot see. John the Evangelist explained, "No one has ever seen God, but God the One and Only, who is at the Father's side, has made him known" (John 1:18). It is also a challenge because everything we can see with our natural eye has been created. But God was not created; he is the Creator. Nevertheless, throughout history people have tried to make visible representations of deity. The prophets denounced those who worshiped idols that were the work of their own hands and could do nothing to help them. The majesty of the beauty of the earth was also created, but God is not imbedded in his creation. The visible universe testifies instead to a pre-existent Creator who is infinitely greater than all that can be seen.

God's invisibility is a blessing. We find incomparable comfort in knowing that God our Father in heaven transcends everything we can comprehend with our natural senses. His immensity and his majesty overwhelm our comprehension. Yet we belong to our invisible Father in heaven; we do not belong to this visible earth. Our essential bond is with our Father. Even though we battle inclinations that would hold us captive to the earthly sphere where we live, we cling to our heavenly parentage. For this reason Jesus taught God's children to pray the Lord's Prayer each day.

Whenever we offer up this prayer, our foremost concept of God is of a Father relating to his children. Prayer is our entrance into the presence of our heavenly Father. But as essential as this concept of God as Father is, it is not comprehensive. In order to pray properly, we must keep the truth in mind that God our Father is also infinite. He is knowable only to the extent that he has chosen to reveal himself to our finite understanding.

My personal computer illustrates this point. I depend on my computer to perform important tasks. But I have little understanding of the technology that accomplishes the amazing things it does for me. I am content to accept the usefulness of the device without feeling compelled to explore the abstruse technological universe behind it. I may think of God my heavenly Father in a similar manner. I turn to my Father in prayer because he is always accessible, and he has done amazing things for me. God our Father in heaven is above and beyond the parameters of our concepts of him. All who will pray the Lord's Prayer properly are wont to ponder the manifold aspects of our heavenly Father's deity.

God has chosen to disclose himself to us in various ways. It is our responsibility to know him as fully as he has revealed himself to us. In the meeting of the Areopagus in Athens the apostle Paul explained the Lord God to the philosophers:

> From one man he made every nation of men, that they should inhabit the whole earth; and he determined the times set for them and the exact places where they should live. God did this so that men would seek him and perhaps reach out for him and find him, though he is not far from each of us (Acts 17:26–27).

Prayer's Mystery

We cannot pray the Lord's Prayer effectively if the one to whom we pray it is a figment of our imagination. Supplicating a specter of our own fabrication is hardly different from what pagan worshipers do in their temples, surrounded by grotesque images of imagined deities. Our prayer is to the Lord God Almighty revealed to us in the Holy Scriptures.

There is a mystery in praying to our Almighty Father in heaven. What kind of connection do finite beings have with an infinite God? We cannot speak or write to a fellow human being without having a fairly accurate mental concept of the person addressed. When I speak by telephone to someone I know, I have a clear picture in mind. I can "see" the person. If the person is a stranger I have at least a vague concept of a woman or a man, approximate age, perhaps nationality, or the person's mood—all based on the sound of the voice. Interpersonal communication involves a mental image. To some extent, however, social media have changed our mindset. It is now possible to correspond in an impersonal but intimate manner with people we have never met, nor do we see or hear.

People used to keep in touch with pen pals they had never met personally. Having a pen pal illustrates the way some of God's children relate to him. They communicate regularly, but are satisfied to have only scant knowledge of God to whom they pray. But the Prayer Christ gave to his followers makes no accommodation for a pen-pal-like relationship with God. When Jesus taught his followers to pray he told them to conceive of God as their Father.

How do we speak to God? I used to have a fuzzy concept of a transcendent divine presence that listened to my prayers. My prayers were sincere, but I struggled with the concept of speaking to a Father I could not picture. I found no satisfactory resolution to my struggle in the Scriptures, so I resolved to live with an unanswered question. One of my college professors told us to learn to live with unanswered questions. George MacDonald also addressed this challenge:

"You who know that for which we groan, you whom Jesus called Father, we appeal to you, not as we imagine you but as you see yourself, as Jesus knows you. To your very self we cry—help us! Be our Father.[45]

Peniel

In the spring of 2007 Liz and I spent a week at SonScape Retreat Ministries in Woodland Park, Colorado. One day, on a ridge in view of Pike's Peak, I knelt to pray. For several hours I wrestled in prayer about addressing a God I believed in and I loved, but I could not see or imagine. Out of the intimacy of that holy rendezvous with God came this prayer:

Almighty God in heaven, my Father, coming to you is precious to me. It is not a duty or a chore. But I have difficulty conceptualizing that I am somehow in the presence of God who is more than I am able to imagine or conceive of—and God who sees through me completely. I cannot pretend anything when I am in your presence. The things I think in order to convince myself that you are attentive to my prayer—like what you are doing while I am praying—may or may not be true. Father, I just want to be genuine with you, because that is the sincere desire of my heart. I want to be with you, and to know it is real. I don't ask you for anything, except for everything that I should have in order to be near to you. I don't know what those things are, but I think of contentment—not feeling that something important is missing in my relationship with you. When I am contented with you, then you—and only you—decide what else is necessary.

You as my God and my wise, loving Father decide what else I should know, or experience, or see, or feel, or lose, or receive, or change. Please help me to want nothing more than the contentment of being with you. When I am contented with you, I have no fear. Give me the strength to accept what you choose to do and the wisdom to see nothing more than your presence behind it. I don't need to understand why.

That place on the mountain between two large rocks became my *Peniel. Peniel* means "face of God." After Jacob struggled with God all night, ". . . Jacob called the place [of that meeting] *Peniel,* saying, 'It is because I saw God face to face, and yet my life was spared'" (Genesis 32:30). I did not share Jacob's encounter by seeing God face to face, but my experience was similar. It spared me further perplexity about my Father's presence when I pray.

As God's children we pray to our heavenly Father in the context of a genuine relationship with the infinite God who is incomprehensible to our finite understanding. But he has revealed himself sufficiently so that as mortal beings we can speak intelligently about knowing God. We address him as "Our Father."

Praying to Jesus

Can praying to Jesus instead of praying to the Father resolve this problem for those who still try to visualize God when they pray? Is substituting Jesus Christ an acceptable alternative? Is it appropriate to advise someone, "Just pray to Jesus Christ, because then you can picture God as a person when you pray"? After all, didn't Jesus tell Philip that anyone who had seen him had seen the Father? (John 14:9) Doesn't the Bible say that Jesus Christ is "the image of the invisible God"? (Colossians 1:15) John wrote, "No one has ever seen God, but God the One and Only, who is at the Father's side, has made him known" (John 1:18). May we picture God the Son Incarnate as a first century middle-eastern male? Would that be an appropriate mental image of our Father in heaven?

If we so desire, it is acceptable to address prayer to Jesus Christ. But Jesus himself told his followers to pray to their Father in heaven. He made a distinction between himself and the Father, even though he also made it clear that he and the Father are one (John 17:11, 22). This is no trivial matter, as we see in John Stott's comment on the Lord's Prayer:

> The entire formula is less concerned with the proper protocol in approaching Deity than with the truth of who he is, to establish within the believer the right frame of mind.[46]

We can understand God only to the degree that he has chosen to reveal himself. He intends his children to know him primarily as our Father in heaven.

The Indispensable Name, Father

Consider this question: What if Christ had not given his disciples the specific designation "Our Father" for their prayer to God? What if he had merely instructed his followers: "When you pray to God Almighty, start by saying 'Hallowed be your name'"? What name do you suppose they might have chosen to address the one to whom they prayed? Perhaps they would have begun by saying, "Your Eternal Majesty, hallowed be your name." That seems fitting, because much is said in Scripture about God's incomparable greatness and glory. But Jesus specifically instructed them to pray to "Our Father." Surely a more august title could be applied to the Almighty God than the familiar term "Father." Given the plethora of options, "Father" seems too common.

In Britain, the honorific "Sir" is conferred upon a person knighted by the reigning monarch. The nation is apprised of the exploits that merited the grand title. The name testifies to a compelling attribute of the person. Similarly, when Jesus taught his disciples to address God as "Our Father," he implied that from the perspective of his followers, God's supreme attribute is "Father." It is the hallmark of God's dealings with mankind. Nothing else that we know about God matches his Fatherhood. Yes, God is our King; God is our Judge; God is our Creator; God is our Master; but above all, God is our Father. Why is God's Fatherhood preeminent? Not because he created us to be part of his awesome universe, nor because of his absolute authority over every aspect of our being, but because he made us in his own image and likeness.

Superbly Human

Both the prophet Isaiah (6:1–4) and John the Revelator (Revelation chapters 4, 5, and 19) describe the heavenly beings surrounding the throne to worship God. The actors and the venue are awe inspiring, beyond earthly counterpart. The scene portrays Almighty God in his glory adored by heavenly beings. But none of those splendid heavenly creatures is as precious to God as mankind. In the late nineteenth century Johnson Oatman, Jr. composed a hymn that celebrates mankind's unique status:

There is singing up in Heaven
such as we have never known,
Where the angels sing the praises
of the Lamb upon the throne,

Their sweet harps are ever tuneful,
and their voices always clear,
O that we might be more like them
while we serve the Master here!

Refrain
Holy, holy, is what the angels sing,
And I expect to help them
make the courts of Heaven ring;
But when I sing redemption's story,
they will fold their wings,
For angels never felt the joys
that our salvation brings.[47]

After God created everything on earth, God created mankind in his image and according to his likeness. In the entire universe mankind alone bears the image of God. We alone have the opportunity to call God our Father. We are close kin to God himself. This intimate relationship constitutes us human. British historian Paul Johnson wrote:

. . . by cutting the umbilical cord with God, our source of ethical vitality would be gone. Morally we would become nothing better than a species of fantastically clever monkeys. Our ultimate fate would be too horrible to contemplate.[48]

Among all the earthly creatures mankind alone possesses some features that are not controlled by the limitations of time and space. The foremost feature of human nature is the capacity to commune with the eternal God. There is a spiritual dimension that sets mankind apart from all other creatures. Solomon gave this summary of his ponderings:

I have seen the burden God has laid on men. He has
made everything beautiful in its time. He has also
set eternity in the hearts of men; yet they cannot
fathom what God has done from beginning to end
(Ecclesiastes 3:10–11).

The uniqueness of having eternity in our hearts qualifies
us to address God meaningfully as "Father." To pray to God
as our Father is to pray with heightened intelligence and
feeling.

A Holy Intimacy with God

There is, however, a greater purpose in addressing God
as our Father than having a way of relating that is intelligible
to us. God created mankind in his likeness so that he and his
highest creation might enjoy an intimate relationship like
that of a father with his children (cf. Psalm 8:5). The apostle
Paul told the Roman Christians that those who live according
to the sinful nature will die, but those who live by the Spirit,
putting to death the misdeeds of the body, will live (Romans
8:13). Then he explained,

. . . because those who are led by the Spirit of God
are sons of God. For you did not receive a spirit that
makes you a slave again to fear, but you received
the Spirit of sonship. And by him we cry, '*Abba*,
Father.' The Spirit himself testifies with our spirit
that we are God's children (Romans 8:14–16).

He wrote in a similar vein to the Galatian believers:
"Because you are sons, God sent the Spirit of his Son into
our hearts, the Spirit who calls out '*Abba*, Father'"
(Galatians 4:6). It is the presence of the Holy Spirit—the

Spirit of Christ—in our lives that validates our identity as children of the heavenly Father. We are, therefore, entitled to call out to God, adding the familiar Aramaic word for father—*abba* (Mark 14:36; Romans 8:15: Galatians 4:6). So we pray "*Abba*, Father" and "Our Father in heaven."

My grandson Wrigley and granddaughter Lucy call me "Pops." Few joys can compare with my delight when my twin grandchildren greet me as Pops. The fact that God chose to be known as Father implies that he experiences divine bliss when his children who bear his "image" address him as "*Abba*" or "our Father." Christ instructed his followers to address God as Father because God has chosen fatherhood to be his attribute of intimacy with those he created in his image. God created mankind so that he would experience something unique, a relationship found nowhere else in his vast creation.

In this regard it may be necessary to adjust our concept of God. Do not think of God as the all-powerful, infinite, eternal, sovereign, holy Creator who deigns to let us call him Father. I consider the opening clause in the Lord's Prayer to be our response to God saying, in effect, "call me Father." One of the reasons why God created humankind was so that he might define fatherhood and delight in it.

When Liz and I took our grandchildren on an outing we had to remind them over and over to hold our hands. They were young and they tended to rush ahead of us to explore a myriad of attractions awaiting them. When my grandson reached up to take my hand without me having to tell him, my pleasure was indescribable. I imagine the joy to my heavenly Father when I reach out to him and say "*Abba*, Father" just because I want to. I cannot imagine the grief to our heavenly Father when his children stubbornly refuse to depend on him and willfully wrench their hands from his safe clasp to run off and do what they want. When children call out to their earthly father, it is often an appeal to the father to comfort, to defend, or to provide. Helmut Thielicke points out that what we ask of a father is that he should act as a father should.[49] God is the consummate definition of fatherhood. But if we make an earthly father the model according to which God's fatherhood is fashioned in our thinking, we weaken the bond we have with God our heavenly Father.

The Ultimate Definition of Fatherhood

There are some points of correspondence between a good earthly father and our heavenly Father. But God alone is the definitive standard of fatherhood. God is holy. He is radically and essentially "other." The fact that our Father is in heaven underscores his holiness—his transcendent uniqueness. God overwhelms the most superlative expressions of earthly fatherhood. Our heavenly Father outdoes every description we use to try to define him. Our best explanations of God are grounded in the truths he himself has revealed to us. Even our efforts to apprehend God according to what he has revealed about himself are inadequate. They fall woefully short of grasping the fullness of his divine fatherhood.

Our Father in heaven gives meaning to life. Everything separated from God has lost the fullness of its intended purpose. The apostle Paul said concerning Christ who is the image of the invisible God, ". . . in him all things hold together" (Colossians 1:17). Disconnected from God, life falls apart. People who have no connection to God are adrift. That describes sin's effect. It separates people from God. Life as we see it all around us is at any given moment a snapshot of the consequences of being disconnected from the one in whom all things hold together.

The gospel of God is the good news of the way people, alienated from God because of sin, may be reconciled with God. The gospel reveals how people become qualified to address God as "Our Father in heaven." The good news of what God has done for helpless mankind recalibrates people's lives to be in harmony with God. All who have come into a relationship with God through faith in Jesus Christ have the privilege and the obligation to address God as Father. The Apostle Paul wrote to the Ephesian church: "For this reason I kneel before the Father, from whom his whole family in heaven and on earth derives its name" (Ephesians 3:14–15). The phrase, his "whole family" translates *pasa patria.* It incorporates all who have a common ancestor. It is the total family of God, not only on earth but also in heaven. It comprises the Father's children here, and those who have passed on to their eternal inheritance with the Father.

Our Father's Uncompromising Standards

Many who pray to God the Father have not made their relationship with him their highest priority. Their most cherished relationships are earth-bound. They do not recognize that God must be principal in their thoughts and affections—otherwise they pray amiss. God described himself as a jealous God. He will not forever tolerate granting to another the affection that is rightfully his alone. Moses instructed Israel, "Love the Lord your God with all your heart and with all your soul and with all your strength" (Deuteronomy 6:5). The mercy of God our Father is great beyond comprehension, but he does not indulge the misbehavior of his children. Through the prophet Nathan the Lord spoke to King David concerning his offspring who was to succeed him as king:

I will be his father, and he will be my son. When he does wrong, I will punish him with the rod of men, with floggings inflicted by men. But my love will never be taken away from him, as I took it away from Saul, whom I removed from before you (2 Samuel 7:14–15)

This insight helps us to understand God in his divine role of Father. "Father" is the dominating motif of his relationship with all who have placed their trust in Jesus Christ, who is God the Savior.

During Israel's early monarchy God warned the king of severe repercussions for wrongdoing. God has not become more lenient with time. We have no grounds to expect our heavenly Father to indulge wrongdoing by his children in the modern era. William Barclay insisted, "We must never use the word Father in regard to God cheaply, easily, and sentimentally."[50] A good father on earth commands the respect of his children. He, in turn, demonstrates unconditional love for them. When we pray, "Our Father," a reverent fear of dishonoring our Lord is the proper attitude with which we approach God.

Picture a child in ancient times whose father is a good king. The young prince enters the throne room with a solemn respect for the sovereign on the throne. At the same time he knows that he will receive a loving welcome from his father. In obeisance he approaches no closer than the footstool, knowing that the king will reach out and draw him into a warm embrace. Jesus likewise speaks of the Father being benevolent and kindly disposed toward his children.

I heard a speaker at a men's breakfast tell of an incident when he was a young father. He was trying to feed his infant daughter in her high chair. She would not cooperate. She kept spitting out the food and throwing it on the floor. He eventually lost his temper and screamed at her with a string of expletives. The doorbell rang. It was the next-door neighbor. The kitchen window was open and he had heard it all. He asked if everything was okay, wanting to be certain before calling the police to report child abuse. As I listened to him I was grateful that our heavenly Father never loses his temper with us, no matter how defiant and stubborn we are. He is patient; his heart is kind beyond all measure.

Jesus encouraged his disciples to offer petitions to God their Father—to ask, seek, and knock (Matthew 7:7–8). Then he added, "If you, then, though you are evil, know how to give good gifts to your children, how much more will your Father in heaven give good gifts to those who ask him!" (Matthew 7:11) Note the qualification in the clause above, "though you are evil." Was it Christ's assessment that his disciples were wicked men, or was he indicating the spiritual condition of fallen humanity? New Testament commentators (R. V. G. Tasker,[51] William Hendricksen,[52] and D. A. Carson[53]) favor the latter interpretation.

The Lord's Prayer is unambiguous. God is "our Father in heaven." He does not permit this truth of his divine nature to be corrupted by any negative notions of father that may have been ingrained into our psyches.

The Family of God

The Hebrews were the people of God. But slavery in Egypt for 430 years (Exodus 12:40–41) had dimmed their knowledge of the God of their forefathers. In the Passover and the Exodus God revived their identity as his people by delivering them from slavery (Exodus 12:1–51). Through Moses, God instructed his people to commemorate the Passover throughout their generations (Exodus 12:17). The Passover was an ongoing reminder that they were God's chosen people, rescued from bondage.

Jesus Christ inaugurated the Lord's Supper, also known as Communion, in the context of the Passover observance (Luke 22:7–20). The Apostle Paul referred to Christ as "our Passover lamb" (1 Corinthians 5:7). By his sacrifice for our sins on the cross, Christ delivered us from bondage to Satan. We became the people of God and we have the right to be called the children of God. He is our Father in heaven. This theme should be prominent in the regular observance of Communion in our churches. Whenever Christians celebrate the Lord's Supper, they testify that they are the children of God.

God's children are in this corrupt world for a purpose. William Barclay commented, "It will always help us if we regard this world as organized not for our comfort but for our training."[54] Since God made mankind in his image and likeness, the optimum way for mortals to relate to him is as family. We are his children undergoing training as sojourners on earth.

We have the high privilege of calling God our Father. There is an old story, perhaps apocryphal, about a young prince. His parents, the King and Queen had sheltered him since birth from the trappings of royalty. He knew his father only as "Daddy." Then the time came to introduce the child of the king to grand events that would soon become a part of his world. He was taken to a gala where he watched people approach his father with a formality that was foreign to the little prince. They bowed, curtseyed, saluted, and addressed his father with extreme deference. He nudged his mother, the Queen, and whispered, "Why are those people doing that?" His mother answered, "Because your Father is the King. He is more important than anyone else." The prince paused for a moment, then asked, "Is it okay if I still call him Daddy?"

The privilege of calling out to God as our Father includes some boundaries. We must disabuse ourselves of any attitude toward God that smacks of a flippant familiarity. We are children of the King who are welcome in heaven's throne room. But we do not bound casually up to the throne of the Most High, and in utter disregard of his ineffable holiness, plop ourselves in the Father's lap. Rather, with sanctified imaginations we approach God's footstool at the throne of heaven (vis. Psalm 99:5) to adore the Almighty. Because we are his children, our Father reaches out and takes us into his arms. Jason Ingram and Reuben Morgan wrote the lyrics of a song, *Forever Reign,* about intimacy with God. They use the image of a child running to the arms of his father, but the richness of reverence for God is pervasive in the song:

Refrain:
(Oh) I'm running to your arms
The riches of your love
Will always be enough
Nothing compares to your embrace
Light of the world forever reign.

Third Stanza:
You are more, You are more
Than my words will ever say
You are Lord, You are Lord
All creation will proclaim
You are here, You are here
In Your presence I'm made whole
You are God, You are God
Of all else I'm letting go.[55]

The Right to Call God our Father

Does the mere fact of being human entitle a person to call God "our Father"? No, not all are qualified to claim God as Father. Jesus explained that only his followers have God as their Father. John the Evangelist, introducing Christ as the Word, wrote, "yet to all who received him, to those who believed in his name, he gave the right to become children of God—children born not of natural descent, nor of human decision, or a husband's will, but born of God" (John 1:12–13).

In his letters to the churches the apostle Paul says much about being children of God—for example, "You are all sons of God through faith in Jesus Christ" (Galatians 3:26); "Those who are led by the Spirit of God are sons of God" (Romans 8:14); and

> But when the time had fully come, God sent his Son, born of a woman, born under the law, to redeem those under law, that we might receive the full rights of sons. Because you are sons, God sent the Spirit of his Son into your hearts, the Spirit who calls out, *Abba,* Father. So you are no longer a slave, but a son; and since you are a son, God has made you also an heir (Galatians 4:4–7).

William Barclay said this about the Lord's Prayer: "It is a prayer which only one who is committed to Jesus Christ can take upon his lips with any meaning."[56] According to Hendriksen, this is not a debatable matter:

> It is immediately clear that not everyone is privileged to address God thus. This is the exclusive prerogative of those who are 'in Christ' (John 1:12; Romans 8:14–17; Galatians 4:6; 2 Corinthians 6:18; 1 John 3:1–2) . . . this model prayer is for believers in the Lord Jesus Christ, for them alone.[57]

The weight of the Scriptural evidence makes this an incontrovertible tenet of the Christian faith: addressing God in prayer as "our Father" is not the right of all human beings.

Jesus said, "No one knows the Son except the Father, and no one knows the Father except the Son and those to whom the Son chooses to reveal him" (Matthew 11:27). When some Sadducees tested Jesus by asking him about marriage in the resurrection, Jesus explained that "those who participate in the resurrection from the dead do not marry and they can no longer die for they are like the angels. They are God's children since they are children of the resurrection" (Luke 20:34–36). Outside the empty tomb the risen Jesus identified his followers as children of our heavenly Father. He said to Mary, "Do not hold on to me, for I have not yet returned to the Father. Go instead to my brothers and tell them, 'I am returning to my Father and your Father, to my God and your God'" (John 20:17).

One of the implications of being children of our heavenly father is the duty to love our enemies. Jesus told his disciples, "Love your enemies and pray for those who persecute you, that you may be sons of your Father in heaven" (Matthew 5:44–45). The apostle John wrote, "Everyone who believes that Jesus is the Christ is born of God, and everyone who loves the father loves his child as well" (1 John 5:1).

Paul explained to the Ephesian church that we have become children of God by adoption through Jesus Christ (Ephesians 1:4–5). He assured them that we "are no longer foreigners and aliens, but fellow citizens with God's people and members of God's household" (Ephesians 2:19). And what was their status in God's household? It was the status of children who may call God their father. This includes the privilege of being heirs (Galatians 4:7).

Parental Discipline

As God's children we are heirs of God, but we are not exempted from parental discipline. The hardships of our sojourn as aliens in a world controlled by the evil one are divine discipline that proves we are children of the heavenly Father. The writer of the Letter to the Hebrews explained:

> Endure hardship as discipline; God is treating you as sons. For what son is not disciplined by his father? If you are not disciplined (and everyone undergoes discipline), then you are illegitimate children and not true sons (Hebrews 12:7–8).

There is no biblical basis for the notion that our heavenly Father wishes his children to enjoy a comfortable, easy life in this world. We are "strangers in the world" where our enemy "the devil prowls like a roaring lion looking for someone to devour" (1 Peter 5:8). Instead of settling down and relaxing, God's children must live in a constant state of spiritual alertness. This is not accidental; it is intentional. It is intended to produce in us the perseverance, character, and hope that our Father wants to see in his children.

Sons and Daughters by Birth and Adoption

Some may be offended by the reference to sons, with no mention of daughters. But the Scriptures are not sexist in this teaching. Throughout the biblical era, society assigned to females a lower status than to males. This was a reality in the cultural milieu of the first century church. Therefore, the reference to sons of God reflects a cultural sensitivity. All believers in Christ, both females and males, are accorded the full rights of sons in the family of God the Father.

According to God's Word, our place in the Father's family is both by birth and by adoption. How can we be both adopted into God's family and born into God's family? (John 1:13) Our natural condition is depraved children of the evil one. The means of becoming the children of God is a work of God variously called redemption, reconciliation, salvation, adoption, and being born again or born from above. These inspired metaphors enlighten our understanding of God's work in rescuing us from damnation and making us his children for eternity. The apostle Paul gives the succinct explanation that, "We are God's workmanship, created in Christ Jesus to do good works" (Ephesians 2:10).

Were it not for Jesus Christ's teaching about God the Father, our prayers would be like those of the people of Athens who worshiped in their pantheon an "unknown God" (Acts 17:23). Not so when God's children pray. There is a divine and transcendent quality to our knowledge of God our heavenly Father. Those to whom Christ the Son reveals the Father gain an intimate understanding beyond merely knowing about God. Thielicke remarked,

> The main thing in prayer is not that we present particular petitions but that we enter into communion, into a personal relationship with the Father. If I do nothing else but say from the bottom of my heart, 'Dear Heavenly Father,' the main thing has already happened.[58]

Loving God

As God's children on earth our most important relationship is with our Father in heaven. No other relationship merits our unique affection and allegiance for God our Father. This obligation is implicit in the command the Lord God gave to his people as they prepared to cross the Jordan into the Promised Land, "Love the Lord your God with all your heart and with all your soul and with all your mind and with all your strength." Jesus Christ repeated it in the answer he gave to the question about the greatest commandment (Deuteronomy 6:5; Matthew 22:37; Mark 12:30; Luke 10:27). Our love for our Father in heaven encompasses all our human faculties—heart, soul, mind, and strength. Genuine love for God emanates from every part of us. A lackadaisical attitude toward God is unacceptable. When the apostle Paul addressed the issue of God's children eating food that had been sacrificed to idols, he gave a stern warning:

> No, but the sacrifices of pagans are offered to demons, not to God, and I do not want you to be participants with demons. You cannot drink the cup of the Lord and the cup of demons too; you cannot have a part in both the Lord's table and the table of demons. Are we trying to arouse the Lord's jealousy? Are we stronger than he? (1 Corinthians 10:20–22)

The lesson is unambiguous. The children of our Father in heaven must love him in a manner that brooks no rival. Compare it to the exclusionary principle in the relationship between marriage partners. If a woman is physically intimate with a man not her husband, how can she claim to love her husband? She may explain that she loves him with her mind. She appreciates and admires him as a good provider for her and for their children. Her excuse might be that he does not satisfy all her desires. Such a perspective would be intolerable in our relationship with God. If we claim to love the Lord God because of his amazing grace, but we have a greater passion for all the material stuff he has not supplied, our love for God is not genuine. God has decreed that his people must love him with all their being. Jesus said no one can serve two masters; you cannot serve both God and money (Matthew 6:24; Luke 16:13).

The Sons of Korah sang with a passionate longing for God, "As the deer pants for streams of water, so my soul pants for you" (Psalm 42:1). David's devotion to God infused many of his Psalms with a holy passion. The Apostle John explained the practical power of love for God:

> This is love for God: to obey his commands. And his commands are not burdensome, for every one born of God overcomes the world. This is the victory that has overcome the world, even our faith (1 John 5:3–4).

The Source and Supply of Good

The pronoun "our" in "Our Father in heaven" is pivotal. It is possessive. The Father belongs to us, and we belong to him. He is ours. An intimate connection with God is paramount. The psalmist David grasped this. He said, "I said to the Lord, 'You are my Lord; apart from you I have no good thing'" (Psalm 16:2). In a corrupt world ravaged by evil, God our Father alone is the source and supply of good. David continued:

> As for the saints who are in the land, they are the glorious ones in whom is all my delight. The sorrows of those will increase who run after other gods. I will not pour out their libations of blood or take up their names on my lips. Lord, you have assigned me my portion and my cup; you have made my lot secure. The boundary lines have fallen

for me in pleasant places; surely I have a delightful inheritance. I will praise the Lord, who counsels me; even at night my heart instructs me. I have set the Lord always before me. Because he is at my right hand, I will not be shaken. Therefore my heart is glad and my tongue rejoices; my body also will rest secure, because you will not abandon me to the grave, nor will you let your Holy One see decay. You have made known to me the path of life; you will fill me with joy in your presence, with eternal pleasures at your right hand (Psalm 16:3–11).

Apart from our Father in Heaven we have no good thing. Secular society bears this out. For people alienated from God, all "good things" are circumscribed by this world. The values they hold dear are what Christ warned his followers not to pursue, because earthly treasure is destined for destruction like trash.

A common caricature of "father" is the family buffoon who kowtows to a self-centered, domineering wife and is manipulated by unruly children. Such a boorish familiarity with our heavenly Father is a cosmic insult and is the diametrical opposite of the biblical description of God as Father. Even a healthy relationship with an earthly father is woefully deficient in describing how to associate with our heavenly Father. Our Father in heaven is qualitatively distinct from earthly fathers. In contrast to our earthly fathers, God is called "the Father of our spirits" (Hebrews 12:9). God is our spiritual Father.

For many women, and some men, "Father" is a repugnant concept. Their earthly father was absent or abusive or a drunken oaf that was a perpetual embarrassment to the family. Their experience with an earthly father is a painful recollection. For them the concept of God as Father is revolting. They never knew genuine love or protection by a father.

I am grateful that the concept of God as a Father has been positive for me since childhood. I did, however, fear my heavenly Father as a stern judge. A little children's song may have had something to do with that:

O be careful little eyes what you see,
O be careful little eyes what you see,
There's a Father up above
And He's looking down in love.
So, be careful little eyes what you see.[59]

I was much more mindful of my Father looking down on me than I was of his love. If he became upset with what he saw, I imagined him hollering from heaven, "Hey, John! Cut that out!"

A young woman in our church asked to meet with me. She told me that she could not bring herself to love God if she had to refer to him as her Father. She prayed only to God, not to God the Father. She justified her veto of Christ's directive to address God as Father on the grounds that she had a horrible relationship with her earthly father. Her natural father was a brute who had abused her and told her she was worthless trash. My training in pastoral counseling in seminary had ill-equipped me to deal with her crisis. I do not recall what I said to her; my goal was just to keep her from jettisoning her faith. Her struggle is not unique. She stands in a throng of Christian women haunted by the trauma of what their fathers did to them, or did not do for them. Their odious image of an earthly father has shaped their concept of God as Father, and it is repulsive.

Do we have the right to exempt such people from addressing God as Father because the term is a personal affront to them? Must the Almighty abandon his chosen name with its strong family significance because some fathers have tarnished the earthly image? Should we seek out a less offensive motif as a bypass to God for those who cringe at the thought of having to call him Father? To do so would deny the clear instruction of Jesus Christ. We dishonor our heavenly Father if we expect God to accommodate our qualms by revising his revelation of himself. Such a notion is the ultimate in conceit. There should certainly be an accommodation, not by God, but by the person who struggles with the designation *Father*. People who wrestle with negative concepts of father may need assistance to reshape their severely flawed image when they go to God in prayer. An individual's personal struggle cannot be resolved by redefining God.

The Father's Kindness

Our Father in heaven is the epitome of fatherhood. In him we find the zenith of affection, intimacy, and compassion for his beloved children on earth. We, therefore, pray to our Father who hears us from heaven as we stumble and frequently fall in our pilgrimage as aliens in a hostile world.

In the prayer of the returned exiles after the rebuilding of the wall of Jerusalem they recounted Israel's repeated disobedience and turning from God's way. Then we read this glorious statement, "And when they cried out to you again, you heard from heaven, and in your compassion you delivered them time after time" (Nehemiah 9:28). As sojourners in enemy territory God's people today are like those Israelites. We also succumb to the temptations that lure us from his pathway. Who among us has not snubbed our Father's guidance? However, like the Israelites in hostile territory, we too may call out to our Father who hears from heaven and delivers his people time after time.

Jesus told the parable of the lost son to help us understand God as Father. The son had dishonored his father and had landed in a shameful predicament. But the father was always waiting and watching for his lost son to come home (Luke 15:20). God our Father in heaven watches over his children with compassion. When we turn to God and pray "Our Father" he is eager to welcome his children. Our Father is pleased when his children turn their attention to him and appeal to him for mercy. Many of the "grand old hymns" exult in the love of our heavenly Father toward us. A few examples are Charles Wesley's *And Can It Be* in which he celebrated the amazing love of God; *The Love of God* by F. M. Lehman which stated that "the love of God is greater far than tongue or pen can ever tell"[60]; and *Wonder of It All*, in which George Beverly Shea wrote, "The wonder of it all! Just to think that God loves me."[61] These correspond with what John wrote in his Gospel, "For God so loved the world that he gave his one and only Son, that whoever believes in him shall not perish but have eternal life" (John 3:16). God's amazing love is the reason for our standing as his children.

Those who are righteous are called children of God. The apostle John wrote,

> Everyone who does what is right has been born of him. How great is the love the Father has lavished on us, that we should be called children of God! And that is what we are! The reason the world does not know us is that it did not know him. Dear friends, now we are children of God, and what we will be has not yet been made known, but we know that when he appears, we shall be like him, for we

shall see him as he is. Everyone who has this hope in him purifies himself, just as he is pure (1 John 2:29–3:3).

We become children of God by being born of God. When he appears we will be transformed to be like our Father, seeing him as he is. In the same letter John continued,

> No one who is born of God will continue to sin, because God's seed remains in him; he cannot go on sinning, because he has been born of God. This is how we know who the children of God are and who the children of the devil are: Anyone who does not do what is right is not a child of God; nor is anyone who does not love his brother (1 John 3:9–10).

How do we reconcile John's words with the frequent calls to God's children in Scripture to confess their sins? It is undeniable that God's children do sin, but they are no longer addicted to sin or trapped in sin, nor do they delight in sin. When they sin, their souls are grieved because they have dishonored their holy Father, and they acknowledge their need to repent.

God Knows Us by Name

Our Father in heaven knows each of us by name. None of us is an insignificant number among the hordes of God's children. George Foreman, a former two-time world heavyweight boxing champion and Olympic gold medalist, has twelve children. He named each of his five sons "George." There is George Jr., George III, George IV, George V and George VI. Could a parent do anything more

123

to blur the distinctiveness and individuality of his children? Our Father in heaven's way of dealing with his children is vastly different. He treats each of us as a unique child whom he loves. The Lord's Prayer is for the children of their Father in heaven who knows them individually better than they know themselves. His heart is kind, and he is attentive to his children who need deliverance time after time.

God our Father loves his children and he pays attention to those who love him. To claim to know God, but display no evidence of loving him, is worthless. The Apostle Paul contrasts the arrogance that accompanies knowledge with the blessing that comes with loving God. He writes:

> We know that we all possess knowledge. Knowledge puffs up, but love builds up. The man who thinks he knows something does not yet know as he ought to know. But the man who loves God is known by God (1 Corinthians 8:1b–3).

Thielicke quotes Goethe's remark that one can understand only what one loves.[62] Anyone who claims to know God without being motivated by love for God is, at best, doing theology as an academic exercise. Anyone who professes to love God without heeding what God has revealed about himself, dabbles in the idolatry of those who construct an idol from their own fantasies.

Our Father, the Creator, King, Judge, and Master

In Scripture God has disclosed himself as Father as well as Creator and Sovereign over all that exists. Christ's instruction to pray to our Father in heaven is the primary way God has chosen for us to relate to him. We do not address God as our Creator in heaven when we, his children, pray to him.

What is the significance of praying to God as "our Father" and not as "our Creator?" It challenges our intellectual faculties to wrap our minds around either concept. But our finite minds can appreciate immeasurably more about God as Father than about God as Creator. Our familiarity with the role of father in a human family helps us to conceive of God with the intimacy he has invested in our relationship with him. If God treated us as his creatures rather than his children, our condition would be radically different. A Creator seeing imperfections and corruptions in his creatures might well put an end to them and start over. A potter creating a vase will toss it aside if it cracks, and begin afresh with new clay. After all, the divine image is not stamped into the core of those that are merely part of his creation.

God does not relate to mankind primarily as King. A king regards the people under his rule as his subjects. If they rebel against him he will take action to limit or remove their liberties. Nor does God relate to us as Judge. As it applies to God's children, the role of judge would be superfluous because there is no condemnation to those who are his children through faith in Christ Jesus (Romans 8:1).

Our God wants mankind to be able to address him, not as "our Creator," or "our King" or "our Judge." God wishes to relate to those created in his image as the heavenly Father in fellowship with his children. He created us as his offspring. God's children have "God's seed" in them (1 John 3:9). As our Father he responds to our weaknesses and flaws with love, discipline, and correction. In writing to the Corinthian Church the apostle Paul extolled the compassion of God the Father:

Praise be to the God and Father of our Lord Jesus Christ, the Father of compassion and the God of all comfort, who comforts us in all our troubles, so that we can comfort those in any trouble with the comfort we ourselves have received from God (2 Corinthians 1:3–4).

We do not think of a Creator as being merciful. Nor is mercy the chief trait of a King or Judge. But a loving Father is known for his mercy and kindness, even when his children defy him. The fact that Jesus taught his followers to pray to God as our Father should be a major encouragement to us. When we pray to God in private or in concert with other children of the Father, it is honorable to begin every prayer with the address, "Our Father," or simply "Father" (following Luke's account, Luke 11:2).

Creator

While we focus on God as our Father in heaven, we must not marginalize as insignificant the Scriptural truths about God as Creator. Our Father in heaven is also the Creator. We believe that in the beginning there was only God. C. S. Lewis explained,

Once, before creation, it would have been true to say that everything was God. But God created: He caused things to be other than Himself.[63]

God created the heavens and the earth and all that is in them—*ex nihilo,* out of nothing. God spoke the world and its contents into existence. Our puny mental processors cannot grasp the dynamics of God bringing the universe into existence. Our finite understanding spawns an array of hypotheses and pathetic misconceptions. For example, if at the beginning there was only God, he must surely be greater now than he was before he created! Such thinking is deeply flawed.

When we think of God as Creator, we face the imponderables of a universe measured in distances of thousands or millions of light years. We are flummoxed by the profound mysteries of the structure of matter and the nature of energy. Even the biblical record of creation is accommodated to our limited ability to grasp these esoteric propositions. For us reality is circumscribed by time and space. But God transcends time and space. The apostle Peter explained that God's time scale is entirely different from ours, "But do not forget this one thing, dear friends: With the Lord a day is like a thousand years, and a thousand years are like a day" (2 Peter 3:8). God is eternal and unlimited in all aspects of his essence. How can we grasp all the other spheres of reality in which God may now be involved and has been involved since before the creation of the earth? Even my attempt to explain our limitations is itself fundamentally flawed because of its reliance on terminology that describes our limited grasp of reality.

In pondering God's role as Creator there is a riveting focus on his majesty. We marvel at the wonders of creation. The mountains and oceans are awe-inspiring. We probe the amazing complexities of microbiology and other scientific intricacies. We ponder the unfathomable distances of the stars and their enormity. Earth is located just the right distance from the right size star (our sun), rotating at just the right rate, with a moon of just the right size and distance, orbiting earth at just the right rate—all to support life on planet earth. The ability of tiny butterflies to navigate thousands of miles in their annual migrations, and the facility of some birds to use twigs as tools to dig grubs and insects from their hiding places are examples of the astounding genius in the Creator's design. The better we understand God, the greater our challenge of finding suitable adjectives to affix to his name.

To pray to God as our Creator would keep him remote because of our ignorance of his greatness. With our finite senses we are not equipped to grasp the wonder of all that God has done. Our apprehension of reality is limited to what we can verify empirically. Dinesh D'Souza wrote:

> . . . the religious believer lives in the humble acknowledgment of the limits of human knowledge, knowing that there is a reality greater than, and beyond, that which our sense and minds can ever apprehend.[64]

In the realm of the infinite where God is ruler, there are mysteries we cannot fathom because they lie beyond the plane of what we can grasp within the limits of time and space. Jesus did not instruct his followers to pray, "Our Creator." We may also assume that he did not teach them to address God primarily as "Our Master." These two roles are qualitatively different from each other. Neither term incorporates the concept of God as our Father in heaven.

King Solomon said, "Many curry favor with a ruler, and everyone is the friend of a man who gives gifts" (Proverbs 19:6). The practice of cultivating relationships with wealthy and influential leaders runs rampant today just as it did in the time of Solomon. But with our heavenly Father we do not need to seek privileges. We already have them.

God's essential nature is the province of penetrating theological explorations into what God's revealed word and the wonders of his creation disclose to us. But none can capture the scope of his holiness and majesty. He remains forever the transcendent One, set apart as ineffable. Our heavenly Father is the Almighty, Sovereign, King of Kings, Lord of Lords, the Infinite, Creator, and His Eternal Majesty.

How do these aspects of God's nature, which we are at a loss to define, become evident in God's actions? He delights in being the Father who provides his children with what they need each day. He keeps us gratefully dependent upon him. He invites us to ask him to guide us through tough trials. He wants us to call out to him for protection from the subtle and overt assaults of evil in this fallen world.

The Tragedy of a Lesser View of God

Thielicke said we could never say "our Father" unless the Father had first spoken to us.[65] Praying to God the Father without knowing him is futile. Tragically, this is how millions recite the Lord's Prayer in their empty rituals. When most people turn their attention to God, the concept of Father is probably far from their thoughts. They may say "Our Father, hallowed be your Name." But their thoughts and words are far more likely to be complaints and the assigning of blame to God, as in "Why does God allow the terrorists to wreak their hateful violence upon innocent people? Why did God allow my son to be paralyzed in that accident? Why did God allow that pervert to rape my innocent little daughter? Why does God permit wicked and deceitful people to become national leaders?" Why does God not eliminate the evil behind heinous atrocities graphically portrayed in the media?

Would you wish to decide the level at which God should eradicate evil? Would the evil thoughts and intentions in people's hearts be exempt? Should God intervene only in extreme expressions of evil that are appalling to the majority in society? What we may regard as minor offenses or as extreme wickedness are all affronts to the absolute perfection of our Holy Father in heaven. Our human progenitors in the garden yielded to the temptation presented by the devil which enabled the evil one to usurp divine authority. As a result, the whole world lies in evil. The despicable deeds of mankind are the result of satanic control of our environment. This condition will persist until the end when God the Son, Jesus Christ, will return to judge all evil. Until that happens, mystifying and appalling expressions of evil will assault us.

The tragedy of a jaundiced view of God as unfair or uncaring can be avoided only by a spiritual relationship with God the Son, Jesus Christ. Apart from Jesus Christ as Savior, people launch into the Lord's Prayer as if they are entering an ethereal void without a guidance system. But those who have placed their faith in Jesus Christ as God our Savior are the contemporary counterparts of the disciples. God has delivered them from the dark spiritual domain of the evil one (Colossians 1:13).

Eternal Father

Being the heavenly Father's children is the eternal status of those who belong to God. The earthly motif of a father-child relationship cannot help us to comprehend the magnitude of being a child of God. It is definitely not a fuzzy metaphor of a benevolent father. God is not *like* a father. God *is* our Father in the deepest, most definitive sense; and he is our Father for eternity.

This differs vastly from the earthly stage of life we call childhood. Earthly childhood is transitional. It is not permanent. Children transition from their early state of dependence on their parents, and progress to a more mature relationship. Most children eventually leave their father and mother and are united with a wife or husband. Our mortal life stages are naturally transitional. But the relationship of a child of God to the Father in heaven is different. God as our heavenly Father is and shall ever be our primary relationship.

We never "mature" or move on from an inseparable, dependent bond with our heavenly Father. But this dependence on our Father in heaven in no way conflicts with the myriad of instructions in Scripture to grow up and mature in our faith, to stand firm and not be tossed about like infants in the waves. In relation to our Father in heaven our spiritual maturing and our constant dependence are compatible.

It is common during adolescence and young adulthood to speak of our earthly father without actually having spoken to him for weeks or months. Some children have been alienated from their father for years and do not even know his whereabouts. Sadly, many children do not even know their father—or know who their father is. As a pastor who has officiated at scores of funerals, some of my saddest experiences were dealing with children who had not seen or spoken to their father for years prior to his death. They attended his funeral in an emotional turmoil of guilt and anger focused on a father now gone from them forever.

When we pray to our heavenly Father, let us not allow any disappointing and painful experiences with our natural fathers distort our concept of our heavenly Father. When we pray to our heavenly Father, we must understand that we never outgrow our dependence on him. There is never a time in our lives as God's children when we need our Father in heaven less than we needed him before. Our dependence is constant. He is never absent or too distracted by something else in his vast universe to be there for us.

God did not create mankind to be fatherless. But when Adam sinned in the garden, mankind forfeited the privilege of intimacy with God. Sin caused an estrangement between humans and God the Father. Scripture says the only way to gain the right to be called children of God is by receiving Jesus Christ as Savior and by believing in his name (John 1:10–12). All who pray sincerely and effectively to God as Father in heaven prove that they are not orphans or abandoned children.

If God is not every person's Father, the only alternative is that the devil is the father of those who are not children of God. How did the devil become a father? He did so by deception. In the guise of a serpent in the garden Satan deceived the first couple. They fell for his lie, and as a result the whole creation was cursed.

Some religious people who were determined to kill Jesus told him, "the only father we have is God himself" (John 8:41). Jesus answered them, "You belong to your father, the devil, and you want to carry out your father's desire" (v. 44). Jesus added, "He who belongs to God hears what God says. The reason you do not hear is that you do not belong to God" (John 8: 41–47). Were it not for the atoning and reconciling work on the cross by the one who gave us the Lord's Prayer, we would all be children of the devil. By faith in Christ we are rescued from the horrors of an abusive diabolical father (cf. Colossians 1:13). There are, therefore, only two categories of people—the children of God and the children of the devil.

The Centerpiece of Godly Devotion

The Lord's Prayer is the centerpiece of my devotions in prayer and Scripture. I pray that my attention to the Father will become the default orientation of my affection each day. The words of the hymn, *Holy, Holy, Holy. Lord God Almighty* inspire me to pray, "Early in the morning may my love and may my longing rise to you, our Father."[66]

When we direct our attention to God in the Lord's Prayer, we are part of a great company that shares our privilege of addressing God as Father. Yes, God is my Father in heaven, but I do not relate to God as an only child. There is one who is called the only Son—the only begotten Son, Jesus Christ. So I relate to God as Father in a way that cannot compare with the fullness of the manner in which God the Son, Jesus Christ, relates to God the Father in heaven.

I come to God as one in a multitude, but one who has the assurance that the Father is attentive to my prayer. D. A. Carson wrote, " . . . this is an example of a prayer to be prayed in fellowship with other disciples, not in isolation."[67] Rabbi Skorka explained, "According to our Law, prayers become more powerful if they are recited together by at least ten Jews."[68]

This prayer should probably not be prayed exclusively in isolation, but it may be prayed in private. Whether in concert with others or in private, I do not pray this prayer without recognizing the community of God's children, the heavenly family of which I am part. Immediately before giving this prayer to his disciples, Jesus said, "But when you pray, go into your room, close the door and pray to your Father, who is unseen. Then your Father, who sees what is done in secret, will reward you" (Matthew 6:6). Aside from the plural pronoun "our" in "our Father," there seems to be as much direct biblical support for praying this prayer in private as praying it corporately.

In approaching God as our Father through this prayer, our desire for God must be a consuming passion. Praying to our Father is not a duty to dispense with speedily in order to move on to a more pressing agenda. God is not part of the "furniture" of our lives, always there but in the background, and merely incidental to other matters that compel our attention. Remember the heart-felt longing for God in the song of the sons of Korah:

As the deer pants for streams of water, so my soul pants for you, O God. My soul thirsts for God, for the living God. When can I go and meet with God? (Psalm 42:1–2)

Questions for Discussion and Personal Application

1. In your opinion, do agnostics and atheists lack all sense of spirituality?
2. Thielicke called this world an "un-fatherly place." Give reasons why you agree or disagree with him.
3. When you pray, do you focus more on God or on feeling pleased with yourself for having prayed?
4. Give an example of prodigal love from your experience.
5. Moses established some distinguishing features for the Israelites to set them apart as the children of the Lord God (Deuteronomy 14:1). What are some visible signs people use today to declare that they belong to God?
6. Since God is an invisible personal being, what concept do you have in mind when you pray to him?
7. Do you address your prayers to God the Father, to Jesus as God the Son, or to God the Holy Spirit? What is the reason for your choice?
8. Name some of the implications of mankind's unique status in God's creation.
9. What part does the Holy Spirit play in our relationship with God as Father?
10. List some ways God our Father is greater than the most ideal earthly father.
11. How does a person become qualified to address God as "our Father in heaven?"
12. Tell of an incident when you felt overwhelmed by God the Father's patience and kindness.
13. Can you think of a poem, a song or a hymn that combines both reverence for the Almighty God and intimacy with our heavenly Father?
14. How do you answer those who accuse Scripture of sexism because God's children are called "sons" and not "daughters"?

15. How do you explain what the Scripture says about the heavenly Father's children being born as well as adopted into God's family?

16. How can you clarify what it means to love God with all your heart and with all your soul and with all your mind and with all your strength?

17. Name some affections that threaten our love for God our Father. How do you deal with them?

18. How can you help people to have a positive concept of God as Father if an abusive earthly parent made the concept of father repugnant to them?

19. In Jesus' parable of the lost son in Luke 15:11–32, do you identify more with the older son or with the lost son? Why?

20. Our heavenly Father knows you and everything about you. How does this truth encourage you?

21. List some reasons our prayers are more effective if we address our Father in heaven rather than our Creator in heaven?

22. How can you help people who blame God for bad things happening to them?

23. Cite some basic ways a child of an earthly father is different from a child of our heavenly Father.

24. Jesus told some religious people who wanted to kill him that their father was the devil. How did the devil become their father?

25. Does the address, "Our Father in heaven" require us to utter this prayer in the company of others? If you pray it privately, should you change the wording to "My Father in heaven"?

5. IN HEAVEN

Our God ascends his lofty throne,
Array'd in majesty unknown;
His lustre all the temple fills,
And spreads o'er all th'ethereal hills.,

The holy, holy, holy Lord,
Is by the seraphim adored;
And while they stand beneath his seat,
They veil their faces and their feet.

And can a sinful worm endure
The presence of a God so pure?
Or these polluted lips proclaim
The honours of so grand a name?

Philip Doddridge[69]

Our Heavenly Father is Near to Us

Jesus Christ promised his disciples a place in his Father's house: "Do not let your hearts be troubled. Trust in God; trust also in me. In my Father's house are many rooms; if it were not so, I would have told you. I am going there to prepare a place for you" (John 14:1–2). God's children have a place in the abode of the heavenly Father. That is where we belong.

In his final sermon Stephen quoted Isaiah's prophecy about the Most High God, "Heaven is my throne, and the earth is my footstool" (Acts 7:49; Isaiah 66:1). Our Father is enthroned in heaven. We are on the earth. There is no greater distance than the expanse between the moral decadence that has overtaken our fallen planet and the absolute righteousness of our Father's habitation. This world is in the grip of evil, while our Father is enthroned in unadulterated glory. The implications of us being here and our Father being there are profound.

Nevertheless, God is not an absentee Father with whom we communicate long-distance. God's children need not fear that our heavenly Father is far from us, and we are left spiritually alone to struggle through this world. Our Father always sees and hears us, even when we pray silently in our spirits. There are no strata through which we must ascend by self-abnegating penance to attain the lofty state where our Father may deign to listen to our cry. I have seen elderly penitents on Mt. Royal in Montreal, Canada crawling on hands and knees up the myriad stairs to St. Joseph's Oratory. It is heartbreaking to see the crippled shuffling up the long aisle of the Quiapo Church of the Black Nazarene in Manila, Philippines. Each of these hoped their mortification would win the favor of God. They feared he would not pay attention unless their extreme penance merited his attention in heaven.

On the contrary, God in heaven immediately hears the call of each of his children. His ear is attuned to our cry. Prior to the mid-twentieth century anyone living in a land far from home was painfully aware of the distance from family. Mail might have taken a month or more to arrive via ships on the ocean. By the time the letter arrived the sender's circumstances may have changed markedly. An ailing relative may have died; a newborn child would be old news.

Physical distance is no longer an obstacle. Today we communicate directly and immediately with people anywhere on earth through technological wizardry. On hand-held devices we see and talk in real time with family and friends on the other side of the world. We are on the verge of people's holographic images sitting across from each other and communicating live across a dozen time zones. But physical distance has never been a factor in communicating with God our Father in heaven.

The little phrase "in heaven" does not connote that our heavenly Father is a great distance from us. But many people feel a sense of cosmic isolation. Astronomers use powerful telescopes to probe deep space in their search for any hint of alien life. They speculate that there are among the distant galaxies other solar and planetary systems capable of sustaining life similar to ours on earth. But even if extra-terrestrial life exists, we cannot establish contact because of the distance. The brevity of earthly life compounded by distance measured in thousands-to-millions of light-years makes contact with alien life practically impossible, even if it were to exist. Some propose inter-galactic travel in a human lifetime via so called "worm holes," but this is still considered a far-fetched theory.

The Lord's Prayer assumes our proximity to the Creator who is our heavenly Father, even as we ponder the immensity of his creation. The message of the Bible is about God undertaking to be near to his people. In the Psalms we read "The Lord is near to all who call on him, to all who call on him in truth" (Psalm 145:18).

God's Majestic Presence

We do not know the location of heaven. When the apostles saw Jesus ascend into heaven, how far and how fast did he go? (Luke 24:50; Acts 1:9–11). Perhaps heaven exists in a different dimension whose distance from us cannot be measured in physical or time frames. Could he have intended his visible departure to show that he had transcended earth's time and space constraints? We know that our Father is in heaven, but he is also near to us. He is omnipresent. He is close by to see us and to hear us.

The ancient concept of God's whereabouts was different from what ours may be today. "Heaven" (literally, "the heavens") did not necessarily mean a distant place. It may rather have indicated God's transcendence. Asaph the Psalmist remarked, "We give thanks to you, O God, we give thanks, for your name is near; men tell of your wonderful deeds" (Psalm 75:1). The Lord God made a covenant with his people that allowed them to speak of him as present and benevolently engaged with mankind. The terms of God's covenant with his people in the Old Testament may be summarized under three terms: "My dwelling place will be with them; I will be their God, and they will be my people" (Ezekiel 37:27). The New Testament renewed this rudimentary tenet in God's covenant with his people in the coming of Jesus as *Immanuel*—God with us. God is not absent or far from us. He is near to us; he is with us. Our Father's address is in heaven, but heaven is not the fixed location of God.   Heaven connotes God's majesty and sovereignty. According to the *Catechism of the Catholic Church,* "it does not mean that God is distant, but majestic."[70] We pray to our Father who is within us, and among us in the presence of the Holy Spirit. He is also God in heaven, over all and adored above all. God is both immanent and transcendent.

As humans our most distinguishing feature is the divine image in us. This sets us apart from the rest of creation. We have the capacity to commune with Almighty God, our Father in heaven. The Old Testament presents Israel's Lord God as living and all-powerful. This set him apart from the pagan deities of the surrounding nations. The gods of the nations were idols fashioned by human hands out of stone or metal or wood. God commanded his people not to bow down before any idols, or to tolerate their presence in the land the Lord God gave to his people.

The Ark of the Covenant represented the dwelling of the Lord God among his people. It contained the tablets of the covenant (the Ten Commandments). It was housed in the Most Holy Place in the tabernacle, and later in the Temple in Jerusalem. When the Philistines captured the Ark of God in battle, they placed it in the temple of their god Dagon. The idol of Dagon fell and shattered in the presence of the Ark of the Lord God of Israel. (1 Samuel 6) Serious illness struck the Philistines wherever they moved the Ark. Removing a foreign deity from a nation's territory was thought to deliver the people from the power of that deity. So the Philistines sent the Ark of the Covenant back to Israel.

The Ark represented God's presence, but the Ark was not God. Nothing made by human hands can contain God. But the Philistines considered the Ark to be the actual deity of the people of the Lord God. The pagans believed that deities were localized. A god was the deity of a certain tribe or nation in a particular region. On Mount Carmel the prophet Elijah challenged the priests of the god Baal to petition their deity to produce fire to consume a sacrifice. But Baal was an impotent idol. Then Elijah prayed, "O Lord, God of Abraham, Isaac and Israel, let it be known today that you are God in Israel . . ." (I Kings 18:36) Then the fire of the Lord fell and consumed the offering. "When all the people saw this, they fell prostrate and cried, "The Lord—he is God! The Lord—he is God!" (1 Kings 18:39). It demonstrated that the authority and power of the Lord God was absolute. Elijah proved that the Lord was Israel's God, and that he could do what no man-made god could do.

It has been proposed that one of the reasons for the multitude of dissimilar languages in the relatively small geographic region of Papua New Guinea relates to its mountainous topography. People considered each valley the domain of a local deity that had to be propitiated by the regional population. The tribal people would not venture out of their own valley for fear of coming under the malevolent power of a foreign deity. Fear of hostile gods kept each tribe confined to its own valley for generations. Today an estimated population in excess of six million people speaks over 800 distinct languages. The tribal languages bear little resemblance because the people have long been isolated from each other. Their concept of a god is a spiritual force whose influence is limited to their territory.

The Mystery of God's Abode

God's eternal habitation is in heaven, and his dominion is universal. Heaven is the venue from which God acted to create a vast universe, including this world as the habitation of his highest creation, mankind. We know what it is like to have this earth as our dwelling. We acquit ourselves quite capably in describing our physical world. But we are at a loss to explain the heavenly abode of God our Father. What he has told us about himself in his Word implies that God our Father operates in more dimensions than our minds are equipped to grasp. The apostle Paul identifies God the Son as the Creator,

> He is the image of the invisible God, the firstborn over all creation. For by him all things were created: things in heaven and on earth, visible and invisible, whether thrones or powers or rulers or authorities; all things were created by him and for him. He is before all things, and in him all things hold together (Colossians 1:15–17).

God created everything pertaining to this earthly sphere of reality, and every reality beyond it. From our perspective, God's earthly creation is confined within the dimensions of time and space, with one known exception—mankind. God "set eternity in the hearts of men" (Ecclesiastes 3:11). Yet 'mankind cannot grasp the wonder of what our Father in heaven has prepared for his children beyond the range of our earthly experience. According to Paul, "No eye has seen, no ear has heard, no mind has conceived what God has prepared for those who love him" (1 Corinthians 2:9).

The assurance that we have a Father in heaven—beyond the frame of this world—allays our fears of cosmic isolation. We are not relegated to a tenuous existence on a fragile planet in a solar system fraught with the constant threat of cataclysmic devastation. We may not have discovered out there the existence of any beings like us, but we are not abandoned and alone. Dinesh D'Souza writes:

> Christianity also offers a solution to the cosmic loneliness we all feel. However successful the secular life, there comes to every thinking person the recognition that, in the end, we are alone. Christianity removes this existential loneliness and links our destiny with God.[71]

These fundamental realities about God being our Father in heaven are essential to understanding the Lord's Prayer.

We have a constant need to be in touch with heaven. Therefore, the Lord's Prayer is our daily prayer. We live in a decadent world system that competes for our attention. If we fail to turn our attention to our heavenly Father, we risk becoming captive to this fallen world system. The psalmist wrote, "I will lift up my eyes to the hills—where does my help come from? My help comes from the Lord, the Maker of heaven and earth" (Psalm 121:1–2). The apostle Paul likewise appealed:

Since, then, you have been raised with Christ, set your hearts on things above, where Christ is seated at the right hand of God. Set your minds on things above, not on earthly things (Colossians 3:1–2).

Jesus instructed his followers to pray to our Father in heaven. God delights in adoration offered by his children. But the Father does not need us, or anything from us. We, by contrast, call on our Father whom we love and need. Our Father's power provides everything his child needs for life and godliness (2 Peter 1:3). Let us not suffer the delusion that when we pray to our Father we do something that he needs and that we should be commended for doing so.

What is Heaven, and Where Is It?

One of my earliest recollections of a Sunday School song was:

I met Jesus at the cross roads,
Where the two ways meet;
Satan too was standing there,
And he said 'Come this way,
Lots and lots of pleasures I can give to you this day.'
But I said 'No! there's Jesus here,
Just see what He offers me:
Down here my sins forgiven,
Up there, a home in heaven;
Praise God that's the way for me.'[72]

I heard in church that Jesus arose from the dead and ascended to heaven to build a mansion for us there.

I've got a mansion, just over the hilltop
In that bright land where we'll never grow old

And some day yonder, we'll never more wander
But walk on streets that are purest gold.[73]

This song was based on Jesus' own words to his disciples as rendered in the King James Version of John 14:2: "In my Father's house are many mansions: if it were not so, I would have told you. I go to prepare a place for you." When I looked at the palatial homes of wealthy folk, I wondered how much grander my mansion in heaven would be. But the King James version rendering is misleading. The literal rendering of the Greek text is, " In my Father's house are many dwelling places (rooms) . . ." Jesus' emphasis is not on the grandeur of a heavenly edifice but on the privilege of proximity to our heavenly Father.

Many people, however, believe that everything ends at death; beyond the grave there is nothing to fear or to enjoy. Just nothing. That viewpoint may relieve anxiety about having to give account to God. But if there is nothing after this life, is there any significance to what a person does during a lifetime on this planet? Some say we lose our individuality when our earthly life ends, but death does not end our existence. Instead, we are all absorbed into the infinite whole. Yet others believe in reincarnation or the law of *karma,* namely that after death an eternal soul may occupy a new body, perhaps a lower form of life if you were a bad girl or boy in this life. Spiritualists say that the dead do not really leave us. They are nearby, invisible to the physical senses, but they can communicate with those who have psychic powers.

When we pray to our Father in heaven, we must believe in a real heaven—a place where God dwells and where people can go after this life. Heaven is not a preposterous fantasy—a pie in the sky.

Multiple Meanings of Heaven

What should we know about heaven? The word *heaven* can mean the atmospheric heavens, where the clouds are. In the Bible we read of God shutting up the heavens so that it did not rain. Heaven can also mean the celestial heavens, where from our perspective on earth the planets and all the stars and galaxies have their place in the universe. In the Old Testament we read about God creating the heavens and the earth, and about the constellations Orion and Pleiades (Job 9:9; 38:31; Amos 5:8). The context makes it clear what kind of heaven is meant. For a modest sum of money you can actually name one of those tiny pinpricks of light in the night sky after yourself. You receive a certificate that locates on a celestial chart the star that bears your name. Among the wacky novelties mankind has concocted that has to be one of the daftest!

Jesus taught his disciples to pray, "Our Father in heaven." Is that the address of God's residence? When God made his covenant with his people Israel, he declared that he would dwell among them. The Tent of Meeting, or Tabernacle, during Israel's wilderness sojourn was the visible representation of God's presence with them. But they also learned that the Lord their God could not be confined in an earthly habitation. In Solomon's prayer at the dedication of the temple he said, "But will God really dwell on earth? The heavens, even the highest heaven, cannot contain you. How much less this temple I have built!" (1 Kings 8:27; cf. 2 Chronicles 2:6).

Wilbur Smith elaborated:

> Even though we are told in the Scriptures that the "heaven of heavens cannot contain God" and that God is everywhere present, on earth as well as in heaven (Deuteronomy 4:39; Joshua 2:11),

146

nevertheless, the same Scriptures clearly teach that God does dwell particularly in heaven, a place often designated as his habitation.[74]

Wayne Grudem explained,

God is present everywhere . . . The greatest manifestation of God's presence to bless is seen in heaven, where he makes his glory known, and where angels, other heavenly creatures, and redeemed saints all worship him.[75]

Some people think of heaven as a state of being rather than an actual place. Someone in a state of bliss may gush, "Oh! I'm in heaven!" But heaven is an actual place (2 Corinthians 5:1–3). The New Testament clearly presents heaven as a place. After his resurrection, God the Son, Jesus, ascended to heaven in full view of the apostles, then a cloud hid him from their sight. Two angels came to them and said, "Men of Galilee, why do you stand here looking into the sky? This same Jesus, who has been taken from you into heaven, will come back in the same way you have seen him go into heaven" (Acts 1:11). Jesus left physically, miraculously, and went somewhere—to a place. Before his crucifixion Jesus told his disciples that he was going to a place and he would also prepare a place there for them (John 14:2–3). The New Testament Greek word is *topos,* which means a literal location, a place, a site.

New Heaven and New Earth

Scripture states that a new heaven and a new earth await God's people (Isaiah 65:17; 2 Peter 3:13; Revelation 21:1). This "new heaven" is the atmospheric and celestial heaven, not the eternal dwelling of God. It is what we read about in the first verse of the Bible, "In the beginning God created the heavens and the earth" (Genesis 1:1). When mankind defied God's will in the garden and sin entered the world, the whole creation was cursed. We are living in a corrupted world. But it will be renewed. The apostle Paul wrote:

> . . . the creation itself will be liberated from its bondage to decay and brought into the glorious freedom of the children of God. We know that the whole creation has been groaning as in the pains of childbirth right up to the present time" (Romans 8:21–22).

If God our Father brings about a grand cosmic renewal, what will the destiny of the world be and of the universe be as we experience it? The apostle Peter wrote, "But the day of the Lord will come like a thief. The heavens will disappear with a roar; the elements will be destroyed by fire, and the earth and everything in it will be laid bare" (2 Peter 3:10).

How will this take place? We do not know the details, but it is reasonable to believe that a cosmic cataclysm will occur. We live on a vulnerable planet. We are riding the very thin crust of a huge, dynamic molten ball. Every earthquake, every volcanic eruption is a sobering reminder of our precarious posture. An asteroid or gigantic meteor shattering and burning as it strikes our atmosphere with parts perhaps rupturing the earth's crust could cause unimaginable devastation. There is ample evidence that versions of this have occurred in the history of the earth. Consider all the factors that fit this world as a habitation for us. Scripture indicates that a cosmic cataclysm would not happen by chance. God sustains this fragile world, and regulates all the cosmic forces that affect it. Paul said, "All things were created by him and for him, . . and in him all things hold together" (Colossians 1:16–17). God's superintending power prevents something catastrophic from happening to this world by accident.

How will the new heavens and new earth come into existence? Will this earth be obliterated? Will the new earth be a totally new creation, or will this present creation be renewed? We are not able to explain the process, but we know that there will be what is called a "new heaven and a new earth, the home of righteousness" (2 Peter 3:13). This stretches our imaginations. We attempt to grasp just a small part of what our infinite, eternal, all-powerful God will do, but it lies beyond our ability to comprehend how he will accomplish it.

After the creation of a new heaven and a new earth, God will make his dwelling with his people. The apostle John described it:

> Then I saw a new heaven and a new earth, for the first heaven and the first earth had passed away, and there was no longer any sea. I saw the Holy City, the new Jerusalem, coming down out of heaven from God, prepared as a bride beautifully dressed for her husband. And I heard a loud voice from the throne saying, "Now the dwelling of God is with men, and he will live with them. They will be his people, and God himself will be with them and be their God. He will wipe every tear from their eyes. There will be no more death or mourning or crying or pain, for the old order of things has passed away" (Revelation 21:1–4).

During the present age the distinction between heaven and earth is vast. But in the new order there will be no separation of heaven from earth. The Holy City, heaven, will be on the new earth. The dwelling of God will be with mankind (v.3). God will fulfill his timeless promise to be our God, we will be his people, and he will dwell with us.

Life in the New Heaven

According to Scripture, there will be no darkness or night in heaven (Revelation 21:25). Does that mean there will be no time in heaven? If there is no time, things cannot be done after one another. But the description of events in heaven includes words being spoken—one after another— and events happening, such as a tree of life yielding its fruit each month (Revelation 22:2). We cannot experience eternity as our infinite God does, but we may expect our experience of time in heaven to be similar to the way we understand it here. Wayne Grudem wrote, "As finite creatures, we will rather live in a succession of moments that will never end."[76]

Heaven is a real place where God's children will live after this earthly life.

> Now we know that if the earthly tent we live in is destroyed, we have a building from God, an eternal house in heaven, not built by human hands. Meanwhile we groan, longing to be clothed with our heavenly dwelling, because when we are clothed, we will not be found naked (2 Corinthians 5:1–3).

The Apostle Paul groaned under a burden of hardships on earth. He compared our physical bodies to a tent (2 Corinthians 5:4). For some it may be a pup tent; for others it is a circus tent. A tent was a symbol of something temporary. Our earthly bodies are like temporary tents. Peter said something almost identical:

I think it is right to refresh your memory as long as I live in the tent of this body, because I know that I will soon put it aside, as our Lord Jesus Christ has made clear to me (2 Peter 1:13–14).

Something infinitely better is waiting—a building from God, an eternal house in heaven, not built by human hands (2 Corinthians 5:1).

Christ has prepared a place for God's children where they can be with him forever. We have bodies that are wasting away, but the children of our Father in heaven live on—to receive a new body infinitely grander than the earthly one. We tend to cling to what is earthly and physical, and do not want to let go. All the things we have are temporary. Let us not cling to things that cannot go with us.

Heaven is the destiny of God's children. People who accept the Bible as the inspired, authoritative word of God search therein for answers to questions about heaven. The apostle Paul gives us some helpful insights into the nature of heaven and life after death.

For while we are in this tent, we groan and are burdened, because we do not wish to be unclothed but to be clothed with our heavenly dwelling, so that what is mortal may be swallowed up by life. Now it is God who has made us for this very purpose and has given us the Spirit as a deposit, guaranteeing what is to come. Therefore we are always confident and know that as long as we are at home in the body we are away from the Lord. We live by faith, not by sight. We are confident, I say, and would prefer to be away from the body and at home with the Lord (2 Corinthians 5:4–8).

God made people for a purpose vastly superior to our earthly life. The anticipation of heaven should bring joy to our souls. Charles Haddon Spurgeon, arguably the greatest preacher of the 19th century, was teaching some young preachers to put proper expression into their sermonic delivery. He said, "When you speak of Heaven let your face light up, let it be irradiated with a heavenly gleam, let your eyes shine with reflected glory. But when you speak of Hell—well, then your ordinary face will do."[77]

Attaining Our Heavenly Destiny

How do God's children attain their heavenly destiny? The presence of the Holy Spirit guarantees what is to come (2 Corinthians 5:5). Although we may become increasingly frail outwardly, yet inwardly the Holy Spirit is getting us ready for all that God has prepared for us.

Jesus Christ promised his disciples that he would return to take them to their heavenly abode. (John 14:1–3). His second coming will involve a supernatural intrusion into the earth's natural order. What will be the condition of God's children when the day of the Lord comes? Whatever our location, how will we fare when the heavens and the earth are destroyed by fire? Peter explains that the day of God will bring about the total destruction of the earth and the heavens by fire, and the elements will melt in the heat (2 Peter 3:10–12). He adds that God's people must live holy and godly lives as they look forward to the day of God and speed its coming. Peter does not state explicitly here that God's people will be removed from the earth before this intervention takes place (2 Peter 3:13). But the apostle Paul says Jesus rescues believers from the coming wrath (1 Thessalonians 1:10; cf. 5:9).

Bible scholars interpret these Scriptures through the sieve of their theological grid. Their viewpoint is confined within the parameters of time and space. They hold that God the Father will safely remove his children from the earth before the cataclysmic destruction and the renewal of the heavens and the earth takes place. Scripture testifies to such a removal in what we call the "rapture of the saints" (1 Thessalonians 4:16–17). God's children will then be with our Father in the place Christ prepared for us. But our transformation when Christ returns implies that our removal from the earthly cataclysm and our arrival at our eternal home will take place in a manner that transcends our finite understanding. Furthermore, Peter writes about believers looking forward to the day of God with its devastation, rather than looking forward to our own extraction before the day of God (2 Peter 3:12).

Scripture describes the events prior to the end of this age and Christ's return in terms that make sense to us within our space-time perspective. When Christ returns, however, at the end of the age, God's children will be transformed to be like him (1 John 3:2). It is reasonable to assume that in our new Christ-like state we will experience reality in a manner that is not restricted to a space-time frame of reference. How this will transpire is beyond our present grasp. Paul wrote,

> I declare to you, brothers, that flesh and blood cannot inherit the kingdom of God, nor does the perishable inherit the imperishable. Listen, I tell you a mystery: We will not all sleep, but we will all be changed—(1 Corinthians 15:50–51)

God's children will undergo a physical transformation when Jesus Christ returns at the end of the age. The apostle Paul explained that God's children:

". . . await a Savior from there [heaven], the Lord Jesus Christ, who by the power that enables him to bring everything under his control, will transform our lowly bodies so that they will be like his glorious body" (Philippians 3:20–21).

In his resurrected, glorified body Jesus was not constrained by his physical environment. Locked doors and walls could not prevent him meeting with his disciples so that they could see him and touch him (John 20:19). It is reasonable to suppose that the transformed bodies of God's children may be impervious to the incinerating blast in which the heavens and the earth are destroyed. The physical transformation of Shadrach, Meshach, and Abednego that enabled them to be unscathed in Nebuchadnezzar's blazing furnace may be examples of the condition of God's children at the fiery destruction of the heavens and the earth (Daniel 3:8–28). God's children must not be held captive by physical concepts of time and space in their thinking of end time events. In glorified bodies—like Christ's—God's children will assume residency on the new earth with its Holy City.

There is continuity between our physical bodies that die and our glorified bodies in heaven. It may be compared to the continuity a seed has with the magnificent tree that emerges after the seed is planted. In the lives of God's children this newness has already begun. If you have repented of sin and placed your faith in Jesus Christ as your Savior, you are a new creation; the old has passed, the new has come (2 Corinthians 5:17). You are able to "put on the new self, created to be like God in true righteousness and holiness" (Ephesians 4:24). All that you are meant to be will be fully realized in your glorious transformed body. Before sin entered the world and defiled God's creation, he pronounced it "very good" (Genesis 1:31). When God makes everything new, his entire creation will be perfect. In our glorified bodies God's children will be "very good."

Our Occupation in Heaven

As God's children how will we be occupied when we enter our eternal destiny? God has a future for his children infinitely grander than anything we can experience in our mortal bodies. In John's vision of God upon his throne, heavenly beings are worshiping God. But on earth sin has twisted and corrupted the human race so much that we tend to focus on temporal things rather than on our heavenly Father's glory. To pray, "hallowed be your name" is just the recitation of a ritual prayer for most people. But the sincere adoration of the heavenly Father by his children on earth is our supreme duty. The indescribable joy that accompanies pure worship on this earth is a foretaste of sharing in the exultation, "Holy, Holy, Holy is the Lord God Almighty, who was, and is, and is to come" (Revelation 4:8). That expression by the heavenly beings is the heavenly counterpart of the clause in the Lord's Prayer, "Hallowed be your name." We do not know how our adoration of our heavenly Father resembles the perpetual worship in the throne room of the Lord God Almighty. But when we at last become all we are meant to be, the worship we offer will be what our Father delights in from his children.

How to Prepare for Heaven

The crucial question on earth concerning these truths about heaven is, what do people have to do to get to heaven? Billy Graham told a story from his early years as a preacher. He arrived in a small town for a meeting. He had a letter he needed to mail, so he asked a boy on the street how to get to the post office. The boy told him. Then Graham said, "If you come to the Baptist church tonight, you can hear me telling everyone how to get to heaven." The boy answered, "I don't think so. You don't even know how to get to the post office." Millions of people among the nations can testify that Billy Graham was qualified to tell people how to get to heaven: Jesus Christ is the way. Jesus said, "I am the way and the truth and the life. No one comes to the Father except through me" (John 14:6). Jesus gave not only information; he also gave assurances. He promised to those who follow him an eternal inheritance (Matthew 19:29). He promises that those who overcome will inherit all the blessings of the dwelling of God, where there will be no more death or mourning or crying or pain (Revelation 21:3–7). The hope of an inheritance after this life in the dwelling of God is something people sought and Jesus taught. He said,

> Do not store up for yourselves treasures on earth, where moth and rust destroy, and where thieves break in and steal. But store up for yourselves treasures in heaven, where moth and rust do not destroy, and where thieves do not break in and steal. For where your treasure is, there will your heart be also (Matthew 6:19–21).

This earthly life's purpose is to prepare God's children for eternal life with our Father. In telling about the destruction of the present heavens and earth on the day of the Lord, Peter added,

> Since everything will be destroyed in this way, what kind of people ought you to be? You ought to live holy and godly lives as you look forward to the day of God and speed its coming. . . [That's because] in keeping with his promise we are

looking forward to a new heaven and a new earth, the home of righteousness (2 Peter 3:11–13).

Paul made this appeal:

So we make it our goal to please him, whether we are at home in the body or away from it. For we must all appear before the judgment seat of Christ, that each one may receive what is due him for the things done while in the body, whether good or bad (2 Corinthians 5:9–10).

One day, when I was serving a church in the San Francisco Bay Area, I spied a shiny sports car with this question plastered on a bumper sticker, "How much can I do and still go to heaven?" Jesus Christ will reveal the things we have done in our physical bodies as good or worthless. For God's children it will not be a judgment of condemnation, because we have life in Christ (Romans 8:1). You may have heard the saying: "Only one life, 'twill soon be past. Only what's done for Christ will last."[78] That proverb is not in the Bible, but it is thoroughly biblical in the truth it affirms.

As the children of God we have an eternal inheritance guaranteed for us after this earthly life. But many live as if all that matters is tied to their temporary earthly bodies. Everything they long for is here on earth. But the Father's children are sojourners here. David, the psalmist, gave God's children a gut-check: "O Lord, what is man that you care for him, the son of man that you think of him? Man is like a breath; his days are like a fleeting shadow" (Psalm 144:3–4). By God's mercy a person's life on this sin-cursed planet is of short duration. The giant turtle may live to 177 years, the turkey buzzard 118 years. Near the other end of the spectrum is the mayfly that lives only one day and the tiny aquatic gastrotrich a mere three days. Humankind's earthly life expectancy is toward the longer side of the scale, but in terms of God's purpose, it is like a passing shadow. God has ordained the fullness of life for his children. Our entrance into that perfect state depends upon a vital connection to our heavenly Father. The ultimate folly, therefore, is to ignore our heavenly Father and to clutch the temporal trash that will ultimately be burned up.

Children of the heavenly Father can say with conviction, "the best is yet to come." Therefore, we give to our Father in heaven the honor due him. While we await the consummation of our personal transformation we pray each day, "Our Father in heaven."

Questions for Discussion and Personal Application

1. When you pray to our Father in heaven, do you think of him as listening nearby or hearing you at a distance?
2. List some differences between the Lord God and pagan idols. Which difference do you consider most significant?
3. In Ecclesiastes 3:11 we read that God set eternity in the hearts of people. How does this equip people to ponder the mysteries of God's creation?
4. How has your view of what awaits people after this earthly life changed?
5. How do you refute from Scripture the argument that heaven as the dwelling of God is not a literal place?
6. To what extent will the new heaven and new earth have an effect on the heavenly dwelling of our Father?
7. Describe the consummation of God's dwelling with mankind that Jesus Christ revealed through John.
8. God's children will be in heaven with him for eternity. Explain why some features of time will remain in effect in eternity.
9. Besides a tent, what other figures in Scripture underscore the temporary nature of our physical bodies as dwellings?
10. How do you explain the continuity that exists between our physical earthly bodies and our glorified heavenly bodies?
11. How does the description of worship in the book of Revelation help God's children understand their role in heaven?
12. Give a brief summary of Jesus' teaching about how to get to heaven.

13. How should God's children prepare themselves to give an account to our Father in heaven for the way they have lived on earth?

14. In what sense may the brevity of life on earth be considered a blessing?

6. HALLOWED BE YOUR NAME

It's the song of the redeemed rising from the African plain.
It's the song of the forgiven drowning out the Amazon rain,
the song of Asian believers filled with God's holy fire.
It's every tribe, every tongue, every nation, a love song born
of a grateful choir.
It's all God's children singing, "Glory, glory, hallelujah,
He reigns. He reigns."
It's all God's children singing, Glory, glory, hallelujah,
He reigns. He reigns.

Peter Furler and Steve Taylor[79]

May Your Name be Hallowed

Both Matthew's and Luke's recitation of the Lord's Prayer include the clause, "hallowed be your name." For many years I thought "hallowed be your name," was part of the Prayer's appellation, that is, "Our Father in heaven whose name is hallowed." According to a legend, a little boy was learning the Lord's Prayer. "Hallowed" was a strange word, and he had no idea what it meant. It sounded much like "Harold" to him. He took to praying, "Our Father in heaven, Harold be your name." That made better sense to him.

Before I studied the text, I assumed the verb in "hallowed be your name" was indicative mood. So it indicated that our Father to whom we pray is holy. A fundamental tenet of the Christian faith is that our Father in heaven is assuredly holy in every aspect of his being. But if we interpret this as a statement that God is holy, we misunderstand the opening line of the Lord's Prayer. This is not a declaration that God in his essential being is holy. The

161

verb "hallowed be" is in the subjunctive mood. It expresses a wish, a desire, a longing. It is our plea that our Father's fame, because of the perfection of his attributes, may be extolled as incomparably glorious. The meaning is, "may your name be hallowed."

The first petition in the Lord's Prayer is entirely about our heavenly Father. As God's children we focus our prayers first and foremost on him. An Irish hymn underscores God's primacy:

Be Thou my vision, O Lord of my heart;
Naught be all else to me, save that thou art—
Thou my best thought, by day or by night,
Waking or sleeping, Thy presence my light.

Riches I heed not, nor man's empty praise,
Thou my inheritance, now and always;
Thou and Thou only, first in my heart,
High King of heaven, my Treasure Thou art.[80]

"Hallowed be your name" expresses the heart cry of the heavenly Father's children. We pray, "May your name be acclaimed as holy."

The Meaning of *Hallow*

To hallow means to set apart as holy, or to celebrate holiness. The hallowing of the name of our Father in heaven is our promulgation of the wonders of God's nature. In his ineffable, eternal being God is holy. Hendriksen explains, "To hallow God's name means to hold it in reverence; hence, to hold him in reverence, to honor, glorify, and exalt him."[81]

In the early history of the Israelites' desert journey to the land the Lord God had promised them, Balak, king of the

Moabites bribed Balaam to curse them. He feared that Israel would take over the whole territory. But God did not allow Balaam to curse Israel. Instead, he made Balaam bless Israel. Then the Moabite women seduced the Israelite men and enticed them to worship the Moabite god Baal. The Lord God punished those who had indulged in pagan immorality by having them put to death. While the Israelites were weeping because of what they had done, an Israelite man flagrantly brought a Midianite woman home to his family. Moses and the whole assembly of Israel saw this. Then Phinehas son of Eleazar, son of Aaron, followed the couple into the tent and killed them. Immediately the plague that God had inflicted on Israel for its sin was stopped. God told Moses that he had turned his anger away from Israel because of the action of Phinehas. God explained, "for he was as zealous as I am for my honor" (Numbers 25:11). God does not command his people to exact such extreme retribution for sin today, but Phinehas's action elucidates the meaning of "hallowed be your name." A passionate zeal for the honor of our heavenly Father is integral to extolling God's holiness. God our heavenly Father is honored when his children hallow his name. The highest occupation of mankind is to honor God.

The essential meaning of "holy" is the quality of separateness or utter uniqueness. God is the consummate definition of holiness. Our heavenly Father is absolutely righteous, glorious, and ineffable. Cosmo, a character in a George MacDonald pastoral novel said, "God, you know, Joan, is more than anybody knows what to say about."[82] God is the antithesis of all that is ordinary or impure. Our heavenly Father transcends everything mundane and temporal. In this corrupt world where everything and everyone bears characteristics of imperfection and decay, only our heavenly Father is unspoiled and perfect.

"Our Father in heaven, hallowed be your name" is our prayer for the radiance of God's glory to be extolled among all peoples and created beings. In his divine essence God is majestic beyond our comprehension, as the apostle Paul's grand benediction declares:

> Oh, the depth of the riches of the wisdom and knowledge of God! How unsearchable his judgments, and his paths beyond tracing out! Who has known the mind of the Lord? Or who has been his counselor? Who has ever given to God, that God should repay him? For from him and through him and to him are all things. To him be the glory forever! Amen (Romans 11:33–36).

God is more than we can define or describe. This is intrinsic to our plea, "hallowed be your name."

David said, "Every day I will praise you and extol your name for ever and ever" (Psalm 145:2). God the sovereign Lord said to the Prophet Ezekiel, "I will make known my holy name among my people Israel. I will no longer let my holy name be profaned, and the nations will know that I the Lord am the Holy One in Israel" (Ezekiel 39:7). The Prophet Isaiah expressed the same burden, "Give thanks to the Lord, call on his name; make known among the nations what he has done, and proclaim that his name is exalted" (Isaiah 12:4).

When the High Priest Aaron's sons Nadab and Abihu offered unauthorized fire before the Lord, fire came out from the presence of the Lord and consumed them. God upheld his holiness. Even though Nadab and Abihu did not intentionally flout God's commands, they were not careful to heed the particulars of the Lord their God's decrees.

Moses then said to Aaron, "This is what the Lord spoke of when he said: 'Among those who approach me I will show myself holy; in the sight of all the people I will be honored'" (Leviticus 10:3).

When we pray, "Hallowed be your name," we ask our Father to make himself known in such unmistakable terms that no one will take lightly who he is and what he demands. Our heart-felt longing is that people everywhere will honor God, in their speech, attitude, and conduct. The Prophet Isaiah told how God asserted his holiness among the people:

> For this is what the high and holy [lofty] One says—he who lives forever, whose name is holy: "I live in a high and holy place, but also with him who is contrite and lowly in spirit, to revive the spirit of the lowly and to revive the heart of the contrite" (Isaiah 57:15).

In this corrupt world people blinded in Satan's dark dominion ignore, deny, and mock our Father in heaven. Some are so darkened in their understanding that God is nothing more than the one to blame for their problems and hardships. Against this dark backdrop the Psalmist appealed:

> Ascribe to the Lord, O families of nations, ascribe to the Lord glory and strength. Ascribe to the Lord the glory due his name; bring an offering and come into his courts. Worship the Lord in the splendor of his holiness; tremble before him, all the earth. Say among the nations, "The Lord reigns" (Psalm 96:7–10).

Yet another song in the Psalter expresses the longing that all nations join together in giving God his due honor:

> May the peoples praise you, O God; may all the peoples praise you. May the nations be glad and sing for joy, for you rule the peoples justly and guide the nations of the earth (Psalm 67:3–4).

A. W. Pink wrote, "By praying that God's name be hallowed we ask that he will so act that his creatures may be moved to render that adoration which is due him."[83]

Our Father's Name

There is no distinction between the holiness of God our Father in heaven and the holiness of Jesus Christ who is God the Son. Jesus said, "I have come in my Father's name" (John 5:43). When we pray, "hallowed be your name," it is the name shared by Jesus Christ our Lord when he came to rescue mankind from the devil's dominion of darkness. Jesus Christ shares the holiness and glory of the Father in heaven.

Implicit in the plea "hallowed be your name" is displeasure with the condition of earthly life. It is a refusal to embrace the ungodly attitudes and actions prevalent in society. Pink wrote:

> If we offer this petition from the heart we desire that God's name may be sanctified by us, and at the same time own the indisposition and utter inability to do this of ourselves. Such a request denotes a longing to be empowered to glorify God in everything whereby He makes Himself known, that we may honor Him in all situations and circumstances.[84]

When Moses came down Mount Sinai with the two Tablets of the Testimony inscribed by the finger of God, he saw Israel dancing wildly around a calf idol they had made. In fierce anger he flung the two tablets from his hands, breaking them into pieces. Then God punished his people severely.

Later on God summoned Moses back to Mount Sinai with two newly chiseled tablets.

> Then the Lord came down in the cloud and stood there with him and proclaimed his name, the Lord. And he passed in front of Moses, proclaiming, "The Lord, the Lord, the compassionate and gracious God, slow to anger, abounding in love and faithfulness, maintaining love to thousands, and forgiving wickedness, rebellion and sin. Yet he does not leave the guilty unpunished; he punishes the children and their children for the sin of the fathers to the third and fourth generation" (Exodus 34:5–7).

God disclosed this about the meaning of his name: he is the pre-existent Lord; he is compassionate, gracious, and patient; he abounds in love, faithfulness, and forgiveness of sin. Yet he is perfectly just. When we pray, "hallowed be your name," we pray that people everywhere will magnify these attributes of our Father in heaven and that all mankind will exalt him above everyone and everything.

In the Old Testament the ark of God represented his holy presence among his people. It was called, "the ark of God the Lord, who is enthroned between the cherubim—the ark that is called by the Name" (1 Chronicles 13:6). During its transfer from the home of Abinadab, Uzzah reached out and took hold of the ark to steady it when the oxen pulling the cart stumbled. God struck down Uzzah because touching the ark was an irreverent act (2 Samuel 6:6–7). The Levites were tasked with the sacred duty of carrying the ark. They were not to touch it, but to use poles to lift and move it. God's decree was specific and unambiguous. The holiness of God is inviolable. Even a well-intentioned contravention of God's statute regarding the ark evoked severe retribution.

The Lord God decreed, "My name will be great among the nations, from the rising to the setting of the sun" (Malachi 1:11). If we pray, "Hallowed be your name" in a flippant or irreverent attitude we violate the Third Commandment, "You shall not misuse the name of the Lord your God, for the Lord will not hold anyone guiltless who misuses his name" (Exodus 20:7). God's children pray that his majesty and glory will be feted and never taken for granted. David exemplified a reverent fear of God. He prayed, "Teach me your way, O Lord, and I will walk in your truth; give me an undivided heart, that I may fear your name" (Psalm 86:11). A child of God with undivided devotion can pray to our Father in heaven, "Hallowed be your name." The psalmist's appeal was explicitly the same: "Exalt the Lord our God and worship at his footstool; he is holy" (Psalm 99:5).

The Meaning of the Name

The initial injunction of the Lord's Prayer addresses God's holy name—"Hallowed be your name." God's name signifies what is most distinctive about God. Lloyd-Jones said,

> The name . . . means all that is true of God, and all that has been revealed concerning God. It means God in all His attributes, God in all that He is in and

of Himself, and God in all that He has done and all that He is doing."[85]

My father was notorious for assigning people nicknames, and then calling them by that name to their face. The nickname always reflected something distinctive about the one to whom he applied it. "Bless" was the nickname he gave to Mr. Short who liked to say, "Bless you," and to tell about God's blessings. Another godly man in our church was someone my sisters and I knew as Uncle Willy. During the testimony time in the church service Uncle Willy would invariably stand up and recount a thought that had "flashed" through his mind. You guessed it, to my dad he was forever known as "Flash." An acquaintance of our family often quoted the Greek philosopher Socrates. Sure enough, Dad christened him "Socks." We transpose this practice of naming people by their traits to an infinitely higher and holier purpose by declaring God's name to be Holy. "Holy" is not God's nickname. God's holiness in all aspects of his being is his most distinctive trait.

Stephen Charnock said, "His name, which signifies all his attributes in conjunction, is holy."[86] God's essential being is holy—utterly unique and "other." He is incomparable. This truth about God our Father in heaven is the basis of our confidence in him. Everyone and everything else is temporal and fallible. The Psalmist David extolled God's name in this way, "Some trust in chariots and some in horses, but we trust in the name of the Lord our God" (Psalm 20:7).

Our Father's Multiple Names

The personal identity of most of us comprises three names. There is a given first name, a second given name, and then the surname or family name. British royalty tend to multiply given names and append titles to them. For example, Prince Charles's names are Charles Philip Arthur George. The titles attached to his name are His Royal Highness, Prince of Wales, and Duke of Cornwall. My father had three given names and a surname. He was Edward John Hancock Crocker. Multiple names were common in England where he was born. When we moved to Canada he had to lose his third given name. Official documents provided for only two given names. He preferred to use his initials in correspondence. Mail for him was addressed to E. J. H. Crocker. Anyone seeing only his initials would not know his name. It might have been Eric instead of Edward, James instead of John, and Harvey instead of Hancock.

God's name is not a long chain of initials. God's "name" comprises all his attributes. Combining the lists compiled by A. W. Tozer in *The Knowledge of the Holy,* J. I. Packer in *Knowing God,* and Arthur W. Pink in *The Attributes of God,* God's "name" is Trinity, Self-existent, Self-sufficient, Majestic, Eternal, Infinite, Immutable, Omniscient, Wise, True, Omnipotent, Transcendent, Omnipresent, Faithful, Good, Judge, Merciful, Wrath, Gracious, Jealous, Patient, Loving, and Sovereign. We might say that our heavenly Father's surname is Holy. In each of the names of our Father in heaven he is absolutely, incomparably, perfectly, peerlessly, and gloriously the consummate definition of all the attributes comprising his "name." Grudem explained,

> In the Bible a person's name is a description of his or her character. Likewise, the names of God in Scripture are various descriptions of his character. In a broad sense, then, God's "name" is equal to all that the Bible and creation tell us about God. When we pray, "Hallowed be your *name*; as part of the Lord's prayer (Matthew 6:9), we are praying that

people would speak about God in a way that is honoring to him and that accurately reflects his character. This honoring of God's name can be done with actions as well as words, for our actions reflect the character of the Creator whom we serve (Matthew 5:16). To honor God's name is therefore to honor him. The command, "You shall not take the *name* of the Lord your God in vain" (Exodus 20:7) is a command that we not dishonor God's reputation either by words that speak of him in a foolish or misleading way, or by actions that do not reflect his true character.

Now the Bible does give many individual names to God, all of which reflect some true aspect of his character. Many of these names are taken from human experience or emotions in order to describe parts of God's character, while many other names are taken from the rest of natural creation. In a sense, all of these expressions of God's character in terms of things found in the universe are "names" of God because they tell us something true about him.[87]

This, then, is the awesome freight borne in that little clause, "Hallowed be your name." Our prayer expresses our longing that the absolute perfection of everything pertaining to our heavenly Father be chorused just as the seraphim do it before God's throne: "Holy, holy, holy, is the Lord of hosts."

God's Unspeakable Name

The holy name by which God introduced himself to Moses (Exodus 3:14) was *Yahweh*. Nevertheless, people would not utter this holy name for fear of misusing God's name (Exodus 20:7). Instead they referred to God obliquely by using the term "Name." In my Hebrew grammar and exegesis courses in seminary we adhered to the Jewish practice of assiduously avoiding any pronunciation of the term *Yahweh* wherever it occurred in the text. In its place we substituted the name *Adonai,* meaning *Sovereign Lord.*

After the exiles returned to Jerusalem and rebuilt its wall, the Levites led the people in a prayer to the Lord God, including this remark: "You made a name for yourself, which remains to this day" (Nehemiah 9:10). This part of the Levites' prayer referred to God's dealings with the Egyptians while the Israelites were slaves in their land. By his inimitable power demonstrated in the great plagues, God made a name for himself. The Egyptians would know that he was the God above their gods. The Israelites, God's people, also needed to learn about the Lord their God. After centuries in captivity their knowledge of the true Lord God had doubtlessly faded. So God re-introduced himself to his people in a mighty way at the Passover, the crossing of the Red Sea, at Mount Sinai, and in multiple events that followed.

In a letter he sent to Hiram king of Tyre, King Solomon of Israel spoke of God by using the expression, "Name":

> You know that because of the wars waged against my father David from all sides, he could not build a temple for the Name of the Lord his God until the Lord his God put his enemies under his feet. But now the Lord my God has given me rest [peace] on every side, and there is no adversary or disaster. I intend, therefore, to build a temple for the Name of the Lord my God, as the Lord told my father David, when he said, "Your son whom I will put on the

throne in your place will build the temple for my Name" (1 Kings 5:3–5).

Evidently the people understood that the "Name" addressed the most significant aspect of one's nature and character.

After the Lord arrested Saul on his way to Damascus, he instructed Ananias to go to Saul. Ananias was afraid because Saul had been a notorious persecutor of Christ's followers, and he had come to Damascus to arrest all who called on the Lord's name. The Lord answered Ananias, "Go! This man is my chosen instrument to carry my name before the Gentiles and their kings and before the people of Israel" (Acts 9:15). According to the Lord God, Saul (the Apostle Paul) had a mission from God to "carry his (the Lord's) name." The gospel of God emphasizes the Lord God's "name." So the message God's children take into the world focuses on who God is and what he has done.

An Intimate Prayer

A backstage pass at a popular music concert is a prized privilege. The pass grants the bearer access to the star of the show. People who have been backstage get to tell others some juicy snippets about the famous artist. The Lord's Prayer is like a backstage pass to God Almighty. Jesus Christ granted the pass that guarantees the right of entry into the intimate presence of the star of the universe (Ephesians 2:18). Jesus is the One who presents us before God's glorious presence without fault and with great joy (Jude 24). Furthermore, we have the privilege of remaining backstage. In fact, we become members of God's road crew. More than that, as children of our God and Father we declare his glory to people everywhere. We pray as only those who have a close connection to the Father can pray, "hallowed be your name."

David expressed an intimate acquaintance with God, "Praise the Lord, O my soul; all my inmost being, praise his holy name" (Psalm 103:1). Matt Redman's song, *Ten Thousand Reasons* is based on this Psalm: "Sing like never before, O my soul. I'll worship your holy name."[88] David's call to worship involves "all my inmost being." The Hebrew text literally reads "all within me." No part of who we are is excluded from praising God our Father. God made it clear that his people's love for him was to engage all one's heart and all one's soul and all one's strength (Deuteronomy 6:5). Mark's and Luke's Gospels report that Jesus added the mind to the aspects of our being that worship God—all our heart and soul and mind and strength (Mark 12:30; Luke 10:27).

Emotions are part of our inmost being (all that is within us). In which of these aspects of our being do our emotions lie? Are they anchored in our heart or soul or mind? Perhaps our emotions are to God the fragrance from the fusion of the collective ingredients of our heart and soul and mind and strength. Worshiping God our Father without emotion is incomplete; it does not incorporate all one's inmost being.

The worship of the Lord Almighty by the seraphim in the heavenly throne room includes hallowing God's name (Isaiah 6:2-3). God approved the emotionally-charged worship by David as he danced before the Lord God when the Ark was brought from the house of Obed-Edom to the city of David (2 Samuel 6:14–15). The psalmist called God's people to worship with trumpet and harp and lyre, with tambourine and dancing, and with strings and flutes and cymbals (Psalm 150:3–5). Hallowing God's name in worship engages all our inmost being, including our emotions. It is enthusiastic. Let us not disparage churches that hallow God's name with exuberance. Anorexic worship should have no place among those who hallow the name of their heavenly Father with all their inmost being.

The Priority of "Hallowed be Your Name"

When you pray the Lord's Prayer, you may be inclined to fix your attention on one of the second through sixth petitions. Pink cautioned against glossing over "hallowed be your name." When we pray "hallowed be your name," we broach the theme that is foremost to our Father in heaven. Pink wrote:

> "This petition in the prayer must take precedence, for the glory of God's great name is the ultimate end of all things: every other request must not only be subordinated to this one, but be in harmony with and in pursuance of it. We cannot pray aright unless the honor of God be dominant in our hearts."[89]

Sometimes I help Liz change the sheets on our king-size bed. The fitted bottom sheet always seems to resist proper alignment with the mattress. I noticed the manufacturer's label stitched into a seam on the inside of the fitted sheet. I discovered that the sheet fits properly if the label is on the upper left or lower right of the mattress when facing the headboard. All it takes is getting the corner with the label in the right position, then the whole sheet fits perfectly. This illustrates what happens if the Father's children give "hallowed be your name" its rightful place in our prayer. Then the other components of the Lord's Prayer become correctly aligned in our lives. Our commitment first and foremost to the incomparable perfection of all our Father's attributes places the other five appeals in the right perspective.

"Hallowed be your name" is the most important consideration of God everywhere and always. After the prophecy about the restoration of Israel, the Prophet Ezekiel said,

This is what the Sovereign Lord says: It is not for your sake, O house of Israel, that I am going to do these things, but for the sake of my holy name, which you have profaned among the nations where you have gone (Ezekiel 36:22).

God's name signifies not only how he is to be known; it also indicates his essential nature. He is holy, whether people recognize this or not. The majesty of God our Father transcends our comprehension. The focus in Scripture is on God's honor and glory. It is his will that all people—all nations—know that the Lord alone is God.

The lyrics of Brenton Brown's praise song, *Hosanna* express beautifully and powerfully the longing of God's children for him: "Praise is rising, eyes are turning to you; we turn to you. Hope is stirring, hearts are yearning for you; we long for you."[90] This is akin to the intent of the petition "hallowed be your name." The Prophet Isaiah longed for God to shake the mountains and to do awesome things so that the nations would quake before the Lord (Isaiah 64:1–4). Everything God does is for the sake of his holy name. Our foremost prayer is that the whole world will know God our Father in heaven. Jesus instructed his followers to make this their first petition. God our Father in heaven to whom we pray is holy. Nothing is more important than extolling his holiness.

How the Father's Children Hallow His Name

How then should the children of the heavenly Father hallow his name? In the first commandment God says, "You shall have no other gods before me" (Exodus 20:3). The Lord God required his children's wholehearted love. Love was foremost among the commands, decrees, and laws the Lord God gave to his people Israel. In the exodus from Egypt and during the wilderness sojourn God's people had witnessed his awesome works in the parting of the Red Sea, in the phenomenal demonstrations of his power at Sinai, in the miraculous provision of manna and quail and water, in the parting of the Jordan and in the conquest of the Canaanite people. When at last the tribes of Israel prepared to take possession of the Promised Land, Moses instructed them to teach their children to love the Lord God with their whole being. That generation had to ensure that their children after them would know and love the Lord God who brought them out of Egypt and preserved them in the wilderness (Deuteronomy 6:1–9).

When an expert in the Jewish Law asked Jesus, "Teacher, which is the greatest commandment in the Law?" Jesus replied, "Love the Lord your God with all your heart and with all your soul and with all your mind. This is the first and greatest commandment" (Matthew 22:35–38). Notice the emphatic repetition of "all" in the command: "Love the Lord your God will *all* your heart . . . *all* your soul . . . *all* your strength." Such devotion is not beyond our reach. It is not like "reaching for the stars." My math teacher in high school gave his students the dubious encouragement, "Aim for the stars, and you may hit the top of the telephone pole." The command to love the Lord our God with our whole being is not a hyperbole. It is exact. Our Father will countenance no lesser level of devotion.

There is a singularity in our love for our Father. We do not share it with another. The love we have for God our Father incorporates a commitment to expel all competing affections. A famous sermon by the 19th century Scottish preacher Thomas Chalmers had this intriguing title: *The Expulsive Power of a New Affection.* In it Chalmers said,

> We know of no other way by which to keep the love of the world out of our heart than to keep in our hearts the love of God.[91]

How do we obey God's command to love him with such a comprehensive and expulsive devotion? Has anybody been able to do this? Jesus Christ our Savior and Lord is both God and man. As man he was perfect in loving the Lord God his Father with all his heart and with all his soul and with all his mind and with all his strength.

All of us have felt the strong impulse to fix our affections and dreams on earthly delights that are within our reach. But earthly pleasures eventually leave us empty. Augustine prayed, "Thou has formed us for thyself, and our hearts are restless until they find rest in thee."[92]

Sadly, many of God's children treat our heavenly Father with less respect than they give their earthly parents. Why do they not love him wholeheartedly? I have been appalled by the deplorable way some children treat their earthly parents. Nevertheless, their behavior does not disqualify them from being the children of loving (however indulgent) parents. I must ask myself the disquieting question, has my treatment of my heavenly Father been better than the shameful conduct of children in some human families? Alas, my offenses have been profoundly worse! This sobering reality underscores the immensity of our heavenly Father's grace. Out of his incomparable kindness our Father in heaven gives good gifts to those who ask him (Matthew 7:11).

Only our heavenly Father can keep us steadfast amidst the decadent allurements of a fallen world. The apostolic letters of the New Testament are filled with appeals to discard patterns of thinking and behaving that characterized our old sinful nature. The apostle Paul wrote, "Rather, clothe yourselves with the Lord Jesus Christ, and do not think about how to gratify the desires of the sinful nature [the flesh]" (Romans 13:14).

It is a marvel that imperfect mortals like us may be admitted into the presence of infinite perfection. We must, therefore, be truly humble in both our physical and spiritual posture when we pray the Lord's Prayer. In the Prophet Isaiah's vision of worship before God's throne, the seraphim covered their faces as they called out in antiphonal chorus, "Holy, holy, holy is the Lord Almighty; the whole earth is full of his glory" (Isaiah 6:1–3). The heavenly beings are perpetually agog at the wonder of his majesty. The apostle John was privileged to see a similar scene in his vision of heaven:

> All the angels were standing around the throne and around the elders and the four living creatures. They fell down on their faces before the throne and worshiped God, saying: "Amen! Praise and glory and wisdom and thanks and honor and power and strength be to our God for ever and ever. Amen!" (Revelation 7:11–12)

The stunned prophet Isaiah exclaimed, "Woe to me! . . . I am ruined! For I am a man of unclean lips, . . . and my eyes have seen the King, the Lord Almighty" (Isaiah 6:5).

Sadly, it is common to hear people recite the Lord's Prayer frivolously. The Lord's Prayer is often only a faux balm for religious guilt. Let us heed the Psalmist's counsel for those who would come into the presence of the Lord Almighty: "Exalt the Lord our God and worship at his footstool; he is holy" (Psalm 99:5).

Ezra's sorrowful response to the way the occupants of Jerusalem dishonored their holy God is a fitting example for us:

> Then, at the evening sacrifice, I rose from my self abasement, with my tunic and cloak torn, and fell on my knees with my hands spread out to the Lord my God and prayed: . . . While Ezra was praying and . . . throwing himself down before the house of God, a large crowd of Israelites—men, women and children—gathered around him. They too wept bitterly (Ezra 9:5–6, 10:1).

When we think or speak of our Father in heaven, we should fix our attention on his holiness. God's holiness transcends all the temporal things that amaze or amuse us in this corrupt world.

Sin's Effect on the Hallowing of God's Name

When the first humans sinned in the garden, God expelled them from his presence. Mankind lost the propensity to hallow God—to thrill at his incomparable perfection and glory. The alienation from God, along with the corruption caused by sin, ultimately led mankind to try to fill this void by ascribing glory to God's creatures. The adoration of mere mortals is a byproduct of mankind's fall into sin. People pay homage to fallible human beings who have attained the status of celebrity. A celebrity has a name above other names. The names of celebrities are "hallowed." Some of their fans accord them fame that belongs only to the Lord God. Sadly, many celebrities have lifestyles that are an affront to the holiness of God our Father. They flaunt their arrogance in a variety of awards shows where these mortal "gods" meet to glorify one another, while an adoring world delights at the spectacle of their gods at play. Even some who claim to be our heavenly Father's children are enthralled by all the glitz, just as secular fans are.

Name-dropping is a common practice. It had even become a cause of division in the Corinthian church (1 Corinthians 3:3–4). Ordinary folks who have a passing acquaintance with a famous person "drop" the name in conversations. Fans pay exorbitant prices for event tickets, drive great distances, and wait in long lines just to see and hear the person they have set apart in their hearts as having a name above other names. This practice of anointing celebrities is akin to worship.

How do we demonstrate that we give to our Father in heaven the honor that is his due? Does he hold an attraction for us surpassing all earthly heroes? Our heavenly Father's fame exceeds that of the greatest earthly celebrity, as the light from a forest fire exceeds that from a firefly. If we pray the Lord's Prayer properly we recognize God our Father as the ultimate "celebrity." But we do not need to purchase a ticket or travel a great distance or stand in a queue to be in our Father's presence. We enjoy the privilege of immediate access, as the Psalmist writes, "Exalt the Lord and worship at his footstool; he is holy" (Psalm 99:5).

By addressing God as Father we recognize his nearness to us. But God with whom we enjoy familial intimacy is also holy. The Lord's Prayer combines intimacy with God and awe at his transcendence. Jesus taught his disciples that God the Father exceeds all that is common. These two crucial concepts of God—his presence and his transcendence—go back to the constitution of the nation of Israel as the people of God. God said he would be their God, they would be his people, and he would dwell with them. Jesus Christ personalized these two aspects of the divine nature; he is *Emanuel,* God with us.

The secular culture has no qualms about using the name of God as an expletive. "God" is one of the most frequent words in people's vocabulary. The spontaneous ejaculation, "Oh! My God!" is a common expression of surprise or alarm. But the thoughts of those who say it are far from God. In like manner when somebody is displeased or irritated, he may revile the object of his antipathy as "God-damned."

The Sovereign Lord God told the prophet Ezekiel to explain that his judgment on Israel was for the sake of his holy name that they had profaned among the nations (Ezekiel 36:18–22). God's decree to his people to honor his holy name has not elapsed. Nevertheless, many churches today do as Israel did. They foment feuds, rancor, and hypocrisy that provoke the watching world—those who are not God's people—to mock God's name.

What should we do? In the biblical era, people repented of their sins by wearing sackcloth and ashes. It was a public display of contrition. A fitting counterpart to sackcloth and ashes today would have churches in a community banding together in humility to repent and ask forgiveness of the surrounding community for dishonoring God. A contrite confession of sin would give sobering evidence to the secular world that the heavenly Father's children honor him as holy.

The Danger of Misrepresenting God's Holiness

Ignorance of the true Lord God is the characteristic condition of mankind in this world of spiritual gloom. For this reason God has commissioned his people to make him known among the nations. King David said, "Give thanks to the Lord, call on his name; make known among the nations what he has done" (1 Chronicles 16:8). As we journey for a lifetime through this world that is under the control of evil, with its darkness and deceit, let us make known among the nations what the Lord God has done (1 Chronicles 16:23–31). Let us be lights in the darkness. This is our privilege and our responsibility. As the children of our Father in heaven, our authenticity will ensure that the deceitful murk of a decadent culture does not obscure what God has done.

Many spontaneous prayers betray a disrespectful nonchalance toward God. But our Father is not a cosmic convenience that we turn to whenever we have a wish or a need. God is more than a source of comfort or an infinite repository to satisfy our desires. Many prayers give scant evidence of contemplating the holiness, majesty, and grace of the one supplicated. I have found lovely exceptions to this among our Father's children in Asia and Central and Eastern Europe. They generally exude a diligence and reverence when they pray. They take time to engage their minds and tune their hearts before they open their mouths.

When Mount Sinai quaked and was engulfed in smoke punctuated with thunder and lightning, "everyone in the camp trembled" (Exodus 19:16). Moses said to the Lord God, "The people cannot come up Mount Sinai, because you yourself warned us, 'Put limits around the mountain and set it apart as holy'" (Exodus 19:23). From the birth of Israel as a nation, the people were to revere the Lord God. Both reverential fear and love are essential for treating our Father in heaven as holy. Love without fear breeds familiarity; fear without love produces insecurity.

Familiarity with God seems to have displaced reverence for God among many of his children. Some critics fault our

Father for not intervening to put a stop to terrorism and other atrocities. They do not know God, nor do they realize that the world lies in the control of evil. The gospel of God explains that Jesus Christ came into this world to rescue people from the devil's tyranny and save them from his evil dominion. It was not Jesus Christ's mission to restore the earth to the pristine perfection of everything that God pronounced "good" at creation. That restoration of creation will come with the new heavens and the new earth at the end of this age.

God's well-intentioned children may attempt to cast God in a gentle light. But God's mercy does not mean that our Father in heaven will be soft with a sinful world. If God in heaven does not mete out his judgment against sin during this age, it is because of his patience, not his indulgence.

The children of our heavenly Father often speculate about God's actions. They theorize about how he will deal with illness, injustice, terrorism, and the like. When we ultimately enter God's Kingdom in its fullness, everything will be perfect, without flaws, imperfections, impurities or disappointments. Until that happens, God's children live in a world poisoned by evil. Wickedness becomes progressively overt and detestable. But we do not capitulate to the tyranny of evil. We are distinct from the fallen society. The children of the heavenly Father are to be holy, as the Lord God is holy. The way we live must reflect his holiness.

The Holiness of the Father's Children

The Lord's Prayer is for those who care about personal holiness. They are fools who pray to our Father who is holy while they defiantly live an unholy life. The Lord told Moses to address the entire assembly of Israel: "Speak to the entire assembly of Israel and say to them: 'Be holy because I, the Lord your God, am holy'" (Leviticus 19:2). "You are to be holy to me because I, the Lord, am holy, and I have set you apart from the nations to be my own" (Leviticus 20:26).

The secular culture stands in stark contrast to the community of those God has rescued from the dominion of Satan. Therefore God's call to holiness among his children is most apropos. Separation from ungodliness is a distinguishing mark of a true church. Jesus Christ leveled some of his sternest rebukes against the churches of Pergamum and Thyatira that accommodated the mores of the surrounding pagan society (Revelation 2:14, 20–21).

Many churches emphasize a holiness that focuses on external, visible standards of behavior. Members are expected to conform to a set of rules, written or unwritten. Many of the Pharisees in the New Testament focused on external, visible behavior as the mark of righteousness. Jesus confronted their tendency to ignore matters of the heart. He denounced them as beautiful on the outside, but on the inside full of all kinds of uncleanness (Matthew 23:27). I recall Paul Little of InterVarsity Christian Fellowship (IVCF) explaining that those who focus on rules and regulations both underestimate and oversimplify holiness. Authentic holiness is not as simple as abstaining from certain behaviors, and there is much more to it than merely conforming to rules of conduct. Yes, God's children must turn away from ungodly behavior. There must be no confusion among God's children about the nature of a holy lifestyle. But holiness means being like our heavenly Father, not merely being unlike corrupt society.

Tragically, some of the Father's children have a negative orientation. They judge people who do not exhibit the outward marks of the behavior they approve. They focus on what people *do* and they overlook who they *are*, and who they are supposed to *be*. But holiness is about who we are. What we do springs from who we are. Ironically, in demonstrating how much they are not like the world, some of God's children also reveal how little they are like God. They are not overtly wicked in their visible conduct, nor are they holy like God in their inner nature.

When we pray sincerely "hallowed be your name," we long for our heavenly Father's majesty and glory to be honored everywhere. This longing springs from a passion in our souls to be holy as our Father in heaven is holy.

Questions for Discussion and Personal Application

1. When did you first understand the meaning of "hallowed be your name"?
2. Read the biblical account of Phinehas's zeal for God's honor in Numbers 25. What do you think an equivalent expression of zeal for God's holiness might be today?
3. To what extent does your understanding of God's holiness regulate your thoughts and behavior?
4. When you pray the Lord's Prayer, are you particularly drawn to one of the six petitions in the prayer?
5. How do you deal with affections that compete with the love you should reserve for your heavenly Father?
6. Read Isaiah 6:1–5. How can this description of worship in heaven help you when you pray "hallowed be your name"?
7. Since the term "name" comprises all our heavenly Father's attributes, how does "hallowed" or "holy" help us appreciate God's greatness?
8. After the entrance of sin into the human race, people no longer hallowed God's name. What did people substitute for God? What things do people today put in the place that is reserved for God?
9. How does the Third Commandment's warning not to misuse the Lord's name affect you when you pray "hallowed be your name"?
10. How do you cultivate an intimate relationship with our heavenly Father so that your "inmost being" (Psalm 103:1) praises his holy name?
11. How do you engage your emotions to express enthusiasm when you worship God?
12. How would your life be different if you were to exalt God above any earthly celebrities you idolize?

13. How can children of our heavenly Father effectively dissuade people from profaning God's holy name?
14. What evidence have you seen that the children of God today tend to be more casual than reverent in his presence?
15. How does our personal commitment to holiness as the children of God relate to our prayer "hallowed be your name"?

7. YOUR KINGDOM COME

Come, Thou Almighty King,
Help us Thy name to sing,
Help us to praise:
Father, all glorious, O'er all victorious,
Come and reign over us, Ancient of Days.

Anonymous[93]

The Nature of God's Kingdom

In order to pray intelligently for God's kingdom to come, we must understand the intent of Jesus' words in the Lord's Prayer. As an example, if you had asked someone in 1923 what could be done to improve the preservation of food, the response would likely have been a better icebox or more frequent ice deliveries. If you said, "Wouldn't you like to have a Frigidaire refrigerator?" you would probably have been met with a blank stare. Frigidaire had just produced a compact refrigerator for home use. Few people had heard of it, or if they had, they didn't understand how a refrigerator worked. This illustrates the ignorance of Jesus' disciples about the nature of the kingdom they expected him to inaugurate (Acts 1:6–7). Jesus frequently addressed the theme of God's kingdom in his teaching, but the disciples' concept of the kingdom was as different as a block of ice is from a plug-in kitchen appliance. Even today few people grasp the meaning of the kingdom of our Father in heaven. Their notions are far afield from what Jesus told his followers to pray for.

In the New Testament era religious Jews were looking for the coming of the Messiah to inaugurate the kingdom of God in Jerusalem. Their concept of God's kingdom was a political entity through which the nation of Israel would gain supremacy. Jesus explained, "The kingdom of God does not come with your careful observation, nor will people say, 'here it is,' or 'there it is,' because the kingdom of God is within (among) you" (Luke 17:20–21). If God's kingdom is within us, it cannot be a temporal, worldly government. As God is Spirit, so his kingdom is a spiritual dominion. People can actually become citizens of God's eternal kingdom while living as aliens in a temporal world that is ruled by the devil, the evil one.

In the Greek text of the Lord's Prayer the word translated *kingdom* is *basilea.* Its principal meaning is *kingship, reign,* or *rule.* George Eldon Ladd explained that the Kingdom is the sphere in which God's reign is experienced.[94] Those to whom the kingdom of God belongs are people who live under God's rule. All who have placed their faith in Jesus Christ as their Savior belong to God's kingdom. Whenever we speak of God's reign, we affirm the Lordship of Jesus Christ. When we pray for our heavenly Father's kingdom to come, our plea is that he will assert his reign in this world that is presently under the control of evil (literally, *lies in evil,* 1 John 5:19). God's kingdom is essentially his reign, his supreme rule.

Kingdom of Heaven, or Kingdom of God

In Scripture God's kingdom is called either the kingdom of heaven or the kingdom of God. "Kingdom of heaven" was often the preferred term. Pious people scrupulously avoided the utterance of the holy name of God in common parlance.

God our Father is in heaven and he is holy. Therefore, his kingdom is categorically un-worldly. It is marked by an otherness consistent with our Father's holiness. God's kingdom is greater and more glorious than we can comprehend. In certain aspects it may resemble our loftiest concept of a glorious earthly kingdom without flaws or imperfections. But our most fanciful ideas of heavenly things are pitiful illusions. The Psalmist David would not speculate about matters beyond his comprehension. He wrote, "My heart is not proud, O Lord, my eyes are not haughty; I do not concern myself with great matters or things too wonderful for me" (Psalm 131:1). Even though the Scriptures say much about the kingdom of God or the kingdom of heaven, much of it is a mystery to us.

During the 1980s and 1990s Manute Bol played professional basketball in the National Basketball Association. The seven-foot-seven-inch Manute was from the Dinka tribe in southern Sudan. He was discovered playing in local Sudanese basketball leagues. He moved to the United States in 1983 to study English and to develop his basketball prowess. A journalist visited Turalei, Manute's hometown of mud and wattle huts. His relatives could not conceive of Manute making a living by playing the game of basketball. They offered to help him if he needed their help. One of the village leaders said, "We heard life is good in America. We hear they have a lot of cows. This is progress." Dinka tribesmen had gross misconceptions of life in America. Manute Bol's new world was a humongous mystery—another dimension.

Jesus corrected people's false notions about the Kingdom of Heaven. His followers had a narrow-minded concept of the Kingdom that the Messiah would bring. Luke reports that as Jesus advanced to Jerusalem for the completion of his earthly mission, "the people thought that the kingdom of God was going to appear at once" (Luke 19:11). After his resurrection Jesus appeared to his disciples "over a period of forty days and spoke about the kingdom of

God" (Acts 1:3). Nevertheless, his disciples still held wrong notions about God's kingdom:

> So when they met together they asked him, 'Lord, are you at this time going to restore the kingdom to Israel?'" (Acts 1:6)

Jesus explained that the Kingdom was not what they had in mind. Jesus said to the Roman governor of Judea, Pontius Pilate,

> "My kingdom is not of this world. If it were, my servants would fight to prevent my arrest by the Jews. But now my kingdom is from another place (John 18:36).

The preponderance of Jesus' recorded parables was about the kingdom of heaven (e.g., Matthew 13:1–52; Luke 8:4–15). When Jesus called a certain man to follow him, the man asked to bury his father first. Jesus said, "Let the dead bury their own dead, but you go and proclaim the kingdom of God" (Luke 9:59–60).

God's children today face a dilemma. The earthly model of a kingdom governs our idea of God's kingdom. But God's kingdom spans dimensions beyond our finite frame of reference. God's kingdom will ultimately be visible to our senses, but at present it is invisible. Until Jesus Christ the Lord of the kingdom returns in glory, the kingdom of God remains spiritual and invisible.

Why God's Kingdom Must Come

In the Lord's Prayer Jesus instructed his followers to pray for God's kingdom to come to where we are. We are sojourners in a fallen creation. By choosing to believe the tempter rather than obey the Creator, mankind provided the portal for Satan to enter and to establish residency in God's earthly creation. The devil is an immigrant terrorist among us. The heavenly Father's children are living in a war zone. But God's children share in Christ's victory while on their earthly pilgrimage. The apostle Paul wrote,

> For if, by the trespass of the one man, death reigned through that one man, how much more will those who receive God's abundant provision of grace and of the gift of righteousness reign in life through the one man, Jesus Christ (Romans 5:17).

In April 1986 a cataclysmic meltdown occurred at the Chernobyl nuclear generator in Ukraine. Without a containment facility, the nuclear fallout spread throughout Ukraine and beyond. It poisoned the soil, polluting agriculture for generations to come. It fouled rivers and reservoirs. The radiation poisoning infected millions of people.

In like manner, when the first man and woman sinned in the garden at the beginning, there was a spiritual meltdown at mankind's core. The curse of that fallout has been expansive, contaminating all mankind with its virulent poison. Human nature has run amok. All generations of mankind have been under the curse since that fateful fall in the garden. But all who have received God's grace through faith in Jesus Christ have been delivered from the power of death (Hebrews 2:14–15), and they belong to a new kingdom where life reigns. They are set apart as aliens who do not belong to a world where death reigns.

The apostle John's Revelation described what is yet to come in the unfolding of the curse. "But woe to the earth and the sea, because the devil has gone down to you! He is filled with fury, because he knows that his time is short" (Revelation 12:12). He adds, "Then the dragon [Satan] was enraged at the woman and went off to make war against the rest of her offspring—those who obey God's commandments and hold to the testimony of Jesus" (Revelation 12:17). Our plea in the Lord's Prayer is that God's kingdom would break into this world that lies in evil. It expresses the longing of God's children that his reign will banish the evil one and his foul governance.

The prophet Daniel wrote that the people of God will ultimately possess the Kingdom of God:

> In my vision at night I looked, and there before me was one like a son of man, coming with the clouds of heaven. He approached the Ancient of Days and was led into his presence. He was given authority, glory and sovereign power; all peoples, nations and men of every language worshiped him. His dominion is an everlasting dominion that will not pass away, and his kingdom is one that will never be destroyed (Daniel 7:13–14).

Daniel added, "the saints of the Most High will receive the kingdom and will possess it forever—yes, for ever and ever" (Daniel 7:18). He told of great beasts waging war against the saints and defeating them "until the Ancient of Days came and pronounced judgment in favor of the saints of the Most High, and the time came when they possessed the kingdom" (7:22). He described the consummation:

> Then the sovereignty, power and greatness of the kingdoms under the whole heaven will be handed over to the saints, the people of the Most High. His

kingdom will be an everlasting kingdom, and all rulers will worship and obey him (Daniel 7:27).

During their time with Jesus, his followers did not grasp the nature and scope of the kingdom for which he taught them to pray. The prophet Daniel and the apostle John disclosed the magnitude of God's kingdom that extends far beyond our grasp.

The Eternal Kingdom's Visible Dimension

"May your kingdom come" is not a request that our Father will gain a kingdom for himself. He is the King eternal. He has a kingdom, and his rule is universal. Our prayer is that the Sovereign Lord will come, as Paul prayed, *maranatha* (1 Corinthians 16:22). In the Letter to the Hebrews the writer likewise expresses confidence that the kingdom will come:

> Therefore, since we are receiving a kingdom that cannot be shaken, let us be thankful, and so worship God acceptably with reverence and awe, for our God is a consuming fire (Hebrews 12:28–29).

Paul suffered punishment and imprisonment for preaching the gospel. But he wrote to Timothy, "The Lord will rescue me from every evil attack and will bring me safely to his heavenly kingdom" (2 Timothy 4:18). This is the hope of every child of our heavenly Father who endures hardship or suffers injury in this spiritual war zone. We belong to our Father's eternal kingdom.

The earthly concept of a kingdom is a realm that encompasses a specific geographic area. God's kingdom also entails a visible dimension. Christ's church is an expression of God's dominion in the world. The two are not identical, but there is an affinity between God's kingdom and Christ's church. In Scripture the Church is called the body of Christ. Jesus Christ is its Head. It is a spiritual entity indwelt and vitalized by the presence of God the Holy Spirit. Jesus Christ, God the Son, is Lord of the Church. Jesus Christ gave his church the mission to spread the good news of God's kingdom in a world tyrannized by the devil. It is the good news that God's reign has come in Jesus Christ.

A church building, often identified by a cross or distinctive architectural style, is just the earthly meeting place for a community of God's children. The church comprises God's children who have been called out from the world's ungodly culture. According to the apostle Paul, God said to his people:

> I will live with them and walk among them, and I will be their God, and they will be my people. Therefore come out from them and be separate, says the Lord. Touch no unclean thing, and I will receive you. I will be a Father to you, and you will be my sons and daughters, says the Lord Almighty (2 Corinthians 6:16–18).

When God rescued the Israelites from the Egyptian culture, their new identity was the people of the Lord God. They became more than just the offspring of the Hebrew patriarch Jacob. During their pilgrimage to the Promised Land they learned how to become a company of God's people. The lessons were not easy. Most times the Israelites failed miserably.

Today the sojourn of the Father's children as pilgrims on their journey homeward is perilous. But God has rescued us from the dominion of Satan. We are citizens of God's kingdom. The apostle Paul explained:

> For he [God the Father] has rescued us from the dominion [literally, 'authority,' *exousia*] of darkness and brought us into the kingdom [*basilea*] of the Son he loves, in whom we have redemption, the forgiveness of sins (Colossians 1:13–14).

God's Kingdom has two aspects. First, it signifies God's active rule or reign. Second, it is a realm of infinite range over which God is Sovereign. In God's kingdom everything conforms to his perfect will. Only where God reigns and where his will is done is there perfect righteousness. Carson wrote:

> God's kingdom or reign . . . can refer to that aspect of God's sovereignty under which there is life. That kingdom is breaking in under Christ's ministry, but it is not consummated till the end of the age (Matthew 28:20). To pray, "your kingdom come" is therefore synonymous with asking that God's saving, royal rule be extended in the present age. We pray that multitudes will bow in submission to our Father in heaven and taste the eschatological blessing of salvation. By praying for our Father's kingdom to come we express a longing for the consummation of the kingdom (cf. 1 Cor. 16:22; Revelation 11:17; 22:20).[95]

Where people do not pray for God's rule and they do not submit to his will, we find unrighteousness and moral decadence in all its vile manifestations.

The Presence of God's Kingdom

Where is this kingdom for which the Father's children pray? The kingdom of God is wherever God's reign is exercised and his sovereignty is recognized. We may also say that the kingdom is where Jesus Christ, God the Son is honored as Lord. The redemption of people from Satan's dominion is tied to the coming of God's kingdom. Paul explained to the Galatian church:

> Grace and peace to you from God our Father and the Lord Jesus Christ, who gave himself for our sins to rescue us from the present evil age, according to the will of our God and Father, to whom be glory for ever and ever. Amen (Galatians 1:3–5).

John wrote in the introduction of the Revelation he received, "To him who loves us and has freed us from our sins by his blood, and has made us to be a kingdom and priests to serve his God and Father—to him be glory and power for ever and ever! Amen" (Revelation 1:5–6). Grant Osborne commented:

> In spite of the persecutions and suffering that the saints are enduring, John wants them to know that they already inhabit a high position with Christ before God. The world is now in seeming control, but Christ has already entered the world and as a result of his "love" has "freed" them from the burdens of their sins and made them part of his kingdom, in which they are both royalty and priests. Their reign with him has already begun, even though it is yet to be consummated.[96]

God's kingdom is definitely not evident in the political arena. Our fallen, violent, crime-riddled society has nothing in common with the kingdom of God. Jesus warned his disciples that before the end comes . . .

Nation will rise against nation, and kingdom against kingdom. There will be famines and earthquakes in various places. All these are the beginning of birth pangs. Then you will be handed over to be persecuted and put to death, and you will be hated by all nations because of me. At that time many will turn away from the faith and will betray and hate each other, and many false prophets will appear and deceive many people. Because of the increase of wickedness, the love of most will grow cold, but he who stands firm to the end will be saved (Matthew 24:7–13).

Jesus answered some Pharisees who asked him when the kingdom of God would come, "The kingdom of God is within (or among) you" (Luke 17:21). In what sense was God's kingdom among the people? The kingdom of God was among them because Jesus, the one who spoke those words, was standing among them. The entrance of Christ as God Incarnate into this fallen world marked the entrance of God's kingdom. The King had come, but in lowly state. Mark reports in his Gospel that Jesus went about Galilee "proclaiming the good news of God. 'The time has come,' he said, 'The Kingdom of God is near. Repent and believe the good news!'" (Mark 1:14–15). Jesus proclaimed, literally, 'the kingdom of God has drawn near' (*héggiken*, cognate of *eggus*, "to be at hand"). In his person the kingdom had arrived. Where Jesus Christ is, the kingdom of God is. The kingdom is inseparable from God the Son, Jesus

Christ (Colossians 1:13). In Jesus Christ's presence God's reign has come. Paul wrote to the Corinthian church:

> Then the end will come, when he hands over the kingdom to God the Father after he has destroyed all dominion, authority and power. For he must reign until he has put all his enemies under his feet (1 Corinthians 15:24–25).

The evil one has control in this fallen world (1 John 5:19). When mankind in the garden chose to believe his lie, the devil usurped God's authority. That led to this world's corruption. When we pray for God's kingdom to come, we ask for God's universal rule to envelop this world. We look forward to the coming of Jesus, the victorious Lord, who will hand over the kingdom to God the Father. We pray for God's righteous rule to return to the earth where people have yielded their wills to the evil one. We also pray that people everywhere will acknowledge that Jesus Christ is Lord who reigns in the kingdom of God. We yearn for evil to be eradicated from the world. We long for God's righteous rule to reclaim his earthly creation in all its aspects.

Our petition is similar to Elijah's on Mt. Carmel. Elijah wanted to prove that the Lord God reigns. He wanted the hearts of the people to turn back to the Lord God. Before the fire fell from heaven he prayed, ". . . so these people will know that you, O Lord, are God and that you are turning their hearts back again" (1 Kings 18:32). This motif appears throughout Scripture. In Ezekiel's prophecy it appears 70 times. In essence it means the same as the common refrain to "declare his glory among the nations."

The Presence of the King

The king of a kingdom cannot be present at all times in all his domains. During the New Testament era there was a great kingdom—the Roman Empire. The king, or emperor was in Rome. It was a worldwide kingdom, but the king was not present in every country where the empire had gained sovereign control.

Throughout history there have been kingdoms under the absolute rule of a monarch. But the presence of the ruler does not mean his will is always done throughout his kingdom. Even where a dictator rules with an iron fist, some individuals and factions may oppose the will of the ruler. But God's children who pray for God's kingdom to come yearn for Jesus Christ's sovereign rule as Lord on the earth.

At the 1995 Global Consultation on World Evangelization in Seoul, Korea, I witnessed an amazing celebration of Jesus Christ's universal lordship. Four thousand delegates representing 186 nations participated in the conference. During worship in one of the plenary sessions we sang a simple song declaring that *Jesus Christ is Lord.* The leader invited someone to sing the song in his native language, and we all sang the refrain in our own tongue. Then, spontaneously it seemed, there was a line of men and women "from every tribe and language and people and nation," waiting to step to the microphone to sing in their native language that Jesus Christ is Lord. People around me were weeping or beaming with joy as they entered into the celebration of Jesus Christ's reign. It was probably my most soul-stirring offering of worship to the Lord ever. I viewed it as an earthly foretaste of the worship before the throne of heaven. There the twenty-four elders sang a new song: "with your blood you purchased men for God from every tribe and language and people and nation"

(Revelation 5:9). In his letter to the Philippians, Paul alludes to this laudation of Jesus Christ:

> Therefore God exalted him to the highest place and gave him the name that is above every name, that at the name of Jesus every knee should bow, in heaven and on earth and under the earth, and every tongue confess that Jesus Christ is Lord, to the glory of God the Father (Philippians 2:9–11).

The Kingdom of This World

The kingdom of heaven and the kingdoms of this world are different at the core. The kingdom of heaven is a realm of righteousness under the sovereign Lord God. Earthly kingdoms are marked by rivalry, distrust, deceit, covetousness, violence, and a constellation of other vices. Asaph described this world as a place where ". . . haunts of violence fill the dark places of the land" (Psalm 74:20). The entrance of evil created a chasm between God and mankind. We call it the "fall" of mankind. No realignment of our lives will suffice to remedy the devastation caused by sin in the human race.

The most extreme anomaly conceivable is children of the heavenly kingdom holding residence in a world under the control of evil. As sojourners in this corrupt world, God's children are misfits. We are in the world, but we belong in our Father's domain. This sinful world system is fraught with insidious allurements. God's children must constantly resist the tug to become naturalized citizens of the devil's realm. We are citizens of heaven; we do not hold dual citizenship. We are in transit through hostile territory. The way to orient ourselves properly in this world is to acknowledge each day that this world as we know it is not a right fit for our heavenly Father's children. People who work in an environment poisoned by hazardous fumes must wear protective masks. Miners exposed to coal or silica dust take precautions against black lung and miner's phthisis. God's children must guard their minds and hearts lest the mores of the debauched culture seep into their souls.

The Genesis narrative describes mankind's fall into sin. It gives the account of how the first humans sank into depravity under the control of the evil one—Satan, the devil. The Scriptures also disclose God's plan to save mankind from the curse of sin. God Incarnate, Jesus Christ accomplished salvation by his atoning sacrifice on the cross for our sins. God will consummate his plan in the coming of the Kingdom of God in which Jesus Christ is King of Kings and Lord of Lords.

God is absolutely pure and holy in nature. Sin alienated God from those he created in his image. Sin caused the corruption—but not the obliteration—of the grandeur of God's creation in the human race. After mankind fell from innocence and sinned, the image of God in mankind was effaced, but it was not erased. Amid the foulness of the devil's dominion, the beauty of God's grandest creation still bursts through in myriad expressions.

The juxtaposition of sin's hideousness and divine loveliness may be confusing to the children of our Father. We are inclined to reject people whose conduct is deplorable. Sigmund Freud, the so-called father of psychoanalysis, said, "I have found little that is good about human beings on the whole. In my experience, most of them are trash, ..."[97] But the rottenness of sin is not so ruinous that it reduces any person to human trash. In God's sight all people remain candidates for forgiveness. Christ Jesus came into this world to save sinners. In his appendix to the Lord's Prayer Jesus warned his followers that if they do not forgive people their sins, their Father will not forgive them their sins (Matthew 6:15).

The social, political, and spiritual condition of this world is dismal. Moral decadence is not only tolerated, it is celebrated. This world is indisputably under the control of the evil one. The writer in Hebrews explains, "In putting everything under him [Jesus], God left nothing that is not subject to him. Yet at present we do not see everything subject to him. But we see Jesus . . ." (Hebrews 2:8, 9). God's children live as sojourners in this world that is under the control of evil, but we long for the full expression of God's reign when everything will be subject to him. This is the reason we pray, *"Your kingdom come."*

The Longing of the Heavenly Father's Children

According to Murphy's Law, "If anything can go wrong, it will." The present condition of the world exemplifies Murphy's Law. But in God's kingdom where his will prevails, the "law" is "Everything always goes right." This is the longing of the children of God articulated in Paul's letter to Titus: "we wait for the blessed hope—the glorious appearing of our great God and Savior, Jesus Christ" (Titus 2:13). This is our petition for the fullness of God's reign to be inaugurated in the return of our Lord Jesus Christ. John Stott wrote,

> To pray that his kingdom may 'come' is to pray both that it may grow, as through the church's witness people submit to Jesus, and that soon it will be consummated when Jesus returns in glory to take his power and reign.[98]

This petition, "your kingdom come" expresses a deep desire for God to be the foremost celebrity on earth as he is in heaven. As the children of the heavenly Father our citizenship is in heaven, and we eagerly await a Savior from there, the Lord Jesus Christ (Philippians 3:20). During our pilgrimage as children of the heavenly Father we must be constantly alert. Paul explained: "But the Scripture declares that the whole world is a prisoner of sin" (Galatians 3:22).

God's glorious kingdom will come to earth, not just in the little slice of the earth where we live and work and go to church, but throughout the whole world. Jesus said the good news of this kingdom will be preached in the whole world as a testimony to all nations before the end comes (Matthew 24:14). No part of this world will remain unreached by the Gospel of God.

God's children have been transformed spiritually by faith in Jesus Christ as Savior. They are "new creations" (2 Corinthians 5:17). But the ways of the worldly kingdom insinuate themselves into the desires of our Father's children. We are inclined to envision life in terms of earthly experiences. This is evident in the way many or most Christians pray. Their prayer requests focus mostly on the physical and material matters that dominate their affections and their fears. The apostle John warned:

> Do not love the world or anything in the world. If anyone loves the world, the love of the Father is not in him. For everything in the world—the cravings of sinful man, the lust of his eyes and the boasting of what he has and does—comes not from the Father but from the world. The world and its desires pass away, but the man who does the will of God lives forever" (1 John 2:15–17).

Oh, how unabashedly many who consider themselves children of the heavenly Father love the world and the things in it! We are easily captivated by the secular culture's charms, by the desire to make impressions, and by the allure of fame.

Cutting the Earthly Tether

Who are the people that look forward to the coming of God's kingdom? The answer is, those who have been born anew and are new creations through their faith in Jesus Christ. Jesus told Nicodemus, "I tell you the truth, no one can see the kingdom of God unless he is born again . . . No one can enter the kingdom of God unless he is born of water and the Spirit" (John 3:3, 5).

God's children are sojourners away from our Father's heavenly realm. We do not now enjoy all the benefits of our status. We are royalty in exile. People are the noblest of God's earthly creation. He made mankind "a little lower than God" (Psalm 8:5). In all of God's creation there is no rank of beings situated between God and mankind. People are inferior to God alone. The statement that God created mankind, male and female, in his image, denotes the sanctity and dignity of humankind as God's premier creation (Genesis 1:26–27). Therefore, the culture of God's kingdom should be recognizable in God's highest creation. The apostle Paul implies that there is a divine priority attached to mankind:

> We know that the whole creation has been groaning as in the pains of childbirth right up to the present time. Not only so, but we ourselves, who have the firstfruits of the Spirit, groan inwardly as we wait eagerly for our adoption as sons, the redemption of our bodies (Romans 8:22–23).

God created us in his image for his pleasure. We cannot please God if our aspirations are riveted to this world. Regrettably that is the customary worldview in a culture dominated by the devil. The children of our Father in heaven should not seek satisfaction in the stuff of this fallen world. If our souls do not recoil from the perversity of this age, we are in no condition to pray, "Your kingdom come, your will be done." The psalmist said, "If I had cherished sin in my heart, the Lord would not have listened; but God has surely listened and heard my voice in prayer" (Psalm 66:18–19). James also warned, "When you ask, you do not receive, because you ask with wrong motives, that you may spend what you get on your pleasures" (James 4:3). The prayer Jesus gave to God's children is an unequivocal rejection of the social *status quo*. In the Lord's Prayer, the coming of God's kingdom is fused together with the doing of his will. We are sojourners who have already been rescued from the evil dominion of darkness and transferred into the kingdom of God's Son. We are not like those the apostle Peter says are like a dog that has returned to its vomit (2 Peter 2:22). The Lord's Prayer is a bold plea by the heavenly Father's children who refuse to conform to the values of an evil empire.

The Lord's Prayer clashes with any ambition to find one's greatest delight in the temporal pleasures of this world. The psalmist Asaph confessed that he envied the wicked that enjoyed an abundance of material possessions and the physical health to live a prosperous and long life. During his struggle Asaph "entered the sanctuary of God." There his perspective was recalibrated. The people he envied had nothing more than temporal stuff that held them captive to this world. Asaph then described a worldview befitting the children of God. He rejoiced in being always with the Lord; he desired nothing beside the Lord. He understood that those who are far from the Lord would perish. He concluded, "But as for me, it is good to be near God" (Psalm 73:24–28).

Children of the heavenly Father hold earthly possessions with open hands. They are no longer tethered to this world by the stuff they own or the things they desire. They have embraced Christ's admonition,

> Do not store up for yourselves treasures on earth, where moth and rust destroy, and where thieves break in and steal. But store up for yourselves treasures in heaven, where moth and rust do not destroy, and where thieves do not break in and steal. For where your treasure is, there you heart will be also (Matthew 6:19–21).

Paul addressed similar remarks to the church at Colossae:

> Since, then, you have been raised with Christ, set your hearts on things above, where Christ is seated at the right hand of God. Set your minds on things above, not on earthly things. For you died, and your life is now hidden with Christ in God (Colossians 3:1–3).

He wrote, "If only for this life we have hope in Christ, we are to be pitied more than all men" (1 Corinthians 15:19). This is the reason why we pray for the Father's kingdom to come. God's children do not fix their hope on any aspect of this world. The children of our Father in heaven do not live, hope, or plan "for merely human reasons" (1 Corinthians 15:32).

"Your kingdom come" is the passionate prayer of God's children. We cannot settle comfortably into this world. We belong to our Father's kingdom, which has not yet come in its fullness. Jesus told his disciples:

> If the world hates you, keep in mind that it hated me first. If you belonged to the world, it would love you as its own. As it is, you do not belong to the world, but I have chosen you out of the world. That is why the world hates you (John 15:18–19).

When Jesus blessed his followers, he said, "Blessed are you who are poor, for yours is the kingdom of God" (Luke 6:20). Those who stand steadfast in their allegiance to God the Father in this world will have great rewards in heaven (Luke 6:23). The blessings God's children receive here are but a foretaste of the fullness of the kingdom that will be realized when God's kingdom comes to earth.

When we pray "your kingdom come," we do so as those who already belong to the kingdom of God. We yearn for the intimacy of God's presence that we will enjoy when his kingdom comes in its completeness. This longing gripped David's heart in the desert of Judah. He prayed:

> O God, you are my God, earnestly I seek you:
> My soul thirsts for you, my body longs for you,
> In a dry and weary land where there is no water
> (Psalm 63:1).

Most people like to be pampered. They persuade themselves that they deserve some luxuries. This world's values fashion their desires. God's children deal with the same tug of earthly values. But it is patently naïve to pray the Lord's Prayer if the gravitational tug of this world's values holds us tightly in its grip. As children of our Father in heaven, we set our hearts and our minds on things above, where Christ is seated at the right hand of God (Colossians 3:1–2).

Praying with the Right Motives

What moves us to petition our heavenly Father, "Your kingdom come"? Is it distress over the perversity of society, or the violence that overruns our cities, or the rottenness that rules the political arena? Are these the reasons we plead for our Father's intervention? These are worthy motives, but when we pray for God's kingdom to come, our chief motive is a thirst for God himself. It is a longing for God our Father to be glorified in his entire creation. It is a deep yearning that Jesus Christ be exalted, worshiped and acknowledged universally as Lord of the heavenly kingdom.

Jesus warned, "The man who loves his life will lose it, while the man who hates his life in this world will keep it" (John 12:25). Those who cling to this earth as the storehouse of all their desires are incapable of praying, "your kingdom come" as Christ intended it to be prayed. When we pray for God's kingdom to come and his will to be done on earth, we ask for the most comprehensive change this planet has undergone since sin ravaged it. We gain insights into the future mega revolution in 2 Peter 3:10–13 and Revelation 21, which report the destruction of the present world and the coming of the new heaven and new earth.

As mortals we participate in God's kingdom through a radical transformation of our fallen human nature. Jesus explained that entering God's kingdom requires a thorough change marked by child-like innocence, humility, and submission.

> I tell you the truth, unless you change and become like little children, you will never enter the kingdom of heaven. Therefore, whoever humbles

himself like this child is the greatest in the kingdom of heaven (Matthew 18:1–4).

Helmut Thielicke said, "I say that the gospel contains no prescription for a valid world order but is rather a medicine for our hearts."[99] By our efforts we cannot transform society. Nor can we change the political landscape to inaugurate the kingdom of God. We change the hearts of people by the gospel of God that has the power to rescue people from the dominion of spiritual darkness where Satan reigns, and bring them into the Kingdom of God our Father.

God Our Refuge

God has repeatedly explained in his word that he is our refuge in this world. The Psalmist wrote,

He who dwells in the shelter of the Most High will rest in the shadow of the Almighty. I will say of the Lord, "He is my refuge and my fortress, my God in whom I trust" (Psalm 91:1–2 cf. Psalm 9:9, 46:1, Isaiah 57:13).

A refuge is a place where we can be safe. There is no refuge for God's children in this corrupt world. It is fraught with dangers, and there is no place to hide. If we live recklessly we will be maimed by the evil one. Our refuge is our Father in heaven. We pray for that day when we will no longer have to flee to a refuge in order to find peace and safety.

Many people seek a refuge in unhealthy relationships. Some turn to alcohol or drugs to assuage their torment. But they find no refuge. Even the comfort of a trusted friend or spouse is woefully inadequate. There is no rest for their troubled souls. Some who claim to belong to God's kingdom are merely religious interlopers. They are God's children in name only. They have not had an inner spiritual transformation through faith in Jesus Christ who is God the Savior. Jesus addressed this condition in his kingdom parable of the weeds and the wheat:

> The kingdom of heaven is like a man who sowed good seed in his field. But while everyone was sleeping, his enemy came and sowed weeds among the wheat, and went away. When the wheat sprouted and formed heads, then the weeds also appeared . . . . The owner of the field said to his servants, 'Let both grow together until the harvest. At that time I will tell the harvesters: First collect the weeds and tie them into bundles to be burned, then gather the wheat and bring it into my barn.' . . . As the weeds are pulled up and burned in the fire, so it will be at the end of the age. The Son of Man will send out his angels, and they will weed out of his kingdom everything that causes sin and all who do evil. They will throw them into the fiery furnace, where there will be weeping and gnashing of teeth. Then the righteous will shine like the sun in the kingdom of their Father. He who has ears, let him hear (Matthew 13:24–43).

There are some among God's children in this world who thrive like the weeds in Matthew 13. They are assertive and they assume key leadership roles in the community of God's children. We may wonder why our Father allows them to flourish. But they will be separated from the true children of the Father at the time of the judgment. Jesus taught the same lesson in the Parable of the Net, where good fish are separated from bad (Matthew 13:47–50)

Even though sin has rendered us all damaged goods, we still hope this world will treat us well. According to a popular aphorism, "Expecting the world to treat you fairly because you are a good person is like expecting a bull not to attack you because you are a vegetarian."[100] What we deem desirable will not happen in a world system that is broken down. It has been savaged by the evil one. We live in a spiritual and moral slum; and the slumlord is a tyrant. To pray "your kingdom come" is to ask for God's kingdom to come and displace this fallen kingdom. God has not abandoned his creation. He will redeem it:

> For the creation was subjected to frustration, not by its own choice, but by the will of the one who subjected it, in hope that the creation itself will be liberated from its bondage to decay and brought into the glorious freedom of the children of God. We know that the whole creation has been groaning as in the pains of childbirth right up to the present time (Romans 8:20–22).

The writer of the New Testament letter to the Hebrews says, "Therefore, since we are receiving a kingdom that cannot be shaken, let us be thankful, and so worship God acceptably with reverence and awe" (Hebrews 12:28). God's kingdom is unlike the kingdoms of this world that have been shaken throughout history as warnings from God. Scripture recounts such phenomena in the Great Flood and the temblors at Mt. Sinai. Global catastrophes like volcanic eruptions, earthquakes, tsunamis, hurricanes, and tornados testify to the fragility of the earth. In contrast to a kingdom that can be shaken, God's children are receiving a kingdom that lasts forever. "Your kingdom come" expresses a sincere longing to live as citizens in the kingdom where our heavenly Father reigns as Sovereign.

Do Not Love or Hate This World

Do we have to hate this world in order to pray, "Your kingdom come"? To obey God's command not to love the world does not necessarily mean to hate it in the sense that we customarily use the term. God lavishes his grace on people in this world; he meets our needs in this world; he often endows us with material blessings in this world. We receive God's loving provision in this world with gratitude. We do not love this world; nor do we hate it. Most of our life experiences are shaped by this physical world and by our earthly relationships. We have a deep fondness for much that this world offers. So it is a discipline to pray each day, "Your kingdom come," but it is also a spiritual necessity.

This corrupt world has not been expelled from God's realm. He is the ultimate Sovereign over everything. The original sin brought a curse upon humankind. Sin polluted everything earthly. It alienated the earthly creation from God's benevolent control. But God intervened through Christ's sacrificial death on the cross in our stead. Jesus alluded to this in several of his parables. The father sent his son back to his rightful possession, but wicked tenants seized him and killed him. They intended to claim the property as their possession (Matthew 21:33–41; Mark 12:1–9; Luke 20:9–16). God has provided sinful people the opportunity to be reborn as new creations here in this corrupt world. But most people reject the Savior that God sent to us. Nevertheless, God will consummate his redemptive plan with a new heaven and a new earth. In one of his sermons given while the allied forces were bombing Stuttgart, Helmut Thielicke said,

. . . not until we consider that we live in a world in which men kill and die (and how they kill and how they die!) . . , a world in which only dim traces remain of the glory and the grandeur that God intended for his creation—not until we remember all this can we begin to measure the fervency of that petition, "Thy kingdom come," the fervency of hope and homesickness with which we await the coming of a new heaven and a new earth where God will be all in all.[101]

This is the longed-for consummation for the children of God. Our aspiration is to experience the fullness of God's reign. In the interim, we who have been rescued from the authority of the lord of the darkness can live with the confidence of knowing Jesus Christ as Lord of the kingdom of God. Wherever we are in this world, we declare with confidence, "Christ is Lord!"

The Last Days

We live in an era the Scriptures call the "last days." It is the period of time between the first and second advents of Jesus Christ, who is "God with us." The culmination of God's purposes for his people will occur at "the end." The apostle Paul wrote,

Then the end will come, when he (Christ) hands over the kingdom to God the Father after he has destroyed all dominion, authority and power. For he must reign until he has put all his enemies under his feet (1 Corinthians 15:24, 25).

The apostle Peter speaks about the Day of Judgment and the destruction of the present physical earth (2 Peter

3:11–13). In the Revelation of what will be, John tells of a war in heaven between the archangel Michael and his angels against the dragon [Satan] and his angels. The dragon is defeated and hurled down to the earth. Then a loud voice said, "Now have come the salvation and the power and the kingdom of our God and the authority of Christ" (Revelation 12:10). "Our Father in heaven . . . may your kingdom come. Amen."

Questions for Discussion and Personal Application

1. Explain what God's kingdom means to his children today.

2. What are some of the most disturbing evidences of the curse of sin that you see in the world today?

3. The apostle Paul was confident that God would protect him in this hostile world and would bring him safely into his heavenly kingdom (2 Timothy 4:18). If you share this confidence, what are some of the hostile attacks in which you expect God to protect you?

4. How does the church of Jesus Christ express the kingdom of God in the world?

5. Describe how the sojourn of God's children in the world is like the wilderness pilgrimage of God's people Israel to the Promised Land.

6. Why do we pray for God's kingdom to come while we also affirm that the kingdom of God has come?

7. Explain how the kingdom of God came into this world that is under the control of evil.

8. If you have experienced a "foretaste" of heavenly worship described in the Book of Revelation, tell how it happened.

9. What practical actions can God's children take each day to resist the decadent allurements of the world's culture?

10. Sin did not obliterate the divine image from any human being. How then should we regard people whose lifestyle or conduct is repugnant?

11. Give some examples of the kind of prayer requests we make to our Father in heaven if we "do not love the world or anything in the world" (1 John 2:15).

12. What effect should the fact that you belong to God's highest and noblest creation have on your attitude and conduct?

13. Read Psalm 73. To what extent does your experience parallel that of the psalmist Asaph?

14. God's children aspire to good relationships with people in the secular culture. But godly values and standards often clash with society's mores. How do you deal with the temptation to compromise?

15. What is our chief motive for praying to our heavenly Father "your kingdom come"?

16. God our Father is a refuge for his children on their trek homeward through a world fraught with spiritual dangers. How often do you flee to God as your refuge?

17. Read Hebrews 12:28. What does the writer mean by a kingdom that cannot be shaken?

18. God's command not to love the world does not require us to hate it. In what way is it appropriate for God's children to think well of the world?

8. YOUR WILL BE DONE ON EARTH AS IT IS IN HEAVEN

There are only two kinds of people in the end:
those who say to God "Thy will be done,"
and those to whom God says, in the end,
"Thy will be done."

C. S. Lewis[102]

God's kingdom and God's will are inextricably intertwined. An essential aspect of the coming of God's kingdom is the doing of God's will.

We pray for our Father's will to be done on earth as it is in heaven. We do not expect ungodly people to find it in their hearts to do God's will. Fallen mankind lacks the inclination and the ability to do God's will, let alone do his will as it is done in heaven. We pray that our heavenly Father will do whatever it takes to move mankind on earth to embrace God's sovereign will, as the heavenly beings do. Fallible human beings cannot reform life on earth, regardless of how conscientious our efforts may be. The will of our heavenly Father will not come through a referendum of the human race. Our prayer is that our Father's perfect will in heaven be mirrored on earth. God alone can do it. We cannot make it happen. Our part is to ask.

"Heaven" in this petition is the same as the abode of God our Father in the opening clause of the Lord's Prayer. As God Almighty, our Father in heaven receives the adoration of the innumerable heavenly host. All the subjects of God's realm carry out his will perfectly and consistently. Heaven is the antithesis of the corrupt earth, the dominion of darkness where Satan rules. God Almighty has safeguarded heaven against any power opposed to his will. When the resplendent angel Lucifer rebelled against God's sovereign rule, he was summarily cast down to the earth and banned from the realm where God's authority is absolute and God's will is resolute (Isaiah 14:12–14).

God's Will in God's Realm

How do we know that God hears us when we pray? The apostle John answers, "This is the confidence we have in approaching God: that if we ask anything according to his will, he hears us" (1 John 5:14). A commitment to God's will is the *sine qua non* of effective prayer.

The Lord's Prayer is our strongest plea for the Father's will to prevail. Our ambition as the children of our heavenly Father is to do his will, not our will. His rule is not oppressive. He does not force unwilling subjects to comply with his will. Our Father's will is the norm in heaven. We ask for nothing less on earth. This was undoubtedly what Jesus intended when he taught his followers to pray.

We do not ask our Father to grant our desires. We do not pretend that our wishes must surely be God's will. This request in the Lord's Prayer is completely for God's glory. It is not for our convenience or enjoyment.

In praying for God's will to be done "as it is in heaven," we ask for more than we can grasp. We cannot conceive of a scenario where God's majesty and glory are always dominant. Since God is infinite, holy, and sovereign, the highest value in the universe is God's will. Lloyd-Jones said, "The supreme desire of all in heaven is to do the will of God."[103]

Edward W. Klink III said "for God's children it is not a matter of getting God into our lives (he is already there), but rather of getting our lives into God's."[104] Is that not a fitting description of the state of longing for his will? Paul wrote to the Colossian Church: "For you died, and your life is now hidden with Christ in God" (Colossians 3:3).

D. A. Carson elaborated on the nature of God's will done on earth as it is in heaven:

> To pray that God's will, which is "good, pleasing and perfect" (Romans 12:2), be done on earth as in heaven is to use language broad enough to embrace three requests. The first request is that God's will be done now on earth as it is now accomplished in heaven. The word *theléma* ("will") includes both God's righteous demands (Matthew 7:21; 12:50; cf. Psalm 40:8) and his determination to bring about certain events in salvation history (Matthew 18:14; 26:42; cf. Acts 21:14). So for that will to be "done" includes both moral obedience and the bringing to pass of certain events, such as the Cross. This prayer corresponds to asking for the present extension of the messianic kingdom. The second request is that God's will may ultimately be as fully accomplished on earth as it is now accomplished in heaven. "Will" has the same range of meanings as before; and this prayer corresponds to asking for the consummation of the messianic kingdom. The third request is that God's will may ultimately be done on earth in the same way as it is now accomplished in heaven. In the consummated kingdom it will not be necessary to discuss superior righteousness (Matthew 5:20–48) as antithetical to lust, hate, retaliatory face-slapping, divorce, and the like; for then God's will, construed now as his demands for righteousness, will be done as it is now done in

heaven: freely, openly, spontaneously, and without the need to set it over against evil.[105]

God's Will; Not My Will

In all his ways God is perfect and holy. God pronounced everything he created "very good" (Genesis 1:31). God's will is therefore very good. It is perfect. For this reason the prayer of every child of our heavenly Father is that his will be done on earth. Robert Law's counsel brings our desires into proper alignment with our Father's will: "Prayer is a mighty instrument, not for getting man's will done in heaven, but for getting God's will done on earth."[106]

There are two principal reasons for submitting to the will of another. One is compliance. You submit, perhaps reluctantly, to the demands of an authority. The other reason is commitment. You submit in honor of someone you love and trust. Our prayer to our Father, "your will be done," implies that we trust him completely because his will is right and perfect in every way.

Andrew Murray used the analogy of a writer and a pen to illustrate the necessity of absolute surrender to God's will. The pen must be fully surrendered to the writer's will. If another person holds the pen partly, the writer cannot write properly.[107] God cannot work his work every day and every hour in us if we try to take control. Paul said God works in us "to will and to act according to his good purpose" (Philippians 2:13). Jesus taught, "If anyone would come after me, he must deny himself and take up his cross daily and follow me" (Luke 9:23). To pray for God's will to be done implies a denial of self—of what we "will." It is a repudiation of the prideful self that wants its own way and its desires to be fulfilled.

In parts of Asia the elephant has been domesticated. The elephant's owner wants it to remain mighty but he expects the mahout to control the elephant's might so that it does his bidding. Some people want the Lord God to be like the elephant—tame, but powerful. They have no need of a "wild" God who defies domestication and does not submit to their wishes. Even though it is not on their lips, the prayer of their hearts is "my will be done." But we are not God's mahouts, directing him to use his might as we wish.

This world under the control of evil is not a healthy environment for the heavenly Father's children. But God's children do not acquiesce to the mores of this fallen world. Consider the patriarch Joseph. For much of his life he struggled under adverse circumstances. But he retained his status as an alien and refused to become assimilated into the Egyptian culture. His faithfulness to the Father's will gave him extraordinary opportunities to honor the Lord God (Genesis 41:16).

The Lord's Prayer implies that the petitioner's life is oriented toward God's will. When we pray, "Your will be done," we commit ourselves to doing what is right in the eyes of the Lord. William Barclay wrote, "Prayer must never be an attempt to bend the will of God to our desires; prayer ought always to be an attempt to submit our wills to the will of God."[108] The prophet Isaiah asked,

> Does the ax raise itself above him who swings it, or the saw boast against him who uses it? As if a rod were to wield him who lifts it up, or a club brandish him who is not wood! Therefore, the Lord, the Lord Almighty, will send a wasting disease upon his sturdy warriors . . . (Isaiah 10:15–16).

In this context the Lord promised to deal with Jerusalem for its unfaithfulness, just as he dealt with Samaria and Assyria in their idolatry. The lesson for us is that we cannot manipulate our Father in heaven. As an ax does not raise itself above the one who swings it, so we cannot raise ourselves above God and expect him to do our bidding. Therefore we pray, "your will be done." Nothing lies outside the reach of prayer except that which is outside the will of God.

God's Will Among the Nations

What is God's will that he wants done on the earth? God's will focuses on the jewel of his creation, mankind. It is his will that he be acknowledged as God among all the nations. The Lord God spoke through the prophet Isaiah,

> You are my servant, Israel, in whom I will display my splendor . . . . I will also make you a light for the Gentiles, that you may bring my salvation to the ends of the earth (Isaiah 49:3, 6).

God's people Israel had the responsibility to declare his glory among the nations. Throughout Israel's history the way was open for the Gentiles to join Israel in following the Lord God. This is a consistent stream that flows through Judeo-Christian history. God's people have an obligation to present the Lord God to the nations so that they may acknowledge him as the only true God, and worship him.

The heavenly Father wished his children to maintain a concern for the welfare of the nations. Dinesh D'Souza pointed out that the ancient Greeks and Romans did not care about the suffering of people in other nations. "They held a view quite common among nations today: 'Yes, that is a problem, but it's not our problem.'"[109] To pray that God's

224

will be done on earth—that God's kingdom may come among the nations—is quintessentially Christian. Wherever a vibrant Christian faith has spread (not merely traditional Christian religion), we find enthusiastic outreach to rescue people among the nations from the dominion of darkness and to bring them into the Kingdom of God's Son. We do not wish anyone to perish. I was horrified to hear Bishop Desmond Tutu say in a television interview, "I think the West, for my part, can go to hell."[110] No one who truly belongs to God's kingdom should wish that any person or group would go to hell.

Divine Dictator

In the Lord's Prayer we ask for God's will alone, and for God's will without compromise. Our Father's will does not accommodate contrary preferences. But in most aspects of life people seek compromise. Negotiators try to find no-lose solutions to conflicts. It is commendable to achieve a compromise between opposing parties so that all are winners and none are losers. But God's will permits no negotiation and suffers no compromise. When we pray that God's will be done we countenance no will except our Father's. When our heavenly Father's will is done, there is no room for even a snippet of opposition. God's will is explicit and exclusive.

To pray for our Father's will on earth as it is done in heaven is tantamount to acknowledging that God is our dictator. Our desire is to submit in all respects to the will of our absolute ruler who loves us. A dictator declares his will explicitly and demands that his subjects obey it exactly. But "dictator" is generally a negative concept. So it should be, because no earthly dictator has ever been perfectly righteous. Earthly dictators usually impose their will by force. To oppose the wishes of a dictator often means punishment, prison, or death. Some like Bhumibol Adulyadej (d. 2016), former King of Thailand, could be called "benevolent dictators," but most are evil tyrants who bully the citizens and care mostly about indulging their own desires. Lord Acton said, "Power corrupts; absolute power corrupts absolutely."[111] This appears to be an unavoidable trait of fallible human nature.

For this reason, people who cherish liberty detest dictatorial rule. Liberty is the hallmark of the United States of America and the ethos of the American spirit. The huge statue on Liberty Island in New York harbor is called The Statue of Liberty. At the foot of the statue lies a broken chain. The colossal sculpture is the icon of freedom, welcoming immigrants to the United States, the land of the free. A watchword of the nation is Patrick Henry's declaration of 1775 at the Virginia Convention, "Give me liberty, or give me death."[112]

God's children proclaim liberty as the hallmark of their faith. We have been set free from bondage to the evil god of this world. He is the tyrant over whom Jesus Christ won the victory for mankind. By his atoning sacrifice on the cross and his resurrection from death Jesus broke the bonds that imprisoned us in sin.

How can a divine dictator fit into our theology that trumpets liberty? The fact that our "dictator" is our heavenly Father helps immeasurably. He has disclosed himself to mankind as the perfectly righteous and compassionate dictator. God's children long for whatever it takes for his will to be done on earth. Our part is to submit our wills to our Father's will.

When Satan deceived the first human couple, they rejected God's will. As a result, the evil one usurped control over God's creation. The mass of mankind is subject to the will of the evil one. Jesus said to a group of proud religious people who claimed to be Abraham's descendants, "You belong to your father, the devil, and you want to carry out your father's desire" (John 8:44). Many religious people are in a similar situation. They have family reasons for not resisting the devil. They are blind to the truth of their spiritual bondage. There is no longing in their hearts for God's will to be done on earth as it is in heaven.

When we pray for our Father's will to be done on earth, we know a great deal about God's will. The Father has revealed it to us. God's word declares that he does not want anyone to perish but all people to be saved (1 Timothy 2:3, 4; 2 Peter 3:4). We also know that God wants his children to love one another (John 13:34; 1 John 3:23, 24). Above all, God's will is to be honored and obeyed in his creation. The Scriptures are chock full of the revelation of his will for us.

The Freedom to Choose

God also endowed mankind, the bearer of his image on earth, with the freedom to choose. Since earliest history people have chosen the wrong. They choose hatred and warfare instead of love. The evil ruler of this fallen world has deceived most people. International conflicts are evidence that whole nations routinely reject the Father's will.

When we pray for God's will, we ask for the greatest good. We may not know what our Father will choose to do, but we believe his will is always best. The apostle Paul stated this in his doxology:

> Oh, the depth of the riches of the wisdom and knowledge of God! How unsearchable his judgments, and his paths beyond tracing out! Who has known the mind of the Lord? Or who has been his counselor? (Romans 11:33–34).

The petition for the Father's will to be done means all of God's will, the aspects we do not know as well as those we do know. The greatest act of God's will on earth was the death and resurrection of Jesus Christ. Jesus came to do the Father's will. He told his disciples, "My food is to do the will of him who sent me and to finish his work" (John 4:34). He said to the crowd that had been searching for him, "For I have come down from heaven not to do my will but to do the will of him who sent me" (John 6:38). In Gethsemane Jesus prayed to the Father, "Yet not as I will but as you will." (Matthew 26:39) Before he expired on the cross "Jesus said, 'It is finished.' With that, he bowed his head and gave up his spirit" (John 19:30). He had done the Father's will.

Our Father has revealed to us another aspect of will. It is called the "mystery of his will." It is God's will to bring all things to a consummation:

> And he made known to us the mystery of his will according to his good pleasure, which he purposed in Christ, to be put into effect when the times will have reached their fulfillment—to bring all things in heaven and on earth together under one head, even Christ" (Ephesians 1:9–10).

Jesus accomplished the Father's will by his victory over the evil one. Satan can no longer enforce his diabolical will throughout the earth. In the person of Jesus Christ God's kingdom entered this fallen earthly creation. All who have believed in Jesus Christ as Lord have become citizens of God's kingdom and children in God's household. The children of God are not subject to the devil's will. We live in a world that lies in evil, but our citizenship is in heaven (Philippians 3:20). We are pilgrims journeying through the devil's dark domain to our Father's home where Jesus Christ has prepared a place for us.

The children of the heavenly Father have the liberty and the ability to do God's will. We choose to obey our Father because we love him. The apostle John wrote, "And this is love, that we walk in obedience to his commands" (2 John 6). The consummation of our plea for the Lord's will is the realization of our Father's universal rule. Everything that is contrary to God's reign will be squelched. Satan will have dominion nowhere. The world will be liberated from its bondage to decay (Romans 8:21).

The awful devastation that sin continues to wreak in the world was the result of disobeying God's will in the beginning. Someone might object, "The punishment does not fit the crime! Isn't God too harsh? Eating forbidden fruit is a minor misdemeanor." But there is no such thing as a minor contravention of God's will. The weight of the violation does not rest on the nature of the offense, but on the One who is violated, namely God. What seems relatively innocuous to us is as blatant an offense as any. It is a deliberate violation of God's revealed will.

The Precision of God's Will

God's will in heaven is perfect, precise, and unalterable. Defiance or rejection of the Father's will is an egregious anomaly in his creation. Anything contrary to God's will is the essence of evil. Being sojourners in a part of God's creation that has been invaded by evil is sobering. Our heavenly Father's will is not the norm in this world. But in God's pristine creation all things were in accordance with his will. At creation, when God said, "Let there be . ." the result was, "it was so" (Genesis 1:9, 11, 15, 24, 30). To pray for the heavenly Father's will is the foundation of prayer. It is also our loftiest prayer because it transcends all our mundane preoccupations. We ask for our heavenly Father's will, not for our worldly desires.

God our Father's will is always, everywhere, and in every way the order of his created universe. Therefore, we pray for his will. But, alas, frequently our wishes do not line up perfectly with his will. Even God Incarnate Jesus Christ acknowledged that his will was not congruent with the Father's will. When he prayed on the Mount of Olives shortly before he was crucified, he said, ". . . yet not my will, but yours be done" (Luke 22:42).

Do we have any latitude to determine what God's will is, based on what we deem reasonable? Is God's will an ethereal thing? In my youth I heard preachers speak of God's varied wills. According to them, God had a perfect will and something called a "permissive will." The latter was evidently something that God allowed, although it was not his primary intention. So there was some wiggle room in God's will. One could miss God's perfect will, but still be okay by falling within the wider orbit of God's permissive will. You could reject a divine call to missionary service as God's perfect will for your life, and yet avoid the stigma of disobedience by choosing an alternate occupation within the bounds of God's permissive will. That notion implies God's will is like a target. If you do his perfect will, you hit the bull's eye. If you land anywhere within the target's outer edge you remain in good standing with God because of his permissive will.

It is surprising that such an idea could gain traction among those who claim Scripture as their final authority. Perhaps the idea of a permissive will was spawned by efforts to explain why God did not seem to punish his people who disobeyed his will. Perhaps their disobedience did not result in completely missing the target of God's will. Our Father in heaven was construed as approving their chosen alternative.

The correct explanation, however, is that our heavenly Father is patient and merciful.

The clause "as it is in heaven" establishes the precision of the petition. How could anyone seriously countenance the belief that in heaven God's will is flexible? Scripture allows no wiggle room in God's will. William Hendriksen stressed,

> It is the ardent desire of the person who sincerely breathes The Lord's Prayer that the Father's will shall be obeyed as completely, heartily, and immediately on earth as this is constantly being done by all the inhabitants of heaven."[113]

God's will does not bend to accommodate any will in conflict with his. There is no such thing as "second best" in heaven. Second best is inferior to the best. Nothing that is inferior has a place in heaven. The idea that God's will is flexible implies that God should prepare himself for surprises—events that were not his intention. But our heavenly Father knows the end from the beginning. Everything in heaven is perfect—precise and deliberate. When we pray for our Father's will on earth as in heaven, we request the exact working out of his purposes, even to the most minute degree.

King Saul behaved as if God's will is flexible. He presumed to interpret God's unambiguous command in a manner that seemed more reasonable to him (1 Samuel 15). God intended to use Saul and his army to carry out the Lord's judgment on the Amalekites for waylaying the Israelites after they came out of Egypt. God ordered Saul to destroy the Amalekites completely, along with everything belonging to them. But Saul spared their king, King Agag, and the best of the sheep, cattle, fat calves, and lambs. Ostensibly, Saul would sacrifice them to the Lord. Saul had carried out the Lord's instructions approximately, but not exactly. The Lord God sent the prophet Samuel to confront Saul. Samuel gave God's verdict:

> Does the Lord delight in burnt offerings and sacrifices as much as in obeying the voice of the Lord? To obey is better than sacrifice, and to heed is better than the fat of rams (11Samuel 15:22).

Saul's arrogance led him to reject the word of the Lord. He heard God's instructions, but he interpreted them as he saw fit. God, therefore, rejected Saul as king. This lesson from the life of Saul illustrates the inflexibility of the Father's will. When we pray "your will be done," we ask for God's will to be done exactly, perfectly, and without any modification to suit our preference or convenience. All who love our heavenly Father will submit to this divine mandate.

For God's children the petition "your will be done" is a pledge of obedience. William Barclay remarked, "the most important words in the world are "thy will be done." He wrote,

> A man may say "thy will be done" in a tone of defeated resignation. He may say it, not because he wishes to say it, but because he has accepted the fact that he cannot possibly say anything else; he may say it because he has accepted the fact that God is too strong for him and that it is useless to batter his head against the walls of the universe.[114]

The prophet Ahijah explained why God approved of David: "my servant David, who kept my commands and followed me with all his heart, doing only what was right in my eyes" (1 Kings 14:8). John wrote, "Dear friends, if our hearts do not condemn us, we have confidence before God and receive from him anything we ask, because we obey his commands and do what pleases him" (1 John 3:21–23). We subordinate all our personal requests to the prayer for God's will to be done. Anything we ask of God our Father is under the umbrella of his will. The prophet Jeremiah prayed, "I know, O Lord, that a man's life is not his own; it is not for man to direct his steps" (Jeremiah 10:23). Our requests should always and above all fall in line with the will of our Father in heaven. The literal rendering of the text is "Let your kingdom come; let your will come about, as in heaven also on earth" (Matthew 6:10). This is a large request. We ask for nothing less than the completeness of God's will here on earth as it is done in heaven.

The Cost of Obedience

God's children groan as part of a creation marked by pain (Romans 8:18–23). We wait eagerly for our redemption as the children of God. Waiting for God's Kingdom and looking forward to the full realization of his will are joyful prospects. Life in this world is not completely an excruciating ordeal. God's children do not have to "gut it out." We can say with the psalmist David, "Even though I walk through the valley of the shadow of death, I will fear no evil, for you are with me; your rod and your staff, they comfort me" (Psalm 23:4). We know the joy of our Father's intervention to rescue us from a dominion controlled by evil. We see God's "fingerprints" in countless answered prayers.

What role do the heavenly Father's children play in God's will being done on earth? Our part is to obey it. When God's people prepared to enter the Promised Land, Moses emphasized their obedience to the commands the Lord God had given them to follow. The controlling command that held all the Lord's decrees and laws together was: "to love the Lord your God, to walk in all his ways and to hold fast to him" (Deuteronomy 11:22). Moses said to the Israelite families as they were about to cross the Jordan River to enter their new homeland,

> Fix these words of mine in your hearts and minds; tie them as symbols on your hands and bind them on your foreheads. Teach them to your children, talking about them when you sit at home and when you walk along the road, when you lie down and when you get up. Write them on the doorframes of your houses and on your gates (Deuteronomy 11:18–20).

Obeying God's will is just as crucial a commitment for his children today. Our obedience to our heavenly Father must be patently evident in our behavior and not just in our words.

When I moved from Africa to Canada as a teenager, each day presented new fascinations. Fresh stimuli bombarded my mind. Try to imagine the experiences of God's people as they crossed the Jordan. Countless new interests and distractions would blitz the people of God in the land of Canaan. But no matter how alluring the novelties were, as individual families God's people had to maintain the priority of God's will.

How does the Father's will take precedence for a child of God who struggles with worldly desires? The apostle Peter offers this godly counsel:

> Therefore, since Christ suffered in his body, arm yourselves also with the same attitude, because he who has suffered in his body is done with sin. As a result, he does not live the rest of this earthly life

for evil human desires, but rather for the will of God (1 Peter 4:1–3).

Suffering prepares God's children to obey God's will. In the Book of Hebrews we read this about Jesus: "Although he was a son, he learned obedience from what he suffered and, once made perfect, he became the source of eternal salvation for all who obey him . . ." (Hebrews 5:8–9). Suffering is an unpleasant prospect. I would rather do God's will without the requisite suffering. It is a sobering fact that the pathway to God's will takes us through difficulties of various sorts.

Jesus said he came to do the will of the Father. Paul urged the Roman believers to devote themselves totally to God so that they could test and approve God's good, pleasing, and perfect will (Romans 12:2). As we travel through this fallen world toward our eternal home, God's children must be visible exhibits of God's will.

On Earth as in Heaven

We ask for our Father's will on earth as in heaven. But earth is not like heaven. Heaven is perfect; we are accustomed to a corrupt world. Conditions in heaven are beyond our ken. We can, however, turn our attention to our heavenly Father who has disclosed himself to us in his inspired word. We know that he is Sovereign of the universe. He is infinite, eternal, and perfect. We do not know heaven, but we know our Father in heaven. Our plea is for the realization of God's reign on this fallen sphere, as it is in heaven.

Liz and I were vacationing with friends in Arizona. One day the men decided to go into the desert on all-terrain vehicles (ATVs). The four-wheelers were sporty and fast. I had not previously driven an ATV. I had no business driving as fast as I did. I had a serious accident. I was rushed to the Osborne Trauma Unit at the Scottsdale hospital with multiple breaks and internal bleeding. Liz held vigil by my bed. My life hung in the balance. The medical staff urged her to leave and get some rest. She later told me that she went to the hotel to pray. She could not frame words to say. On her knees with her arms raised she prayed the Lord's Prayer to her Father in heaven. She prayed "your will be done." That was her way of giving me over to our Father. That is precisely what this petition in the Lord's Prayer implies for those who pray it.

By praying, "your will be done" we surrender everything we have and are to our Father. It belongs to him to do with us as he pleases. When we pray, "your will be done" we do not hold out for the desires of our hearts. That would be a sham. It is a serious matter to pray, "your will be done on earth as it is in heaven," but Jesus said it is necessary. As God's will is done in heaven, so we pray for it to be done in us globally and individually. When I apply the Lord's Prayer to myself, I ask: "Father, may your will be done in me as it is done in heaven."

As beings that bear God's image, we are endowed with the ability and the obligation to choose his will. Each day we make decisions. Most often our choices do not violate God's revealed will. We have the freedom and the intelligence to make what we believe to be the best decision. Sometimes we make self-indulgent choices and declare them to be God's will. We try to persuade ourselves that our desires are aligned with the will of God. It is common to confuse our desires with God's guidance.

How do we discern God's will in the matter of choosing a life partner or a career? Is it entirely up to us to decide? Is it possible to choose a marriage partner or a career that might jeopardize God's will for our lives? Most definitely!

Someone may object that holding to the exactness of God's will in our lives is absurd, if carried too far. But how far is too far? Who decides where to draw the line? Should you seek God's will in determining whether to have corn flakes and fruit instead of eggs and bacon for breakfast? Imagine the guilt of someone who chose frosted flakes and later sensed that God's will for him was oatmeal! A person could starve while waiting for God's will to be revealed. God has given mankind the faculty to be reasonable in making choices that conform to his will. If you habitually eat foods that are detrimental to your physical health, you may compromise your ability to be what God wants you to be.

Whatever It Takes

For most of my life I was hesitant to include the little clause, "Lord, whatever it takes" when praying for his will. To pray in that manner implied the ultimate in desperation—a prayer of last resort. What if I prayed that God would do "whatever it takes" to pressure a stubborn individual to repent and trust in Christ as Savior? What if my prayer were to precipitate a horrible disaster that at last arrested a rebel's attention? It dawned on me in the process of some discussions with my wife Liz that my hesitancy to pray "Lord, whatever it takes" betrayed two things about me: first, insincerity about God's will being done, and second, a lack of complete trust in God.

If we believe that the most important issue in the entire universe and throughout all eternity is God's will being done, then it is always appropriate, even necessary, to pray "whatever it takes, Lord." It should be the underpinning of all our prayers. If we believe that God's will is paramount, it follows that all our desires, no matter how reasonable they seem, must be subordinated to God's will. Is that not in essence how Christ prayed in his agony in Gethsemane? He asked for the cup to be taken from him, but in the same breath he subordinated his request to the supremacy of the Father's will—"nevertheless, your will be done" (Matthew 26:39). If we pray for someone to become a child of God through faith in Christ, our prayer is consistent with God's will. God's Word says he is not willing that any should perish but that all should come to repentance (2 Peter 3:9). In the Lord's Prayer Jesus taught his disciples to pray for God's will. If we pray sincerely for God's will to be done, it is always appropriate to pray, "Lord, whatever it takes."

If we are not willing to say, "Whatever it takes," we demonstrate that we cannot trust our heavenly Father to do what is best. Instead, we wish to reserve the right to decide whether certain extreme measures may be appropriate. It even implies an arrogant notion that we have the authority to withhold from God the permission he needs to do certain things. If God's will is foremost, then we should always be prepared to pray right from the start—and not as a last resort—"whatever it takes, Lord." We minimize prayer if we ask, "whatever it takes" only when we implore God to intervene in a desperate crisis.

God's Dangerous Will

God's will is not always a safe choice for us. On his journey to Jerusalem the Apostle Paul visited Philip the evangelist in Caesarea. There he met a prophet from Judea named Agabus who warned Paul about the danger of continuing on to Jerusalem. He said enemies of the gospel that Paul preached would arrest him and hand him over to the Gentiles—to the Roman authorities. Philip and the others tried to dissuade Paul from proceeding to Jerusalem. But Paul was convinced it was the Lord's will for him to go on. He told them he was willing to die, if necessary, to obey God's will. They eventually gave up and said with sad resignation, "The Lord's will be done" (Acts 21:10–14). Through the centuries many have been willing to lay down their lives to proclaim the gospel of God in obedience to the Father's will. They are living—and dying—proof of the commitment, "whatever it takes, Lord."

Many of our heavenly Father's children yield to his will reluctantly, and only after they have exhausted all other options. But if we pray, "your will be done" our commitment to God's will leaves no room for contingencies. It is a daily prayer of absolute surrender to our heavenly Father. Our petition is immune to the appeals of loved ones who claim to have our best interests at heart, and urge us to take a safe and comfortable course for life. God's children acknowledge that according to his will, God may choose to give or to take away. To pray, "whatever it takes" means letting go. It means renouncing our last impulse to retain control instead of surrendering all to God. The song *I Surrender All* is one of the simplest and yet one of the most profound prayers for all our heavenly Father's children. It means, "Lord, you decide." It is not our prerogative to decide what measures God should take. We do not determine which divine action might be too extreme.

Parents may struggle to accept God's will for their children to serve as missionaries. The implications of their children and grandchildren moving to foreign soil to do God's will are excruciating. God's will and their desires are in a tug-of-war. "Whatever it takes" is a costly offering squeezed from the depth of their souls; but that makes it a sweet sacrifice to God.

We can trust our Father with "whatever it takes" more than we can trust ourselves. Our heavenly Father has a heart that is "kind beyond all measure," because he is the God of all grace and he is full of mercy. This is not a prayer of resignation. We do not throw up our hands in resignation and quit further praying about the matter. It does not mean, "Well, whatever it takes, Lord, Your will be done. I'm done praying about this." In another New Testament pericope on prayer, Jesus said,

> Ask and it will be given to you; seek and you will find; knock and the door will be opened to you. For everyone who asks receives; he who seeks finds; and to him who knocks, the door will be opened. Which of you, if his son asks for bread, will give him a stone? Or if he asks for a fish, will give him a snake? If you, then, though you are evil, know how to give good gifts to your children, how much more will your Father in heaven give good gifts to those who ask him! (Matthew 7:7–11)

Until we reach our heavenly home God's children never forsake the duty to pray. Jesus encouraged his followers to persevere in prayer. Under no circumstances do the Father's children cast aside the Lord's Prayer as an optional exercise for the pious.

The Challenge of God's Will

When the Philistine army assembled to fight Israel, the Israelites were quaking with fear. The prophet Samuel had instructed King Saul to wait seven days before engaging the Philistines. Then Samuel would come to offer a sacrifice. Saul waited until the seventh day. Samuel had not arrived at the prescribed time. The Israelite forces began to scatter, so Saul offered the sacrifice in Samuel's place. The troops were deserting him, so he saw no alternative. What else could he do? The challenge was too great. Immediately after offering the sacrifice Samuel arrived and rebuked Saul for not keeping the command the Lord his God had given him.

Saul's disobedience would cost him the kingdom (see 1 Samuel 13:5-14).

A politician may feel enormous pressure to compromise personal ethical standards to vote for a measure that has some virtues, but also includes some elements that contradict principles of righteousness.

God's Will in a Permissive Culture

Beware of those who claim Christian liberty as the justification for choosing their own way. In Paul's appeal to the Roman church he urges God's people to be alert to anything that might affect our ability to obey God's revealed will:

> Do not conform any longer to the pattern of this world, but be transformed by the renewing of your mind. Then you will be able to test and approve what God's will is—his good, pleasing and perfect will (Romans 12:2).

Paul underscored the exactness of God's will to live pure lives. He said, "But among you there must not be even a hint of sexual immorality, or of any kind of impurity or of greed, because these are improper for God's holy people" (Ephesians 5:3).

Not all who claim to be the children of our Father in heaven are willing to do his will and follow in his way. Some who claim to be God's children modify their standards to accommodate the mores of a permissive society. They do not flinch when unwed couples engage in sexual intimacy in direct contradiction of God's revealed will. The secular culture applauds when unwed young women are proudly pregnant, and many in the Church give tacit approval. Our Father is full of mercy for all who repent of their disobedience, but God's will on these matters remains steadfast in Scripture. It is not a trifling matter to replace what is biblically precise with what is culturally permissive. Some of God's children behave like children of a divorced couple, namely, God the Father and the secular culture. The break-up occurred in the Garden of Eden. In most divorces one parent has custody, the other pays child support and has visitation rights. So there is a sort of sharing relationship between the culture and God. God the Father, to whom they pray, is at a distance. He pays child support, inasmuch as they benefit from his merciful beneficence. But they visit the Father only on a Sunday. That is visitation day. The rest of the time the secular culture has custody. As is usually the case, the one who has custody also has control.

King Solomon discovered the void in a life separated from God. He put everything in the right perspective for pilgrims trudging homeward through enemy territory:

> Now all has been heard; here is the conclusion of the matter: Fear God and keep his commandments, for this is the whole [duty] of man. For God will bring every deed into judgment, including every hidden thing, whether it is good or evil (Ecclesiastes 12:13–14).

In their quest to find fulfillment, most people seem reluctant to admit that the pursuit of material goods and mundane pleasures leaves them empty. Solomon expressed the most crucial point of his findings in his summation. Having searched the whole earthly realm he realized that it was empty, in that it does not fulfill a child of God. Mankind cannot find wholeness apart from a vital connection with God. The Hebrew text does not include the word "duty" in the clause in Ecclesiastes 12:13, "this is the whole [duty] of

242

man." The translators added "duty" in an attempt to provide some grammatical rectitude. "This is the whole of man" is awkward English. Nevertheless, the precise conclusion at which Solomon arrived is, "This is the totality of being a person. This is the fullness of what it means to be human." All the delights this life offers are not sufficient to make you whole. But if you live in reverent fear of God and you obey his will for your life—then, and only then, are you a whole person. This is what you were made for. This is what Solomon meant. If you do not willingly submit to God's will, your life is diminished. If you leave God out, you miss out.

Godly Values

As humans we are tightly bound to this planet. Our experiences are circumscribed by our earthly existence. Even our spiritual life is regularly compromised by earthly values. For God's will to be done on earth, a change of a magnitude beyond our imagination would have to take place. In the Lord's Prayer Jesus Christ instructed his followers, God's children, to pray precisely for this change to come.

The values of heaven are in stark contrast with the values of the world's degenerate cultures. The treasures people crave reveal where their hearts are. The Apostle Paul prayed that the values of God's children in Colossae would be compatible with God's will as it is done in heaven. He wrote, " . . . since the day we heard about you, we have not stopped praying for you and asking God to fill you with the knowledge of his will through all spiritual wisdom and understanding" (Colossians 1:9; cf. Philippians 1:10).

The children of God should recoil from anything that contradicts God's revealed will. God's children must beware of becoming comfortable with Satan's vile machinations. We resist the apathy that neutralizes our longing for the peace and the purity that mark obedience to our Father's will. Jesus Christ gave the sobering warning,

Not everyone who says to me, "Lord, Lord," will enter the kingdom of heaven, but only he who does the will of my Father who is in heaven. Many will say to me on that day, "Lord, Lord, did we not prophesy in your name, and in your name drive out demons and perform many miracles?" Then I will tell them plainly, "I never knew you. Away from me, you evildoers" (Matthew 7:21–23).

The prophet Isaiah related an example of this condition in the obstinate nation of Israel:

These are rebellious people, deceitful children, children unwilling to listen to the Lord's instruction. They say to the seers, "See no more visions!" and to the prophets, "Give us no more visions of what is right! Tell us pleasant things, prophesy illusions. Leave this way, get off this path, and stop confronting us with the Holy One of Israel!" (Isaiah 30:9–11).

The need of intercession for the rebellious people was brought into powerful relief in the practice of Aaron the High Priest entering into the Most Holy Place in the Tent of meeting. He made atonement for the Most Holy Place by sprinkling the blood of the sin offering on the atonement cover.

In this way he will make atonement for the Most Holy Place because of the uncleanness and rebellion of the Israelites, whatever their sins have been. He is to do the same for the Tent of Meeting, which is among them in the midst of their uncleanness. (Leviticus 16:16).

We pray for God's will to be done on the earth. But during the present age we find its antithesis. God's will is not done completely or even approximately in this fallen world where we must live.

In the Book of Nehemiah we see how challenging it was to do God's will. Nehemiah received permission from Persian King Artaxerxes to check on Jerusalem and the welfare of the Jews who had returned from the dispersion (Nehemiah 13). In defiance of his will, God's people had been intermarrying with the surrounding pagan peoples. Nehemiah reinstated and enforced the statutes of God's law. The Israelites had to send away their pagan partners. This caused pain and distress among the people of Jerusalem. It tore the fabric of what had become their society. The timeless lesson in this example is that we must do God's will even when it is difficult to obey. Repenting of sin and obeying God's will may cause major complications. After flouting God's will, re-establishing it may be a monumental hardship.

A holy discontentment with the way of life in this corrupt world is the proper spiritual stance of God's children. God's children live by different values. Peter wrote,

Since everything will be destroyed in this way, what kind of people ought you to be? You ought to live holy and godly lives as you look forward to the day of God and speed its coming (2 Peter 3:11–12).

This is the attitude and conduct of pilgrims who look forward to "the home of righteousness" as they journey through this world that is the home of unrighteousness. They look forward to God's kingdom coming and his will being done.

The Origin and Scope of Disobedience to God's Will

Does prayer for God's will to be done on earth as it is in heaven imply that God's will is done everywhere in the universe except on earth? Rejection of God's will had its origin in the devil. The most resplendent angel, Morning Star son of the dawn (Isaiah 14:12), attempted to assume the place of God Almighty and was cast from heaven to earth. In his earthly role as the devil he and his demonic hordes are actively hostile to our heavenly Father. They are hell-bent on subverting God's purpose in this world, and doubtlessly throughout God's universe.

Disobedience on earth originated in the Garden of Eden. The devil in the form of a serpent was the tempter. The first humans fell to Satan's temptation. They disobeyed God's will concerning the tree in the center of the garden. Since God has not revealed whether he created life forms in any of his other heavenly spheres, our planet bears the tragic distinction of disobedience to the will of the Creator.

Disobedience is defiance. It is the muck that clings to our fallen natures as humans. Children at home disobey their parents behind their backs or defy them to their faces. Citizens may choose to engage in civil disobedience as a matter of conscience. Some civil disobedience is meritorious, as many of history's heroes, including the Apostles, have demonstrated.

God's kingdom and God's will are beyond our full comprehension. For this reason many people become upset with God when he does not fulfill their assumptions about his will. Things that seem right to them do not happen, so they ask, "Why does God allow this? How can this be God's will?" But God's holiness transcends our ability to sit in judgment of it. The nature of our heavenly Father's reign (his kingdom) and his will are not simple or easy to analyze and categorize.

We cannot imagine the peace and the pristine perfection of heaven where God's will is done as the *sine qua non* of his realm. The benediction in the New Testament Book of Hebrews is an appeal that God would fit us to do his will:

> May the God of peace, who through the blood of the eternal covenant brought back from the dead our Lord Jesus, . . . equip you with everything good for doing his will, and may he work in us what is pleasing to him, through Jesus Christ, to whom be glory for ever and ever. Amen (Hebrews 13:20–21).

Jesus would not have directed the disciples to pray the Lord's Prayer if God's will were in fact being done throughout the earth. The prayer implies that earth is not the realm of God's rule. Helmut Thielicke commented,

> For, after all, we should not have to pray at all that God's will be done, if it were really being done among us and if we ourselves and the whole world were not living our life in a constant boycott of his will.[115]

The Apostle Paul gave an explicit depiction of life in this world where people do not seek the Lord:

> As for you, you were dead in your transgressions and sins, in which you used to live when you

followed the ways of this world and of the ruler of the kingdom of the air, the spirit who is now at work in those who are disobedient. All of us also lived among them at one time, gratifying the cravings of our sinful nature, and following its desires and thoughts. Like the rest, we were by nature objects of wrath. But because of his great love for us, God, who is rich in mercy, made us alive with Christ even when we were dead in transgressions—it is by grace you have been saved. And God raised us up with Christ and seated us with him in the heavenly realms in Christ Jesus (Ephesians 2:1–6).

We grieve the condition of the world that God created for his glory. The natural condition of people "on earth" is "without hope and without God in the world" (Ephesians 2:12). It has become the accepted norm to conform to the mores of a sinful culture in gross violation of God's will.

In the history of Christendom there have been futile attempts to inaugurate God's kingdom on earth. The misguided efforts of the Crusades to realize God's kingdom upon the earth and the decree of the Roman Emperor Constantine are two examples. Jesus taught his followers that God's kingdom and his will are a matter of prayer to our heavenly Father, not the result of human scheming.

The Realization of God's Will on Earth

But how will God's kingdom come, and how will God's will be accomplished on earth? Daniel explained:

In my vision at night I looked and there before me was one like a son of man, coming with the clouds of heaven. He approached the Ancient of Days and was led into his presence. He was given authority, glory, and sovereign power; all peoples, nations, and men of every language worshiped him. His dominion is an everlasting dominion that will not pass away, and his kingdom is one that will never be destroyed (Daniel 7:13–14).

Jesus Christ, God the Son, most frequently referred to himself as the Son of Man. We understand the Ancient of Days in Daniel's vision to be God the eternal Father. When was Jesus given authority, glory, and sovereign power so that the whole world worships him, or when will he receive it? We try to comprehend this from our time-space perspective. But the exchange between God and the son of man in Daniel's vision seems to occur in a timeless dimension. There Christ has his dominion and his kingdom.

God's children on earth frequently violate God's will. They cannot do God's will as it is done in heaven. God's will on earth will be realized when God our Father makes all things new. The consummation of God's kingdom and will upon earth will occur in a new heaven and new earth. This corrupted earth is destined for destruction. When we pray for God's will to be done on earth, we recognize that the world will undergo a radical transformation. All forms of corruption in the world will be obliterated when God's will is completely done (2 Peter 3:10–13; Revelation 21). Scripture is clear that the transition from a fallen, sinful world to a new heaven and new earth will not be smooth. It will not come about by incremental improvement of the human condition or by the increase of righteousness. Instead, Scripture declares that conditions will grow worse before the end comes (e.g. Matthew 24, esp. v. 12).

The Restoration of God's Will

The first two chapters of the Bible state God's plan for this world. As the Creator, God made everything perfect. Then mankind rejected God's will, choosing an alternate proposal offered by the devil. As a result, evil permeated the fabric of all that God had made on earth. But God's purpose was never revoked. Evil and death have never had a place in God's purpose. They are contrary to God's will. Those are components of the 'old order' that originated with the Fall described in Genesis chapter three.

All who come to God by faith in Christ have become new creations. The old has passed and the new has come for them (2 Corinthians 5:17). They do not belong to this fallen world. They set their hearts and minds on things above where Christ is seated at the right hand of God (Colossians 3:1–2). They clothe themselves with the Lord Jesus Christ and do not think of how to gratify the desires of the sinful nature (Romans 13:14).

Paul said, "For to me to live is Christ, and to die is gain" (Philippians 1:21). In identification with Christ we have the assurance of being part of the great renewal that God has planned. John described how God will accomplish this:

> Then I saw a new heaven and a new earth, for the first heaven and the first earth had passed away, and there was no longer any sea. I saw the Holy City, the New Jerusalem, coming down out of heaven from God, prepared as a bride beautifully dressed for her husband. And I heard a loud voice from the throne saying, "Now the dwelling of God is with men, and he will live with them. They will be his people, and God himself will be with them and be their God. He will wipe every tear from their eyes.

There will be no more death or mourning or crying or pain, for the old order of things has passed away (Revelation 21:1–4).

This is the fullness for which we pray, "Your kingdom come, your will be done on earth as it is in heaven."

Synopsis

The first three petitions in this prayer constitute a compass setting for the Father's children. It can keep them from being led astray by the evil one's deceit. It keeps us directed to the ultimate of what is true and right.

- We are in a world under the control of the evil one, but our Father who guides us is the Almighty Sovereign God. He is holy; there is no God beside him.
- Our Father rules. This is the order of his universe. Our daily prayer is for this world to yield completely to his reign.
- In the consummation of his eternal purpose his will alone will be done. We pray for the realization of that blessed condition when each day and everywhere no will contrary to our Father's will prevails.

This daily prayer is, therefore, an alert and purposeful review of the ultimate order of God's universe.

Questions for Discussion and Personal Application

1. What role do God's children play in accomplishing the heavenly Father's will on earth as it is done in heaven?

2. Do you think God listens to the prayers of people who always ask for what they want and do not pray for God's will?

3. To what extent do your prayers reveal that you think of God as "domesticated"? How has God revealed that from our perspective he is more often wild than tame?

4. Explain what God's will is that he wants done on earth.

5. What may we assume about anyone who tells a person to "go to hell"?

6. Why is it appropriate to consider God a dictator?

7. What was the mystery of God's will? What was Jesus Christ's role in it?

8. The penalty for eating the fruit of the forbidden tree was a curse upon mankind and alienation from God. How do you answer the objection that the punishment was too great for such a minor offense?

9. Why is the notion that our heavenly Father has a permissive will inconsistent with what Scripture reveals about God's will? Give a biblical example of the exactness of God's will.

10. What is God's will above all else that he commands his people to obey?

11. Do you think suffering could be part of God's will for you? Do you see any value in it?

12. Tell about an occasion when you were in a difficult struggle and you prayed to our Father "your will be done."

13. Give examples of the kind of choices you feel free to make without specifically seeking God's will.

14. When you pray for God's will, can you readily add "whatever it takes, Lord"? Give the reason for your answer.

15. Have you prayed a prayer of surrender to God's will and then suffered for it? Share.

16. How should God's children relate to those who claim to be God's people but have adopted secular values that violate the standards of Scripture?

17. According to Solomon's insights in the Old Testament Book of Ecclesiastes, what does it take to be all you are meant to be?

18. Read Ezra 10 and Nehemiah 13. Give a contemporary example of God's will causing major changes with severe complications.

19. Where did rejection of God's will originate, and how did it spread to mankind?

20. Why is our prayer for God's will a request for something that extends beyond our comprehension?

21. When and how will our heavenly Father's kingdom be realized on earth?

9. GIVE US TODAY OUR DAILY BREAD

From thee, great God, while every eye
Expectant waits the wish'd supply,
Their bread, proportion'd to the day,
Thy opening hands to each convey;
In every sorrow of the heart
Eternal mercy bears a part.

James Merrick[116]

Our Incompleteness

The petitions, "Your kingdom come; your will be done on earth as it is in heaven" move directly to the request for daily bread. God's children who pray for his kingdom to come and for his will to be done also look to their heavenly Father for their daily provision.

After the Soviet Union (USSR) collapsed in 1991, most of the people in its former republics did not know how to embrace their new freedoms. After generations of subjection to tyrannical oppressors, people lacked the confidence to claim their rightful privileges. They had become imprinted with a mindset of subordination. Many continued to fear repercussions if they asserted their rights.

They serve as an analogy of life in this world for many of God's children. God has rescued them from the dominion of darkness (Colossians 1:13), but they have not learned to live joyfully and confidently as children of the heavenly Father emancipated from the devil's tyranny. Many have defeatist attitudes. They do not factor their new identity into the equations of life. They do not have the faith that turns them toward their heavenly Father to ask, "Give us this day our daily bread."

Change of Focus

At this point the Lord's Prayer turns from the heavenly Father to his children. The pronouns change from "your," addressing our Father in heaven, to "our," focusing on the needs of God's children. As sojourners in a hostile world we have needs our Father alone can meet. God's children look to their heavenly Father for provision and protection. Even though our heavenly Father will bring us to his home in heaven, we remain vulnerable to the devil's schemes on earth.

God created human beings without defect. But they were not complete in themselves. God purposely created people with an incompleteness. In the garden he communed daily with the beings he had created in his image and likeness. He enjoyed an intimate relationship of perfect fellowship with them. God never intended his children on earth to get along without him. Andrew Murray said,

> Adam was created to have fellowship with God and enjoyed it before the Fall. After the Fall, however, there came immediately a deep-seated aversion to God, and he fled from Him. This incurable aversion is the characteristic of the unregenerate nature and the chief cause of our unwillingness to surrender ourselves to fellowship with God in prayer.[117]

Remember Pascal's maxim that an inner God-shaped space is part of the constitution of every human? God reserved that space exclusively for himself. Because it is God-shaped the devil cannot fit comfortably into it. Where Satan has taken control of people's lives, there humanity is in a grim state of malfunction.

The plea for daily bread is consistent with God's plan for mankind since creation. Asking is an integral part of our relationship with our Father. We do not wait until a serious crisis arises before we ask our heavenly Father to provide what we need.

We may be fairly comfortable asking for help from people with whom we do not have, nor do we necessarily seek, a close relationship. For example, Jane, a young mother asks her neighbor Connie to help her with childcare for a few hours. Connie is pleased to oblige. Jane expresses her gratitude for the help. Connie assumes that they have now become friends. She seeks a deeper relationship, but Jane is not interested in a close friendship. She is grateful for the help given by the kind acquaintance, but she does not wish to pursue anything further.

Many people regard God in a similar fashion. They are not interested in a relationship with God, and they do not have a place for God in their life. God is just an acquaintance of convenience. A cartoon I saw had a small boy going upstairs to bed. He asked his family, "I'm going up to say my prayers now; anybody need anything?" Sadly, some people seek out God only if they have a need. That is their motive for praying, "Give us this day our daily bread."

Jesus placed this request for daily bread from our Father after the plea that God be accorded the honor due him—"hallowed be your name." The daily request for divine provision springs from a relationship with God marked by love and reverence. This is the backdrop for asking our Father, "give."

Sin's devastation of mankind is not the chief reason for our dependence on God. Even if there were no evil in the world, God designed us to need him. This request for daily bread is equally applicable to God's children who have little, and those who have more than they need of worldly goods. We cannot manage from day to day without that which our heavenly Father alone can supply. This component of the

Lord's Prayer is not for occasional use. Each new day we depend on our heavenly Father.

The incompleteness of people and the heavenly Father's provision form a strong bond between the Father and his children. If God had not created mankind with an incompleteness, his children would rely on their own resourcefulness for fulfillment. With no felt need of God, people would have no inclination toward God. People who do not know the Lord God are likely to worship inanimate things or celestial objects.

The prophet Hosea reminded the people of Israel how they had worshiped a lifeless idol: "But when they came to Baal Peor, they consecrated themselves to that shameful idol and became as vile as the thing they loved" (Hosea 9:10). When they worshiped an idol they became less like a being in God's likeness and more like the thing human hands had made.

The difference between domesticated and wild animals serves as an illustration. Domesticated animals depend on humans for food and other daily provisions. This dependence forges an attraction in the animal toward its human master. But wild animals have no sense of dependence on humans. Instead of an attraction, there is a strong avoidance. If we did not recognize our need of God, we too would be wild. It is impossible for people to eradicate completely the divine likeness in which we were created. If we reject God we become savage toward God. To be all we were created to be demands our conscious dependence on God our Father each day. This is a human distinctive that sets us apart from all the animals.

The Myth of Self-sufficiency

When we ask for daily bread, our Father in heaven knows exactly the kind of bread his children need each day.

Jesus had just told his followers, "For your Father knows what you need before you ask him." (Matthew 6:8) We do not have to embroider our petition in order to persuade our Father that our need is valid.

Many of God's children have no concern about sufficient food for each day. They have sufficient goods to take care of their material needs. If you are in such a situation, does it obviate your need to ask God the Father for daily bread? Is daily bread a trifling matter for some of God's children?

As children grow up they naturally become less dependent on their father and mother, and rely more on themselves. As God's children, however, we never attain a level of maturity where we need our heavenly Father less. We do not hastily discard the request for daily bread so that we can move on to the more compelling issue of forgiveness in the Lord's Prayer. The dark backdrop behind our appeal for daily bread is the motif of God's children as resident aliens in a world under the control of the evil one.

Needs and Wants

Our Father in heaven does not deny his children all earthly pleasures. All the good things that come to us are from our Father, not just some of them (James 1:17). But the pursuit of material gain or temporal delight is an unworthy goal for God's children. If we covet mundane pleasures, we cease to be pilgrims in transit. Instead, we become squatters intent on settling down.

The distinction between need and want is easily blurred. Children try to convince their parents that they need the latest fashions. How do parents distinguish a valid need from a vain desire? As a pre-teen our son "needed" a popular brand name of shirt rather than the generic sort. He wanted to have what most of his friends were wearing. Liz and I decided this fell into the category of a need. He needed to know that his parents were sensitive to the situation he dealt with each day. But sometimes it is necessary to deny a request because it is frivolous.

Many of the things we appeal to our heavenly Father to give us would do more harm than good. As our wise Father, he knows exactly what each child needs at any moment. Jesus Christ told his disciples, "Do not be like them (the pagans), for your Father knows what you need before you ask him" (Matthew 6:8). This is the theme of a popular worship song by Matt Maher:

> Lord, I come, I confess
> Bowing here I find my rest
> Without You I fall apart
> You're the One that guides my heart
> Lord, I need you, O I need you
> Every hour I need you
> My one defense, my righteousness
> O God how I need you.[118]

Our Father in heaven is the consummate micro-manager. He sustains all things he created. The most minuscule element in the universe is under his watchful eye. In most organizations micro-management is disparaged. The military exemplifies an organization that decries micro-management. It is inviolably committed to established strata of accountability. A private in the army does not have access to a general. In between are sergeants, lieutenants, majors and colonels. Organizational structures are designed to allow those at the top of the chain of command to focus on the big picture while the underlings take care of the minutiae. As Warren Bennis and Burt Nanus put it, "Leaders do the right thing; managers do things right."[119] In the business realm an entry-level employee reports to a supervisor, who in turn reports to someone higher. Attempting to bypass the immediate supervisor by an end-run is grounds for dismissal.

For the people of God there are no strata of separation from our heavenly Father. He is the CEO (Chief Executive Officer) of his vast universe, and the perfect micro-manager. He does not assign any aspect of his oversight of his pilgrim children to an underling. Our Father sees our needs thoroughly. When we pray, "Give us this day our daily bread," our Father does not need our detailed description. We pray directly and with confidence to our heavenly Father. He can provide anything, to the tiniest detail.

God provided what the Israelites needed in the desert. But they were not content. They craved the savory cuisine of Egypt that had been their staple during their slavery there. They complained, "But now we have lost our appetite; we never see anything but this manna!" (Numbers 11:6). God's children today, sojourning as aliens in a hostile world, may also lose their appetite for God's provision. Have we not all at some time gazed longingly at the allurements of the corrupt society in which we were once held in spiritual bondage? We are well acquainted with the tug of the old life's dissolute excitations.

I was raised in a Christian fellowship where I often heard the word "backslider." It was a term our church applied to God's children who slid back into the sinful way of life from which God had rescued them. Desires stirred afresh in them for something the community of God's people did not offer. Practically every church has had its share of backsliders. The Apostle Paul admonished the Galatian Christians, "I am astonished that you are so quickly deserting the one who called you by the grace of Christ and are turning to a different gospel—which is really no gospel at all" (Galatians 1:6). Paul urged church members,

"Brothers, if someone is caught in a sin, you who are spiritual should restore him gently. But watch yourself, or you also may be tempted" (Galatians 6:1). Sadly, many prefer to gossip about "backsliders" rather than rush to rescue them from the peril to their souls.

Our Greater Needs

Our earthly bodies are marvelous exhibits of our Creator's glorious handiwork. When God made mankind in his image and likeness he furnished physical bodies to be the temporal habitation of our eternal spirits. The consequences of sin exacted a heavy toll on our earthly flesh. Death had no place in God's pristine creation. But when the first humans sinned and fell from innocence, the human body was defiled and diminished. Scripture likens human life on earth to grass that withers or flowers that soon fall (Isaiah 40:6–7; 1 Peter 1:24). The Apostle Paul used the metaphor of the human body as a temporary tent. He said we groan and are burdened as we live in this earthly tent. We wish that we could be clothed with our heavenly dwelling, "so that what is mortal may be swallowed up by life" (2 Corinthians 5:4).

You are worth incomparably more than the "tent" you live in. Does this mean your earthly body—your temporary house—is of little value? Most of us consider our earthly homes of mortar and lumber to be essential to our welfare. In like manner, God provided physical bodies for those who bear his image. As the treasures in a locked safe are of greater worth than the safe itself, so people in their essential being are of infinitely greater value than the bodies they inhabit. Nevertheless, even the children of God are prone to focus their needs and wants on their mortal bodies.

The Nature of the Bread

Most of our needs that our Father addresses are not related to our physical bodies. Jesus frequently used the term "bread" in a metaphorical rather than a literal sense. The request in the Lord's Prayer for daily bread undoubtedly includes provision for our physical needs. Physical need, however, is but a tiny part of what our Father's bread satisfies.

When the crowd asked Jesus for a sign, they cited as an example the manna in the desert as the bread God gave from heaven. In response, Jesus identified himself as the true bread of life that gives eternal life to all who partake of him. He said,

> I tell you the truth, it is not Moses who has given you the bread from heaven, but it is my Father who gives you the true bread from heaven. For the bread of God is he who comes down from heaven and gives life to the world (John 6:32, 33).

> Then Jesus declared, "I am the bread of life. He who comes to me will never go hungry, and he who believes in me will never be thirsty" (John 6:35).

He continued,

> "I am the bread of life. Your forefathers ate the manna in the desert, yet they died. But here is the bread that comes down from heaven, which a man may eat and not die. I am the living bread that came down from heaven. If a man eats of this bread, he will live forever. The bread is my flesh, which I will give for the life of the world." (John 6:48–51)

There is a marked difference between the daily bread in the Lord's Prayer and the bread of life. We do not ask for the bread of life each day. As the bread of life, Jesus satisfies forever. The bread of life is like the living water he offered the Samaritan woman at Sychar (John 4:10). Jesus explained, "Whoever drinks the water I give him will never thirst. Indeed, the water I give him will become in him a spring of water welling up to eternal life" (John 4:14).

Eating bread that came down from heaven is a figure of speech for believing in Jesus Christ. But Jesus Christ is not the daily bread mentioned in the Lord's Prayer. Christ as the bread from heaven is a metaphor of his sacrifice for the sins of mankind. Communion, the Lord's Supper, includes partaking of bread that Jesus spoke of as a symbol of his body (Luke 22:19). He said it was a memorial of his atoning sacrifice on the cross for our sins. In his teaching about the Lord's Supper Paul referred to Christ as the Bread:

> Is not the cup of thanksgiving for which we give thanks a participation in the blood of Christ? And is not the bread that we break a participation in the body of Christ? Because there is one loaf, we, who are many, are one body, for we all partake of the one loaf (1 Corinthians 10:16–17).

Why do God's children ask for daily bread? We ask because we have a hunger that our Father alone can supply. It is a daily yearning that we dare not ignore. If we look elsewhere for the satisfaction of this basic daily need, our appetite will soon become corrupted. Our taste will soon turn from a daily longing after God to a nagging greed for earthly pleasures and possessions.

The request for daily bread in the Lord's Prayer expresses a daily dependence on our heavenly Father for needs beyond the physical or material. The bread our Father gives is more than a dietary provision. In *The Message* paraphrase of the Bible, Eugene H. Peterson renders this clause in the Lord's Prayer, "Keep us alive with three square meals."[120] But Peterson's interpretation is like listening to a symphony and hearing only the part of the piccolo. Our need of physical nutrition is part of our request in the Lord's Prayer, but it is only a tiny fraction of our needs.

The petition for daily bread most likely addresses all the needs of God's children. There is ample biblical support for identifying physical, spiritual, and emotional needs as the purview of the petition. The bread you need most for today may be peace and faith because you are struggling with anxiety or doubt. William Hendriksen argued, "It is clear, of course, that the term 'bread' should not be taken too literally. Whatever is necessary to sustain physical life is meant."[121] In my opinion, Hendriksen does not go far enough. The sustenance of the Father's children on their pilgrimage requires more than physical provisions. The intent of the plea for daily bread is that we maintain a daily solicitous dependence upon our heavenly Father.

The Singularity of the Request for Daily Bread

The first three requests in the Lord's Prayer pertain to our Father in heaven. The final three requests—for daily bread, for forgiveness, and for protection—are the only appeals for our personal benefit. The last two are clearly non-material in nature, but they do not address directly all our emotional, social, and spiritual needs. The petition for daily bread is, therefore, the only category in the Lord's Prayer under which other non-material needs might be subsumed. For example, for the Father's children who struggle with depression, daily bread fortifies them with strength and peace.

At the Sychar well, when Jesus' disciples urged him to eat something, he told them, "I have food to eat that you know nothing about. . . My food, . . . is to do the will of him who sent me and to finish his work" (John 4:31–32, 34). The food Jesus spoke of related to his mission. In a similar vein, the daily bread for Christ's followers may include our Father's provision to do his will.

When Jesus taught his disciples to pray, "Give us this day our daily bread," he had more in mind than the product of a baker's craft. As in all the petitions in the Lord's Prayer, it was a provision that could come from our Father in heaven alone. The daily bread from our Father in heaven is what God's children need for their sojourn in a corrupt and hostile world. Martin Luther understood that the "bread" was a symbol for "everything necessary for the preservation of this life, like food, a healthy body, good weather, house, home, wife, children, good government, and peace."[122]

The stuff of this world cannot meet our fundamental needs. Our heavenly Father does not provide *hors d'oeuvres* or dessert as a tasty supplement to the main course we prepare for ourselves. By praying for daily bread we look to the Father for sustenance in all aspects of life.

The Problem of Greed

Jesus declared that self-indulgence has no place in those who follow in his steps. He said,

> If anyone would come after me, he must deny himself and take up his cross daily and follow me. For whoever wants to save his life will lose it, but whoever loses his life for me will save it. What good is it for a man to gain the whole world, and yet lose or forfeit his very self? (Luke 9:23–25).

Jesus Christ frequently used the metaphors of bread and yeast together. On one occasion he warned the disciples to be careful, to watch out for the yeast of the Pharisees and of Herod. They thought Jesus' remarks were in some way related to the fact that they had forgotten to bring bread with them. Aware of their discussion, Jesus asked, "Why are you talking about having no bread? Do you still not see or understand? Are your hearts hardened?" (Mark 8:14–17). Jesus used yeast as a symbol of corruption. His warning was about the spread of corruption by the Pharisees. Paul used the term yeast in contrast with good bread. He wrote, "Therefore, let us keep the festival, not with the old yeast, the yeast of malice and wickedness, but with bread [made] without yeast, the bread of sincerity and truth" (1 Corinthians 5:8). Daily bread from God was wholesome and life giving, but the bread of religious leaders was putrefied and noxious. The Apostle John reports that after Jesus had fed the crowd of more than five thousand, the people he had fed came to him on the other side of the lake. In his interchange with them Jesus contrasted food that spoils with food that endures, which he would give to them (John 6:26–27).

Luke recounts Jesus warning a large crowd about greed and the folly of being fixated on materialistic prosperity. He said life should not be defined in terms of what we possess (Luke 12:15). Benjamin Franklin said, "I conceive that a great part of the miseries of mankind are brought upon them by the false estimate they have made of the value of things."[123] This is precisely the perspective of countless millions of people. Wealth and health are their chief pursuits.

Greed, even when respectably outfitted in the garb of ambition, is still greed. Mankind's great peril lies not in having material resources but in pursuing them as the passion of life. Greed is a weight that can crush your devotion to God. Instead of placing your trust in God your Father, you trust in yourself to provide not just enough for today, but "plenty of good things laid up for many years" so that you can "take life easy; eat, drink and be merry" (Luke 12:19).

A characteristic of secular society is to seek security in money rather than in God. Many who have bountiful provisions are prone to ask, "Who needs faith if you have lots of money?"[124] Many regard money as the solution to every problem. In a family breakup, money often makes the divorce rancorous. A lifetime is not long enough for some people to learn that money can create more problems than it solves.

Greedy people cannot pray the Lord's Prayer with sincerity, because they are preoccupied with hoarding more goods than they need. Jesus emphasized the peril of relying on earthly riches. He said greed characterized the pagan world: "for the pagan world runs after all such things, and your Father knows that you need them" (Luke 12:30). "Jesus said to his disciples, 'I tell you the truth, it is hard for a rich man to enter the kingdom of heaven. Again I tell you, it is easier for a camel to go through the eye of a needle than for a rich man to enter the kingdom of God'" (Matthew 19:23–24). Jesus taught the right attitude: "But seek his kingdom ('your kingdom come'), and these things will be given to you as well" (Luke 12:30–31). Paul wrote that Christians must live as "those who use the things of the world, as if not engrossed in them. For this world in its present form is passing away" (1 Corinthians 7:31).

I can testify from my long experience as a pastor that money does not solve problems for God's children. Money may provide a temporary balm in a crisis, but as a long-term solution, money tends to exacerbate problems. A humorist said, "All I ask is a chance to prove that money can't make me happy."[125] God our Father in heaven wants his children to depend on him daily while they are aliens in enemy territory. God is glorified and exalted when his children fix their hopes on him during their trek through this dangerous world.

Day-to-day dependence on our heavenly Father does not prohibit us from enjoying the good things God created. Many years ago someone gave me a little plaque with this caption, "Man does not live by bread alone. He needs a little peanut butter and jelly on it too." This imperfect world holds many pleasures for God's children. These blessings are ours for more than just a day—sunshine and rain, magnificent flowers and marvelous creatures, majestic mountains, soul-stirring music, and countless other sensory delights. The pleasure of friends and family and intimate relationships are long-term gifts from our heavenly Father. But when we pray for daily bread, we do not ask for the enduring blessings he has already granted. We ask for something we need each new day, and which God alone can provide.

Asking is the Rule of God's Kingdom

Asking has never been easy for me. My parents taught us children not to get into the habit of asking for things. They provided all we needed. We always had good food, comfortable shelter, and adequate clothing. But we did not have much left over for extras. The milieu in which I was raised was mid-twentieth century South Africa. My family was part of the English-speaking community. I grew up in a conservative and proper British culture. A manufacturer's label on clothing meant nothing to me as a young boy. Sometimes I envied those who flaunted their luxuries, but it was just a passing infatuation. The basics were usually adequate.

The unspoken rule in our family was "do not ask." It was part of the ethos of the Crocker family. Asking people for anything was considered gauche. This was a governing axiom whenever we visited the homes of relatives and friends. To this day, my sisters and I delight in giving, but it is not easy for any of us to ask or to receive. Our spouses joke about this "Crocker trait. "

We moved from Africa to Canada in the mid-1960s. The cultural clash of South Africa with North America on this matter of asking was staggering. I was horrified to hear children disrespectfully demanding stuff of their parents. They seemed to consider it their right to have all their whims satisfied. I discovered that parents often aided and abetted the greedy behavior. The end result of this, I suspect, is the prideful manner in which people today boast about being "high maintenance." They spend inordinate sums proudly indulging their profligacy.

I am grateful to my parents for the benefits of the "don't ask" dictum that was ingrained into my psyche. But the rule also produced an undesirable result. Sometimes I am hesitant to make requests of my heavenly Father. I have frequently pondered whether it is honorable to request anything for myself. But Charles Spurgeon insisted, "Whether we like it or not, asking is the rule of the kingdom."[126]

In the two New Testament passages where Jesus taught his disciples the Lord's Prayer, he followed up with personal applications. In Matthew 6 Jesus added a lesson about forgiveness. Luke's account began with the disciples asking Jesus to teach them to pray. Jesus then gave them the Lord's Prayer, after which he stressed the importance of persisting in asking. He urged them to ask and seek and knock—to persevere in making requests of God (Luke 11:9–10; cf. Matthew 7:7–11). We do not quit asking our Father.

Jesus compared it with the practice of an earthly father giving good gifts to his children when they ask him (Luke 11:11–13). In our relationship with our Father in heaven any reluctance to ask is incongruous with the ethos of God's household. Asking and receiving are rudimentary in our relationship with God. The prophet Isaiah relayed God's message to his people,

> Come, all you who are thirsty, come to the waters; and you who have no money, come, buy and eat! Come, buy wine and milk without money and without cost. Why spend money on what is not bread, and your labor on what does not satisfy? Listen, listen to me, and eat what is good, and your soul will delight in the richest of fare (Isaiah 55:1–2).

God our heavenly Father knows what is good for his children. He invites us to ask him for what we need each new day. We must never become weary of asking, because our Father is never weary of giving. Jesus gave this encouragement:

> "If you then, though you are evil, know how to give good gifts to your children, how much more will your Father in heaven give the Holy Spirit to those who ask him!" (Luke 11:13).

James explained that we do not have because we do not ask God (James 4:2). A hesitancy to ask our Father is the reason we may forfeit some of his choice blessings. If our motives are right (see James 4:3), asking is essential to life in the family of God and in the kingdom under God's reign. We do not pretend to God that we are without needs and problem free. We ask confidently for the "daily bread" from his gracious provision.

What gift does the Father bestow on those who ask? Jesus identified the chief gift: "how much more will your Father in heaven give the Holy Spirit to those who ask him!" (Luke 11:13). Our Father in heaven does not intend to lavish worldly possessions upon his children. He gives us the Holy Spirit. The Holy Spirit is the Spirit of God himself. God gives Himself to us. This is the most precious gift from God. All other possessions pale in comparison. Our heavenly Father may not give us what we have in mind when we ask him for daily bread, but he will grant us each day the provision he has prepared for us.

Our Heavenly Father's Surprising Provision

God's provision may come to us sideways, rather than head-on. Our heavenly Father may provide in a manner we never considered. How often have we realized in retrospect that God provided daily bread for us, even though at first we doubted he had heeded our petition? We didn't see the Father's answer because we were looking in the wrong direction, expecting to receive something we had set our hearts on.

Some children away from home, attending a university, may look to their parents for financial help. As an example, when a young man squanders the funds intended for tuition and board, he sends an appeal: "Dear Dad, I have run out of funds. Please send money now." The wise father knows that his son has been fiscally irresponsible. His response is, "My dear son, I checked the classified ads in your town. The Acme Janitorial Service is hiring people to clean offices at night. I suggest you apply for a job there to earn what you need." The father's response would be considerably better than what the son hoped for.

The daily bread from our Father in heaven for one of his children who needs to mature may be an opportunity rather than a direct material provision. The bread from our Father may not be a sumptuous feast. It is a staple, not a gourmet delight. When we ask for daily bread from our Father we expect palatable provision. Jesus told his disciples that their Father in heaven would not substitute a stone for bread or a snake for fish (Matthew 7:9–11)

This petition in the Lord's Prayer is not an encouragement to ask for a specialty loaf. Jesus said immediately before giving the Lord's Prayer to his followers, "your Father knows what you need before you ask him." (Matthew 6:8) Our Father in heaven often gives his children bread that has no peanut butter and jelly on it.

In some impoverished lands people live in shanties close to the city's garbage dump. The powerful stench of rotting refuse constantly assaults their nostrils. But a particular home may emit the delightful aroma of freshly baked bread. In a foul atmosphere it is prudent to stay close to the bread. When they go back outside, the nauseating odor of rancid swill once again attacks their senses. The fresh daily bread from our Father's supply provides a wholesome repast for us, but it does not shield God's children from the fetidity of the fallen world where we must live.

Daily Dependence

Is Jesus' instruction to pray for daily bread as applicable to a mature child of the Father as to a struggling infant? Have you noticed that the longer you are a child of God the easier it is to live up to the Father's standards? Me neither! It is a dangerous delusion to suppose that the more we mature spiritually, the less dependent on our Father in heaven we become. The prayer for daily bread is essential both for the established believer and for the spiritual novice. God's children are sojourners in a dangerous world with pitfalls both seen and unseen. Paul gave a sobering depiction of such a worldly culture divorced from the heavenly Father:

> Furthermore, since they did not think it worthwhile to retain the knowledge of God, he gave them over to a depraved mind, to do what ought not to be done. They have become filled with every kind of wickedness, evil, greed and depravity (Romans 1:28–29).

The New Testament letter of James gives this warning: "You adulterous people, don't you know that friendship with the world is hatred toward God?" (James 4:4). Corrupt earthly society has removed every thread of heavenly culture from its fabric. For this reason every child of the Father must be wary of seeking satisfaction in the mores of the secular society.

The sequence of "today" and "daily" indicates an emphatic redundancy in our plea to our Father. Werner Foerster of Munster explained,

> It might also be pointed out that in the ancient world the day began the evening before, so that even later in the day it might well refer to the new "day" which was shortly to begin.[127]

He added,

> And it is of the very nature of faith, from which the request springs, that it expects God's help and counts on it for the very time when it is needed, and not before.[128]

Foerster gave another helpful insight:

> The truth seems to be that *epiousios* (*'daily'*) is not an indication of time but of measure. . . But in view of the foregoing discussion there can be little doubt that its (the term, *epiousios*) force is adequately brought out in the rendering: 'The bread which we need, give us today (day by day).'[129]

The daily bread of the Lord's Prayer is an allusion to the manna that God gave his people each day during their wilderness sojourn. The Israelites were in a barren wasteland. They could not provide what they needed each day. If the Lord God had not supplied their needs, they would all have perished in the desert. So Jesus Christ taught his followers to ask their Father in heaven for that without which our souls would starve. The sum of everything we accumulate in this corrupt world of our sojourn will render our souls anorexic.

The "daily bread" that our Father supplies is without preservatives. The manna in the desert was a daily provision that could not be stored up. Likewise, our sustenance from our Father is not stored up in case it is needed later. Our Father has not given his children a pantry of provisions infused with preservatives. We live for today, not for tomorrow. Jesus said, "Therefore do not worry about tomorrow, for tomorrow will worry about itself. Each day has enough trouble of its own." (Matthew 6:34) We cannot manage even one day without depending on God. Agur, son of Jakeh, underscores the necessity of daily dependence on God:

> Keep falsehood and lies far from me; give me neither poverty nor riches, but give me only my

daily bread. Otherwise, I may have too much and disown you, and say, "Who is the Lord?" Or I may become poor and steal and so dishonor the name of my God (Proverbs 30:8, 9).

The lyrics of a song in the popular musical *Godspell* emphasize the importance of daily prayer: "Day by day, day by day, O Dear Lord, three things I pray—to see thee more clearly, love thee more dearly, follow thee more nearly, day by day."[130] That is what our Father intends for his children. A day-by-day worldview shapes God's children's perspective on life. Our link to this earth is tenuous. Our appeal is, "Father, I cannot 'do today right' without depending on you."

"Daily bread" advances the basic dimension of time. As humans we function within a time-space continuum. By God's design in creation we are constituted to live out our lives in successions of days. We cannot fathom existence outside these constructs. We are perplexed by the concept of reality outside the dimensions of space and time. The total number of our days is our earthly lifetime. Our days are clustered into years. We celebrate the advancement of our lifetime in "birthdays." God created a world regulated by time. In teaching us to pray, Jesus Christ accommodated our worldview by recognizing time as an indispensable factor for us: "Give us this day our daily bread."

Our request is narrowed to a small slice of time: "this day . . . daily." It is not, "Give us this year our annual provisions." If it were the latter, we might assume that an annual prayer to God our Father in heaven would suffice. We might offer the prescribed prayer, and thereafter live devoid of any sense of dependence upon our Father for the remaining 364 days of the year. The daily time frame is an advantage for us. In this fallen world the devil is unrelenting in his assault on the children of earth who belong to the Father. Each day's dawning should be a fresh reminder to depend on the love, care, and protection of our Father in heaven. The beloved Swedish hymn, *Day by Day* (*Blot en Dag*), affirms the blessings of daily dependence on God:

Day by day, and with each passing moment,
strength I find to meet my trials here;
Trusting in my Father's wise bestowment,
I've no cause for worry or for fear.
He whose heart is kind beyond all measure
gives unto each day what he deems best—
lovingly, its part of pain and pleasure,
mingling toil with peace and rest.

Every day the Lord Himself is near me,
with a special mercy for each hour;
all my cares he fain would bear and cheer me,
He whose name is Counselor and Pow'r.
The protection of his child and treasure
is a charge that on himself he laid;
"As your days, your strength shall be in measure,"
This the pledge to me he made.

Help me then in every tribulation
so to trust your promises, O Lord,
that I lose not faith's sweet consolation
offered me within your holy Word.
Help me, Lord, when toil and trouble meeting,
e'er to take, as from a father's hand,
one by one, the days, the moments fleeting,
till I reach the promised land.[131]

Our heavenly Father provides for "this day"—one day at a time. In his commentary on the Gospel of Matthew, Robert Gundry wrote that the intent of this prayer is that "no room remains for anxiety over tomorrow."[132] In contrast, those who do not have God as their heavenly Father are seldom satisfied. They crave more of this world's goods to allay their fear of tomorrow.

Many of God's children living in developed countries are amply supplied with this world's goods. But some have been entrapped by the deceitfulness of riches. They look for satisfaction in something other than what our father provides each day. They delight in displaying their treasures and telling about their exotic adventures abroad. They believe they can amass everything needed to secure a comfortable future. But unless they receive what their Father alone can provide each day, the paucity of their hoarded resources will yield only spiritual starvation.

I have had the pleasure of knowing some affluent children of our Father in heaven who hold the world's goods lightly. They reject the impulse to pursue gratification in the accumulation of wealth. Their lifestyles demonstrate that there is greater joy in giving than in getting. While they do not practice asceticism, they are content with what our Father provides. They live modestly instead of extravagantly, and they give generously to worthy causes. They have invested in the values of eternity.

The Passage of Time

Time permeates every aspect of earthly life. Time brings us face to face with our hopes and fears. In living things time fosters growth or decay. Until the Father's children realize their ultimate destiny as members of God's household, they must deal with the vicissitudes of time. Prior events, though past, are not gone. We struggle today to live up to the commitments of yesterday. Herein lies one of the chief reasons why we fail and sin miserably. With the passing of time, a powerful and passionate pledge often fizzles out.

King Joash of Judah served God faithfully under the godly tutelage of the priest Jehoiada. He rebuilt the temple in Jerusalem that had been profaned by the wicked sons of Athalia. But after Jehoiada's death Joash abandoned the temple and allowed the restoration of pagan worship. Zechariah, son of Jehoiada, warned the people not to disobey the Lord's commands. King Joash then ordered Zechariah to be stoned to death. Joash's reign that began honorably ended ignominiously (2 Chronicles 24:1–25). Joash's life is a tragic testimony to the spiritual corrosion that time may bring. A covenant to turn away from sin and to obey the will of the Father may dissipate. As the Apostle Paul lamented, "For what I want to do I do not do, but what I hate I do" (Romans 7:15). We are deluded if we think we have within us the requisite fortitude to remain sinless and live up to a spiritual resolve that recently stirred our souls.

According to the Second Law of Thermodynamics, disorder [entropy] always increases, or *an isolated system's ability to do work decreases over time.* God did not create people to be "isolated systems" that break down over time. It was sin that isolated mankind from our heavenly Source. Mankind's greatest need is to be reconciled to God. Without fresh infusions of spiritual virtue through prayer, our ability to flourish as children of the Father is sapped. Long periods of prayerlessness plunge us into a foolish self-reliance. The Apostle Paul told the Corinthian Christians that the hardships he endured in Asia "happened that we might not rely on ourselves, but on God, who raises the dead" (2 Corinthians 1:9). Relying on ourselves spiritually over any period of time leads to a fall. The occasions when sin has wrecked my resolve to honor my Father have almost always been a consequence of my neglect of prayer. We risk serious spiritual injury if we factor God out. Paul wrote: "Now it is God who makes both us and you stand firm in Christ" (2 Corinthians 1:21).

Most people have long-term plans for life. We expect a new day to dawn for us tomorrow. Financial planners market their services to help people prepare for their future. In an earthly economy financial planning is prudent. In the economy of our heavenly Father, however, we depend on daily provisions. We pray for fresh daily provision according the Father's perfect knowledge of our needs. How our Father may choose to provide is not ours to determine, but we may have the peaceful assurance that he will heed our requests.

Not One-a-Day Prayer

The request for bread "this day" and "daily" does not restrict the Father's children to one-a-day prayer. The Apostle Paul told the Thessalonian Christians to "pray continually" (1 Thessalonians 5:17). We pray daily—multiple times each day. We may suffer spiritual asphyxia if we pray to our Father only once per day.

Daily bread is a divine endowment to live counter-culturally in this fallen would with its deceptive charms. We need the right perspective as aliens passing through a world inhospitable to the children of God. Most of us will still be on this journey tomorrow. But we are not able to guarantee our own safety or the necessary provisions for our journey. Paul urged, "Devote yourselves to prayer, being watchful and thankful" (Colossians 4:2).

The Lord's Prayer is a "quality control" prayer. We enhance our spiritual vitality by bringing to our Father each day the requests that comprise the prayer. An automobile requires regular servicing by a qualified technician—

changing the oil and replacing worn parts—otherwise it will eventually break down. For a car once every three months or every six to nine thousand miles may suffice. But for God's children a spiritual tune-up is a daily need. Nuclear-powered aircraft carriers have sufficient fuel aboard to power all their systems for more than 20 years. They have no need of regular refueling. But God did not design us with the capacity to navigate this life without regular reliance on him for spiritual vitality. Only if we are filled from our Father's provision do we have power to pass through a dangerous world where the evil one has usurped control. Paul prayed for the Ephesian Church: "—that you may be filled to the measure of all the fullness of God" (Ephesians 4:19). God made us to be dependent on him at all times. If we detach ourselves from our Father, we become mired in the filthy slime of this fallen world.

Over a period of thirty-three years I served as the senior pastor of three churches. Then I took on a new role as an interim pastor for an additional ten years. The interim pastorate was a radical change from the way of life to which I had long been accustomed. Liz and I had been used to having roots in a local community and feeling a sense of belonging. Then we moved from community to community for as brief a time as three months and as long as sixteen months. Temporariness rather than permanence became more characteristic of our perspective on pastoral ministry. We were separated from most of our earthly possessions and found that we did not depend on them. I had been used to long-term planning. In my new role my long-range thinking could be measured in months instead of years. My interim experiences helped me appreciate the day-by-day orientation of God's children. One of the many benefits of interim pastoral ministry is that it gave Liz and me a greater appreciation of the petition, "Give us this day our daily bread."

The Risk of Repetition

Someone might ask if the daily repetition of the Lord's Prayer diminishes its potency for God's children. A daily recitation can easily become an empty ritual. For countless religious folks this prayer has degenerated into vain repetition. But the tragic abuse of this prayer does not annul its diligent use. Is the checklist of specific functions to be reviewed before takeoff a mindless operation for an airline captain because he repeats the practice with each flight? If so, millions of passengers' lives would be in jeopardy. The pilot of the airplane understands the importance of giving his undistracted attention to the checklist. A surgical team in a hospital must apply the same diligence to its operation. Driving a car, and a myriad of familiar functions in our homes and in industry demand our concentrated attention. The daily prayer Jesus Christ gave is integral to the spiritual vitality of God's children. It demands and deserves our earnestness.

How often have we thought, "I wish this day were over" or "I can't wait until tomorrow"? God's children toil in a hostile environment. Sometimes we long for the sun to set. The words of the psalmist recalibrate our perspective: "This is the day the Lord has made; let us rejoice and be glad in it" (Psalm 118:24). The day to which we awake is a gift from our Father in heaven. He graciously supplies the sustenance we need for the day's demands.

Some sundials have this verse engraved on their faces, "Count none but the sunny hours." But we cannot discount the dark and stormy hours. They also come from our Father who does not spare us painful tests. Each day the Father's children encounter challenges and pitfalls. We feel the allurement of unsavory enticements and may succumb to temptation. Our feelings of guilt impel us to pray to the Father for forgiveness and cleansing. Our sense of need stirs us to pray for daily bread.

Gratitude for the Father's Provision

The Lord's Prayer is a fresh daily exercise for God's children on our trek through hostile territory to our heavenly Father's home. God's people Israel endured hardships in the wilderness before they reached the inheritance he had promised them. They suffered for their own sins. They dealt with serious threats from enemies intent on destroying them. The Israelites of that generation and the generations to come had to learn to depend on God day by day. Even today the nation of Israel is alert to the daily threat from neighboring nations intent on its destruction. The sojourn of God's people Israel is analogous to the pilgrimage of God's people today. Until our earthly pilgrimage is ended and we realize the fullness of God's kingdom we will depend on our Father in heaven for our daily bread.

The Lord's Prayer is a brief component of Jesus Christ's lengthy "Sermon on the Mount." In his address Jesus admonished his listeners not to be anxious about the future. He said, "Therefore, do not worry about tomorrow, for tomorrow will worry about itself. Each day has enough trouble of its own" (Matthew 6:34; cf. Luke 12:22ff.). Worry is antithetical to a daily dependence on God our Father. The Lord's Prayer is, therefore, also Jesus Christ's gift of an antidote to worry.

The psalmist's words are particularly applicable here: "Your word is a lamp to my feet and a light for my path" (Psalm 119:105). God's word is a lamp for where we are standing or walking at the moment. It is not a searchlight to enlighten our future and reveal what awaits us tomorrow. It is for now—the present. Similarly, God's bread is for us today. It is not intended for future sustenance.

Let us be certain to give thanks to God for his daily provision. We take what God in his munificence provides for his children. But we often fail to turn back to him with our deep thanks. In the account of the ten men who had leprosy Jesus emphasized the importance of expressing heart-felt gratitude. Jesus healed them all, but only one turned back to praise God and to thank Jesus. Jesus deliberately drew attention to the gratitude of the one and the neglect of the nine (Luke 17:12–19).

Synopsis

As God's children traversing perilous territory we learn the following lessons from the petition, "Give us this day our daily bread."

1. First, we live in a fallen world that is under the control of the evil one. Therefore, things "go wrong" as the evil one assaults our faith and attempts to neutralize our confidence in our heavenly Father's provision.

2. Second, God alone is absolutely reliable. He is the only sure anchor for our hope during the storms of life. When everything else breaks loose, God alone is immovable and worthy of our trust. Our heavenly Father may not grant us each day what we ask for, but he will give what we need when we need it.

Questions for Discussion and Personal Application

1. Why do many of God's children not receive what they need from their father each day?
2. To what degree does the exclusion of God from people's lives affect the condition of society? Give some examples.
3. What are some of the ways people treat God as a useful acquaintance instead of the heavenly Father?
4. How do you distinguish between wants and needs when praying to our heavenly Father?
5. Tell about an urgent request you made to God, but later you realized it would have done more harm than good if God had granted it.
6. How do you think God's children should deal with one of their own that slides back into the former sinful ways?
7. What is our chief need that daily bread from our heavenly Father meets?
8. What is the difference between the daily bread from our heavenly Father and the bread that represents people's cravings and greed?
9. How would God's children be different if they were to rely on the daily bread our Father provides instead of devoting themselves to accumulating this world's goods?
10. Was asking for things an issue in your family as you were growing up, and how has it affected your relationship with your heavenly Father?
11. What is the specific gift our heavenly Father delights to give to his children who ask? Why do you think Jesus cited this gift?
12. Tell how your heavenly Father provided daily bread for you in a way you did not anticipate.

13. How does daily bread from our heavenly Father sustain you while you are surrounded by the unpleasantness of a corrupt society?
14. How have you learned that God's provision that nurtured your soul yesterday is not sufficient for today?
15. What does holding the things of this world lightly, or with open hands, mean to you?
16. How have you dealt with the tendency to renege on commitments you previously made to your heavenly Father?
17. What lesson have you learned about what happens to you if you neglect regular prayer?
18. What can you do to keep the Lord's Prayer from becoming stale?
19. How have you learned that sincerely praying to our Father in heaven for daily bread can be a cure of anxiety?

10. FORGIVE US OUR SINS AS WE ALSO FORGIVE THOSE WHO SIN AGAINST US

Do not consider yourself as irredeemably sinning,
because God's will to forgive is
even greater than your power to sin.

Pinchas Lapide[133]

The Obliteration of Offenses

What is forgiveness? Forgiveness means excusing someone for an offense. The one who has granted the forgiveness considers the fault to be null and void. It is no longer a cause of friction or division between the parties. The New Testament Greek word meaning "to forgive" is *aphiemi*. Its primary meaning is *to let go, send away* or *dismiss*. In Matthew 13:36 this verb in its participial form reports Jesus *sending away* the crowd after telling them various parables. If we say our sins have been forgiven, we can rightly claim, "my sins are gone." Forgiveness is freighted with the rudimentary concept of eradication. If a dentist extracts an abscessed tooth, the tooth is discarded. When our heavenly Father forgives us, our sins are removed and no longer attached to us.

Debts, Transgressions, Sins

The word "debts" or "trespasses" in some translations of the Lord's Prayer can be misleading. In modern parlance these terms mean something entirely different from what Jesus intended in the Lord's Prayer. Jesus did not mean debts as financial obligations or trespasses as encroachment misdemeanors. Tasker explained,

> "Debts" is a Jewish way of regarding sins, and, as we do not in English use the word in this connection, Knox felt justified in using here the word "trespasses" even though the Vulgate rendering is *debita*.[134]

In the account of the Lord's Prayer in Luke's Gospel (11:4), the petition is "forgive us our sins" (*hamartiai*, in the Greek text). In conversation Jesus would have used an equivalent Aramaic term to denote offenses or transgressions for which we must seek the forgiveness of our Father in heaven. As with the other requests in the Lord's Prayer, only our heavenly Father can grant this forgiveness.

Whichever term is used, whether "debts," "trespasses," or "sins," in both Matthew 6:12 and Luke 11:4 Jesus is clearly speaking of sins. These are the debts we owe to our Father in heaven. This term, "debt" is translated as "obligation" in Romans 4:4—a man's wages for working are an obligation. In the Lord's Prayer the same word "debts" means failures in our obligations to God. Could anything be more definitively the essence of sin? Willard D. Ferrell commented, "It says something about our times that we rarely use the word *sinful* except to describe a really good dessert."[135] Any "debt" or "trespass" against our Father in heaven is an offense against the perfection and holiness of God.

The Gravity of Sin

This petition in the Lord's Prayer is for God's children who confess that they are sinners. We do not resort to euphemistic terms for sins, like "mistakes" or "ethical lapses." There is no such thing as a trivial offense against God. As corrupt human beings, we have always been powerless to save ourselves from the devastation caused by sin. In mankind's early history God dealt with the horrific sin that had overwhelmed the whole earth. He sent a flood to judge and to purify the human race. Robert Orben quipped that when God said there would be a flood, Noah had to build the ark; he didn't go out and buy a sponge.[136] God's extreme action proved the gravity of sin.

In remarks immediately following this prayer, Jesus showed that by debts or trespasses he meant sins. He said, "If you forgive men when they sin against you, your heavenly Father will also forgive you. But if you do not forgive men their sins, your Father will not forgive your sins" (Matthew 6:14–15). The Apostle Paul also urged the Colossian Christians to heed this principle. He wrote, "Bear with each other and forgive whatever grievances you may have against one another. Forgive as the Lord forgave you" (Colossians 3:13).

The Lord's Prayer focuses first and foremost on God our Father in heaven. Jesus Christ established the sequence of the petitions in the Lord's Prayer. The focus of the first request is our heavenly Father's utterly holy nature. The next appeal is for the advent of God's reign. Then we pray for the execution of his will upon earth as it is done in heaven. The fourth petition addresses our daily reliance on our Father for all our needs. The penultimate plea is for forgiveness of our sins.

Sincere Request for Forgiveness

Forgiveness can have different meanings, depending on the context. The request to be forgiven may arise from a heart-felt regret for a major wrong, or it may be nothing more than a perfunctory apology for a minor inconvenience.

289

In the latter case, the response may be, "No problem," or "Think nothing of it." Sometimes the cost of forgiveness is enormous. The plea for forgiveness enjoined by Jesus in the Lord's Prayer issues from a broken heart. Behind the child of God's plea for forgiveness is shame and sorrow because of sin's affront to the heavenly Father's holiness. We do not claim as Lear cried out in Shakespeare's *King Lear,* "I am a man more sinned against than sinning."[137] Rather, as children of our heavenly Father we acknowledge the seriousness of our sin and repent of it. Repentance is a deep sorrow for sin and a turning from it to follow and obey Christ Jesus as Lord.

There is yet another category of so-called forgiveness that is especially detestable. It is a faux forgiveness—a grudging submission to someone who has demanded an apology. Jesus Christ told his followers to ask the Father to forgive their sins. Is this not similar to a parent ordering a child, "say you are sorry!"? The child complies and says it, but doesn't mean it. But in the Lord's Prayer the plea for forgiveness is a cord of love that ties our hearts, minds, and souls to our heavenly Father. A child of the heavenly Father who does not take seriously the need of God's forgiveness will increasingly conform to the corrupt pattern of this world (Romans 12:2).

The Lord's Prayer is intended for devout children of God. A child of God is someone who is saved by God's grace through faith in Jesus Christ as Savior and Lord (Ephesians 2:8; Romans 10:9–10; John 1:12). But the spiritual condition of God's children is impaired. None of us has completely escaped moral rot. Nevertheless, there is nothing that can separate us from the love of our heavenly Father and the fullness of all he has prepared for his children.

God's children here live in the "already, but not yet" stage of salvation. John explained:

> Dear friends, now we are children of God, and what we will be has not yet been made known. But we know that when he appears, we shall be like him, for we shall see him as he is (1 John 3:2).

Until the end of this age we will struggle with the constraints of fallen human nature. Charles Spurgeon said that God never allows his people to sin successfully. If our heavenly Father's children sin, there is an uneasiness that moves them to deal with it

Scripture warns God's children to beware of the devil who seeks to devour us (1 Peter 5:8–9). This world lies in the control of the evil one (1 John 5:19). We are vulnerable to the devil's deceitful schemes. Paul implores God's children to stand firm in the faith, to live by the Spirit, and not to indulge the sinful lusts of the fallen fleshly nature (1 Corinthians 16:3; Philippians 1:19; Galatians 5:16). If there were no danger for the children of the heavenly Father, there would be no warnings to be alert. There is great peril in living recklessly. It is as absurd as a man jumping from the top of a tall building, and he is heard to say as he plummets by the third floor, "so far so good." God's children cannot persist in sinning with impunity. They will have to give account for their conduct before the judgment seat of Christ (2 Corinthians 5:10). Begging for the forgiveness of our heavenly Father is, therefore, a part of our daily spiritual exercise.

God's Children as Sinners

Should God's children, who have been forgiven and delivered from the control of evil, still admit that they are sinners? If not, how do they explain Jesus Christ's injunction to his followers in the Lord's Prayer to ask the heavenly Father's forgiveness for their sins? Dr. Alexander Whyte served as Principal and Professor at New College, Edinburgh in the early twentieth century. The saintly preacher and scholar did not shrink from attaching the term "sinner" to himself, as the following report reveals:

> Dr. Alexander Whyte years ago staggered the fashionable and starchy congregation at St. George's West, Edinburgh, on Sunday, by saying in solemn tones and grave, that he had discovered that week who was the greatest and vilest and most notorious sinner in Edinburgh. And he was going to name him. [There was] noticeable movement, and a shuffling and clearing of throats among the lawyers and businessmen in the congregation. Then in an awful silence of expectancy that reigned over that beautiful church, the preacher said, "His name is Alexander Whyte." Next morning in New College, of which he was Principal, someone said, "Did you hear about Whyte's outburst in St. George's yesterday?" "Oh, I did," was the reply, "and I'm glad it was him that said it!"[138]

Scripture does not state that God's children have been delivered from all inclinations to sin. In the teaching of Jesus Christ and in the writings of his apostles we find that God's children have a recurring sin problem that we must not ignore. The Apostle John tells God's children to confess their sins, and God is faithful and just to forgive confessed sins (1 John 1:9). The Apostle Paul actually called himself a sinner (1 Timothy 1:15).

In God's sight, however, his children are not guilty of sin. There is no guilt in those who have placed their trust in Jesus Christ, and therefore there is no condemnation (Romans 8:1). Condemnation from God is reserved for those who are guilty of sin.

In our earthly life God's children continue to be capable of sinning. We lie to ourselves if we do not admit this. John states, "If we claim to be without sin, we deceive ourselves and the truth is not in us" (1 John 1:8). But God's children do not seek forgiveness in order to be justified before our holy God. Justification is an event that occurs once-for-all when we repent of our sins and place our trust in Jesus Christ as our Savior. Grudem explained:

> The prayer, "Forgive us our sins," therefore, is one in which we are relating not to God as eternal judge of the universe, but to God as a Father. It is a prayer in which we wish to restore the open fellowship with our Father that has been broken because of sin (see also 1 John 1:9; 3:19–22).[139]

Why should God's children make this petition for forgiveness? Is it because we have trusted in ourselves and have failed to acknowledge our failures? Yes, it is! Is it because we have sinned and feel guilty as a result? Yes, it is! But even more so, it is because we disobeyed God and did not behave as children of our Father in heaven. George MacDonald wrote, "It is when people do wrong things willfully that they are more likely to do them again."[140]

Who would ever believe that we are children of God if they could see all our thoughts and deeds? When a parishioner congratulated the Scottish preacher Robert Murray M'Cheyne for his saintliness, he responded, "Madam, if you could see in my heart you would spit in my face!"[141] We pray, "forgive us our sins" knowing that we cannot hide them from our Father. Our options are to flaunt our sins in the face of God, to pretend that we do not sin, or to beg sincerely for our Father's forgiveness.

The Entrance of Sin

Mankind is the crown of God's creation on earth. How, then, did sin become a deadly scourge for the human race? The Apostle Paul explains that mankind was the conduit through which sin came into the world:

> Therefore, just as sin entered the world through one man, and death through sin, and in this way death came to all men, because all sinned, . . . Consequently, just as the result of one trespass was condemnation for all men, so also the result of one act of righteousness was justification that brings life for all men (Romans 5:12, 18).

Satan was powerless to contaminate the human race with evil when he entered God's earthly dominion. At the time of the temptation in the garden, God's creation was pristine and perfect. Satan could do nothing in his own power to spoil what God had created. The only way the evil one could establish residency and authority on earth was through mankind as the portal. Of all God's creatures, mankind alone had been enfranchised. Only God's highest creation could make moral choices. The first humans voted the devil into office. Sin came into the world through our initial ancestors who rejected God's will and chose instead to believe Satan's campaign rhetoric in the garden.

In the creation account, this refrain is repeated after God's sequential acts of creation: "And God saw that it was good" (Genesis 1:4, 10, 12, 18, 21, 25, etc.). The whole creation was God's work, and he declared it "good." Satan would have no legitimate authority in God's earthly creation unless it were granted to him. Because mankind was created in God's image and had eternity in his heart, the enemy sought a 'portal' to take control of God's earthly creation. The account of mankind's fateful choice is related in Genesis chapter three. Satan the interloper in the garden gained authority through the permission of the first human couple. That is how the evil one gained control as ruler of this world.

Among all living creatures, mankind alone bears the image of God. A signature of God's image is the freedom of choice. The first humans had the liberty to disobey God and to choose an alternative to his revealed will. Thus by God's permission—and this itself is a great mystery—the image of God in mankind was the means by which a curse came upon all creation, including mankind.

Jesus Christ became the "second Adam." By his atoning sacrifice on the cross he became a curse for us. He suffered the punishment for sin in our stead. In his victory over sin and death he exposed the deceit of the evil one, breaking his control over mankind and removing the curse of sin. Paul explained, ". . . just as sin reigned in death, so also grace might reign through righteousness to bring eternal life through Jesus Christ our Lord" (Romans 5:21).

Satan's place in the world today is that of a usurper. He has assumed authority that belongs rightfully to God. The craft of the devil in the garden was deceit. By his atoning sacrifice on the cross Christ broke Satan's power. The devil, therefore, has no authority over God's children. His power lies in deception.

Why God's Children Sin

Why do God's children sin? Consider the following analogy: a child stays close to his father as they walk through a dangerous neighborhood. They are surrounded by evil and filth. If the child strays from his father he may be lured into peril and suffer injury. So in this hostile world God's children never attain a self-sufficiency that allows us to let go of dependence on God our Father. Paul warned, "So, if you think you are standing firm, be careful that you don't fall!" (1 Corinthians 10:12)

It is imperative that the heavenly Father's children not take sin lightly, as if it were something to toy with. In South Africa we lived on a small farm just a couple of miles outside of town. It was what today might be called a "hobby farm" for my father. Among the few animals he kept were a few thoroughbred Jersey cows. They were his delight. One day my father brought home a young registered Jersey bull. It was a handsome little fellow. My dad named him Prince. He used to hold it by the horns and spar with it. But Jersey bulls may develop an aggressive streak. As Prince grew up the time came when my father was the only one who could safely enter the field that was Prince's domain. He had become a menace. He was too dangerous for the servants or me to venture near to him. Prince illustrates the insidiousness of sin. At first something may seem harmless to us, and we play with it. But it grows into something large and dangerous. Eventually that apparently harmless indulgence has become a monster that terrorizes a child of God. If we are not vigilant each day we suffer serious injury.

Asking for forgiveness is a daily necessity, just like the daily request for bread. The two petitions appear to be temporally connected. No true child of the Father would maintain that our need of forgiveness deserves less attention than our daily need of God's provision. Hendriksen states,

"We do indeed, sin daily. . . . He (Christ) never even hinted that there might be a time before death when this petition should be omitted."[142] In October 1517 the Rev. Martin Luther placed his famous ninety-five theses in Latin on the door of the Castle Church in Wittenberg where he was a lecturer in Sacred Theology. The first statement read, "Our Lord and Master Jesus Christ, when he said *Penitentiam agite* ("Repent ye"), willed that the whole life of his believers should be repentance."[143] Penitence is a mark of the mien of our heavenly Father's children.

The Location of Sin

Where do we find sin? Is sin located in a particular object or event? Do we discover sin in a laboratory that manufactures hallucinogenic or addictive drugs? Is sin located in brothels or pornographic book stores?

We are fearful for little children who will grow up in the modern era. The overt expressions of depravity are more evident in society today than in the days of our grandparents. Does this mean there is more sin today than there was in the past? No! Previous generations were just as susceptible to sin as the youth of today are. The curse of sin has infected every person because we are part of the fallen human race. It is noble to do our utmost to protect little ones from being ravaged spiritually by the evil in the world, but it is unrealistic to suppose that we can do anything to keep them free of sin. Even in a puritanical culture people struggled with sin asserting itself in myriad expressions. We are mistaken if we think adolescents are more vulnerable to sin today than we were in our youth. Sin is an internal condition, not an external influence.

In the Garden of Eden, did Adam and Eve sin because the fruit of the forbidden tree was evil? Was sin located in the tree? No, the proto-couple sinned when they disobeyed the Lord God's command not to eat the fruit of the tree of the knowledge of good and evil (Genesis 2:17). As a consequence of their disobedience, sin took root in their lives.

In this regard Jesus said,

> Listen to me, everyone, and understand this. Nothing outside a person can defile [make a person unclean] them by going into them. Rather, it is what comes out of a person that defiles them. After he had left the crowd and entered the house, his disciples asked him about this parable. "Are you so dull?" he asked them. "Don't you see that nothing that enters a person from the outside can defile them? For it doesn't go into their heart but into their stomach, and then out of his body." (In saying this, Jesus declared all foods clean.) "What comes out of a person is what defiles them. For it is from within, out of a person's heart, that evil thoughts come—sexual immorality, theft, murder, adultery, greed, malice, deceit, lewdness, envy, slander, arrogance and folly. All these evils come from inside and defile a person (Mark 7:14–23).

We cannot evade our guilt of sin by blaming something outside ourselves, whether a person, a thing, or a social trend. We are responsible because the sin is within us. We all bear sin's defilement. For this reason we need to be born anew in our inner spirit; we need to become new creations. Christ Jesus came into this world to seek and save the lost (Luke 19:10). Christ's followers are also well acquainted with sin. Therefore, we pray to the heavenly Father, "Forgive us our sins."

Marked by Forgiveness

Forgiveness is a distinctive mark of God's children. It is our daily habit—seeking it and granting it. Repentance and forgiveness are inextricably linked in our involvement with our heavenly Father and with any people we have offended or who have done us harm. Jesus Christ prescribed forgiveness for relationships strained or severed by sin. Those who receive the Father's forgiveness must pass it on.

Sin spawns within us a prideful self-reliance. When we are filled with pride we marginalize our heavenly Father and we feel no need of his forgiveness. We factor God out. Haughtily we redefine the God-given values of Scripture to justify our indulgence in temporal allurements of a depraved culture. That is in essence a resurrection of the sin of Adam and Eve in the garden. They marginalized what God had decreed and thus opened themselves to the deceit of Satan.

Jesus Christ taught his followers to pray, "Forgive us our sins" (Luke 11:4). He did not say, "Prevent us from sinning." Sin is inevitable. In his prayer of dedication King Solomon said, " . . for there is no one who does not sin" (1 Kings 8:46). We must address and confess sin in our daily prayers to our heavenly Father. Throughout the Bible we find that God our Father is patient with sinners and stands ready to forgive the penitent.

In his letter to the Roman Christians the Apostle Paul declared unequivocally, "There is therefore now no condemnation to those who are in Christ Jesus" (Romans 8:1). The prophet Micah exulted,

Who is a God like you, who pardons sin and forgives the transgression of the remnant of his inheritance? You do not stay angry forever but delight to show us mercy. You will again have compassion on us, you will tread our sins underfoot and hurl all our iniquities into the depths of the sea (Micah 7:18–19).

The prophet Jeremiah explained the blessings of God's new covenant with his people:

"This is the covenant I will make with the house of Israel after that time," declares the Lord. "I will put my law in their minds and write it on their hearts. I will be their God, and they will be my people. No longer will a man teach his neighbor, or a man his brother, saying, 'Know the Lord,' because they will all know me, from the least of them to the greatest," declares the Lord. "For I will forgive their wickedness and will remember their sins no more" (Jeremiah 31:33–34).

David wrote from his regular experience of God's forgiveness:

He [the Lord] does not treat us as our sins deserve or repay us according to our iniquities. For as high as the heavens are above the earth, so great is his love for those who fear him; as far as the east is from the west, so far has he removed our transgressions from us (Psalm 103:10–12).

David does not imply that God our Father practices a benign leniency, as if to say "boys will be boys." He exults instead in the magnanimity of the Father's forgiveness of those who fear the Lord. The Lord is a forgiving God. Those who humble themselves before God need not fear that he will spurn their repentance. Their Father in heaven will not reject and abandon them. Such is the nature of divine forgiveness. Sins forgiven by our heavenly Father are buried and never exhumed. Jesus Christ came into the world for this very reason—so that lost sinners may be forgiven. God's Word tells us, "But God demonstrates his own love for us in this: while we were still sinners Christ died for us" (Romans 5:8). God looks at sinful people with a longing to forgive.

God's patience and kindness toward his children changes our manner of dealing with people. Paul wrote, "So from now on we regard no one from a worldly point of view (literally, *according to the flesh*) . . . Therefore, if anyone is in Christ, he is a new creation . . ." (2 Corinthians 5:16–17). As God's children we view wicked and ungodly people in a new light. They are what we used to be before we became new creations who call God *Abba,* Father. This affects the way we treat anyone who has sinned against us.

Genuine Confession

The prayer for forgiveness is *de facto* a confession of sin. All of us have sinned and failed to measure up to God's standard of righteousness. We cannot compensate for our sins. We can do nothing sufficiently virtuous to claim that we are "even" with God. A cartoon pictured a woman meeting with her pastor. The caption had the woman saying, "I've never been good at repentance, Pastor. I'll just let you use my condo during August, and God can call it even."[144] No quantity of good works can compensate for our sins. Our only hope is in forgiveness through the atoning sacrifice of Jesus Christ for our sins. We appeal to our Father for mercy: "Please forgive me, Father. I have sinned and I cannot make things right with you."

Mere compliance with Jesus Christ's command to ask our Father to forgive our sins is inadequate. Our fallen nature may blunt our plea for forgiveness. A petition that is only a few words in a liturgical rite is futile. It does not come from the heart. Sorrow for sin is the *sine qua non* of genuine confession. Brennan Manning wrote, "The men and women who are truly filled with light are those who have gazed into the darkness of their own imperfect existence."[145] A sincere plea for God's forgiveness demands our spiritual recoil from the vile thoughts and actions that have marked us. Without remorse for sin, a prayer for forgiveness is a sham.

Enmity and Forgiveness

The serpent in the garden deceived the first couple and they chose to disobey God's stated will. Then the Lord God said to the serpent, "I will put enmity between you and the woman, and between your offspring and hers." (Genesis 3:15). God deliberately placed hostility between mankind and the devil. He would not permit mankind to thrive in a world under the control of the devil. Throughout the ages of mankind this enmity has been playing out in a dearth of peace on the earth. People and nations constantly exhibit the horrific evidence of diabolical corruption.

People who are not children of God are enemies of God (Romans 5:10). Jesus told those who opposed him that their father was the devil (John 8:44). Their father the devil was also their enemy. The familiar saying "The enemy of my enemy is my friend" is not true of them. The devil is God's enemy, as are people who reject God. But that does not mean the devil is a friend of people who are at enmity with God. Sooner or later they learn that the devil is not their ally. The devil is the ultimate enemy of all humankind. He schemes incessantly to deceive and defile all beings created in the image of God.

Adherents to the world's religions are tormented by fear of hostile evil spirits. They scrupulously perform religious rituals, some repulsively grotesque. They hope thereby to assuage the hostility of their gods. The spiritual entities they fear are real, not imaginary. The Apostle Peter warned God's children to be alert to the real threat posed by our spiritual enemy (1 Peter 5:8).

The people of this world are not the enemy of God's children. If we act with enmity against people who do us harm, we compromise our alertness to the designs of our enemy the devil. If we refuse to forgive those who sin against us, we feed our hostility against a fellow human being. We do the devil's work for him. Our enemy's machinations against mankind become increasingly successful if we refuse to forgive.

Enmity between people is a key element in the devil's strategy to bolster his control over God's creation in this world. Scripture identifies the devil as "that ancient serpent called the devil, or Satan, who leads the whole world astray" (Revelation 12:9). Wherever God's children refuse to forgive, and become embroiled in church conflicts, the devil's work succeeds. In this manner our enemy has dealt a deathblow to many churches.

Jesus Christ on the cross was our consummate model of forgiveness. He who needed no forgiveness forgave those responsible for his crucifixion. He prayed, "Father, forgive them, for they know not what they are doing" (Luke 23:34). The Apostle Paul closely tied forgiveness to our strategy for dealing with Satan:

> If you forgive anyone, I also forgive him. And what I have forgiven—if there was anything to forgive— I have forgiven in the sight of Christ for your sake, in order that Satan might not outwit us. For we are not unaware of his schemes (2 Corinthians 2:10– 11).

If we do not forgive each other, our enemy wins.

The people we forgive may also need to forgive us because we have sinned against them. The condition, "as we also have forgiven those who have sinned against us," applies universally. In the selfsame context in which our Lord gave this instruction on prayer, he told his followers,

But I tell you, do not resist an evil person. If someone strikes you on the right cheek, turn to him the other also. And if someone wants to sue you and take your tunic, let him have your cloak as well (Matthew 5:39–40).

He also said, "But I tell you: Love your enemies and pray for those who persecute you, that you may be sons of your Father in heaven" (Matthew 5:44–45). It is futile to seek the favor of our Father in heaven and simultaneously act in a malicious way towards our earthly brother. I admit that I have prayed the Lord's Prayer sincerely and then behaved in an unloving manner toward people who inconvenience me, or who flaunt values in contrast to my own. This is not a trifling matter. Jesus cautioned his disciples, "But if you do not forgive men their sins, you Father will not forgive your sins" (Matthew 6:15). The Apostle John also drew attention to the seriousness of this offense:

If anyone says, "I love God," yet hates his brother, he is a liar. For anyone who does not love his brother, whom he has seen, cannot love God, whom he has not seen. And he has given us this command: Whoever loves God must also love his brother (1 John 4:20–21).

Therefore, it is a worthless exercise to pray, "hallowed be your name," while being actively hostile to a fellow human being. Hostility or ill will toward our brother cancels good will toward God our Father.

Forgive as We Have Been Forgiven

Divine forgiveness is thoroughly an act of mercy. Forgiveness is not an act of justice. God's forgiveness is his mercy in action. Our forgiveness of others is disingenuous if we forgive reluctantly. In order to forgive those who sin against us it is imperative that the children of the heavenly Father understand the nature of true forgiveness. Forgiveness is an act of mercy as the evidence of love. When you forgive, you do not ask, "Can you give me a good reason why I should forgive you?" The one who grants forgiveness knows there is a good reason. It is mercy. If we are reticent to forgive, we can be certain that our Father is not. He is eager to forgive. His "heart is kind beyond all measure."[146]

The children of God belong to the kingdom of heaven. Our citizenship is in heaven (Philippians 3:20). Forgiveness certifies our citizenship. The stamp of divine forgiveness and our forgiveness of others are embossed upon our souls. Without it we have no part in the kingdom of God. Paul underscored the importance of forgiveness in the churches. He wrote: "Be kind and compassionate to one another, forgiving each other, just as in Christ God forgave you" (Ephesians 4:32).

This petition in the Lord's Prayer is two-sided. The heavenly Father's children have an obligation to forgive as we have been forgiven. There is a correspondence between the way our Father forgives us and the way we must forgive others. Our Father's forgiveness of us is the pattern for our forgiveness of others. No one has ever sinned against me nearly as grievously as I have sinned against God—and he has forgiven me. How dare I withhold forgiveness from others? If the comparison were reversed—if God's forgiveness were modeled after our forgiveness—we would be in spiritual peril.

Immediately after giving this prayer to his followers, Jesus explicitly instructed them to ask for forgiveness from the Father. He said the heavenly Father's forgiveness is conditioned upon their forgiveness of others who sin against them (Matthew 6:12, 14–15). Christ's warning is clear; if we are unwilling to forgive others, we should not expect God to forgive us. This is a sobering admonition. But many of God's children still hold grudges against those who have sinned against them.

Some who profess to forgive do so with festering resentment. Many even flout their refusal to forgive, as if it were their right to withhold mercy. The *Catechism of the Catholic Church* offers this crucial insight: "In refusing to forgive our brothers and sisters our hearts are closed and their hardness makes them impervious to the Father's merciful love; but in confessing our sins, our hearts are open to his grace."[147]

God is not obligated to forgive us because we have forgiven others. A. W. Pink remarked, "We are to be imitators of God, but He does not imitate us in pardoning offenders—it would fare ill with us indeed if God were to forgive no better than we forgive one another."[148] The verb "forgive" in the Greek text of the Lord's Prayer is in the aorist tense, which has no temporal significance but denotes an action simply as occurring.[149] This suggests a correspondence between God's forgiving and our forgiving, rather than God's forgiveness depending on whether or not we have first forgiven. Hendriksen explained:

This certainly cannot mean that our forgiving disposition earns God's pardon. The forgiveness of our debts is based not on our merits—how could we have any?—but on Christ's, applied to us. Consequently, from our point of view, forgiveness is based on God's unmerited (not merited by us) favor, that is, on divine grace (Ephesians 1:7), compassion (Matthew 18:27), and mercy (Luke 18:13). Nevertheless, our own forgiving disposition is very important. In fact, without it we ourselves cannot be forgiven. For us it is the indispensable condition of receiving the forgiveness of sins.[150]

Forgive Without Limit

Jesus said, "So in everything, do to others what you would have them do to you, for this sums up the Law and the Prophets" (Matthew 7:12). A. W. Pink explained, "if we who have so little grace find it possible to be magnanimous, how much more so shall the God of all grace exceed the creature in this!"[151] Our Father knows our recidivism. Many of us have returned repeatedly to committing the same sins against him. But he forgives, and he forgives "seventy times seven." This is a biblical idiom meaning without limit.

The forgiveness the Father grants to those who trust Christ is complete. The way we forgive those who sin against us must also be complete. The way we treat a person after granting forgiveness must prove the genuineness of our forgiveness. There is no residue of resentment that smudges the relationship. The forgiver treats the one forgiven as if there had never been an offense. If you are the offended person, you will probably never erase completely a grievous offense from your memory, but you determine not to allow the memory of the past to poison the present. Thielicke asked,

What is forgiveness? At all events it cannot mean that we cover up a fault with the 'mantle of charity.' Divine things are never a matter of illusions and deception. On the contrary, before the sin is forgiven the mantle with which it is covered must be removed.[152]

True forgiveness does not require us to forget the offense. In fact, the memory enhances the strength of the forgiveness. Thielicke offered this insight,

> . . . forgiveness . . . is a miracle, and [that] therefore one should never mention the words 'forgive' and 'forget' in the same breath. . . Forgiveness therefore cannot mean to be chemically cleansed. It means rather that my sin no longer separates me from God, that it can no longer be a chasm that cuts me off from the Father.[153]

Does the clause "Forgive us our sins as we forgive those who sin against us" imply that the way others sin against us is the same as the way we sin against God? Not at all! The difference is immense. Any similarity lies in the forgiveness, not in the sin. The impact of the sin of others against us is vastly inferior to the implications of our sin against our Father in heaven.

Jesus elaborated on the nature of genuine forgiveness. In one of his parables a merciful king forgave a servant who owed him much and was unable to repay. But that servant refused to show mercy to a fellow servant who owed him a small amount compared to what he had been forgiven. The king then turned over to jailers the man who refused to forgive. Jesus concluded the parable: "This is how my heavenly Father will treat each of you unless you forgive your brother from your heart" (Matthew 18:21–35).

In Matthew's account of the Lord's Prayer, why did Jesus give special attention to forgiveness afterwards? (Matthew 5:13–14). Jesus knew that God's children would struggle with forgiveness. We cannot grow beyond spiritual infancy unless we resolve this crucial issue of forgiveness. Jesus Christ explained forgiveness clearly in the Lord's Prayer and in his postscript to the prayer. We cannot bypass forgiveness. We cannot get over it, under it, or around it. We must go through it. We must "forgive men their sins."

Someone may object, "I have tried to forgive, but I cannot." Resentment and bitterness have taken hold with clutches of steel. But the Lord Jesus Christ told his followers to forgive. Forgiveness may lie beyond our natural ability. But no child of the Father is ever excused from the obligation to forgive. Our heavenly Father will hear his children who sincerely cry out to him for help to let go of a grudge. God provides what we need to do his will. Perhaps an ingredient of our daily bread from our Father is the strength to forgive others in obedience to his command. The strength to forgive may not come from our pluck or perseverance, but from the Father's merciful enabling.

Unconditional Forgiveness

God's manner of forgiving seems to involve repentance. God forgives those who repent. The Apostle Peter said to the crowd on the Day of Pentecost, "Repent and be baptized, every one of you, in the name of Jesus Christ for the forgiveness of your sins" (Acts 2:38). According to a Japanese proverb, forgiving the unrepentant is like drawing pictures on water. On the cross, however, Jesus prayed for those who crucified him, "Father, forgive them, for they do not know what they are doing" (Luke 23:34). Jesus Christ prayed to the Father to forgive people who gave no sign that they had first repented. God the Father and God the incarnate Son agreed on all things. We cannot hold, therefore, that our heavenly Father attached a condition to forgiveness. Likewise, we have no permission to wait until we are satisfied that the person who has sinned against us has repented. Most people who sin against us do not know what they are doing. We forgive as Christ forgave. Our forgiveness of others is unconditional. As the incensed Sanhedrin, the Jewish ruling council, was stoning Stephen to death, he prayed, "Lord, do not hold this sin against them" (Acts 7:60). Those members of the Sanhedrin were engaged in a murderous act—the extreme opposite of repentance. So we forgive others even if they do not confess their wrong. Forgiveness is unconditional. We forgive others because we need to forgive and because we also need forgiveness.

We should not be astonished when wrong is perpetrated against us. Jesus said this would happen. If we accept the fact that we will suffer from the wrongdoing of others, it will mitigate our penchant for vengeance. We forgive as our heavenly Father has forgiven us. A response of outrage is out of character in God's children. It demonstrates that we have not taken to heart Christ's instruction or his "heads-up" warning to anticipate opposition. Children of the heavenly Father must leave no foothold for retaliation or revenge in thought or behavior.

Forgiveness is a distinguishing feature of God's children. It is also one of the most challenging aspects of godly behavior. We tend to harbor malicious thoughts against those who have done us wrong or who have perpetrated vicious mischief against people we cherish or against the nation we love. Imagining retribution upon the culprit can be delectable. How many of us experienced more than a twinge of joy upon learning that a team of Navy Seals had shot to death the terrorist Usama ben Laden in Pakistan? We juxtaposed his demise with the collapsed World Trade Center towers in New York City where thousands perished because of his vile machinations. Many wished that he had been made to suffer slow torture in death. Few of God's children would admit such a barbaric desire, but it was in their heart. Thielicke offered this perspective on such matters:

> . . . if I myself am not a pardoned sinner, living by the grace of forgiveness, I cannot forgive. Then I can only suppress and control my anger. But this only leads to the storing up of more bitterness and spite, until one day it is vented in a sudden explosion.[154]

The Apostle Peter asked Jesus how many times to forgive a brother who sins against him. Jesus indicated there is virtually no limit to the number of times we must forgive. Nonetheless, many who claim to be God's children are reluctant to forgive. Our resentment may fester against someone who has grievously wronged us. We may consider the perpetrator of the offense our enemy. Jesus does not allow this option to the children of the Father. To nurse a grudge against someone defies Christ's mandate to forgive.

If others sin against us, we tend to consider them entirely to blame. I had to deal with this personally. A few influential members of a church I was serving influenced others of their ilk to oppose my leadership. I had no personal ambition to have my way, but I had proposed some modifications to help the church focus more deliberately on its biblical mandate. This was evidently perceived as a threat by the oligarchy. After fifteen years as the senior pastor it became apparent to me that I was no longer able to lead the church to which God had called me. I resigned the church I dearly loved. Months later, while praying the Lord's Prayer and pondering afresh the matter of forgiveness of sins, I recognized that the sin did not lie entirely with the offenders. My attitude toward them had become bitter. I repented of my sin and by God's grace was ushered into the freedom of forgiving and loving them. I was able to pray that our Father would use them for his glory. William Law said. "There is nothing that makes us love a man so much as prayer for him."[155] But I confess that memories occasionally provoke me to indict afresh those I believed to have done grievous wrong. Forgiving others can be a recurring struggle.

The Greatness of Forgiveness

The Apostle Paul taught that godly sorrow moves us to repentance (2 Corinthians 7:9–10). After his resurrection Jesus Christ said,

> This is what is written: The Christ will suffer and rise from the dead on the third day, and repentance and forgiveness of sins will be preached in his name to all nations, beginning at Jerusalem. You are witnesses of these things (Luke 24:46–48).

We have noted that the forgiveness of sins is the only component of the Lord's Prayer that Jesus chose to underscore with a commentary immediately afterward (Matthew 6:14–15). Jesus deemed the element of forgiveness in the prayer to be in need of further elaboration.

In Luke's account of the Lord's Prayer, the verb "forgive" in "for we also forgive" (Luke 11:4) is present indicative tense. This indicates that forgiveness is a lifestyle. Forgiving someone is not a gesture we use as currency to procure God's forgiveness after we have sinned. Jesus Christ advocates a way of life marked by authentic forgiveness. Robert H. Gundry remarked, "Forgiveness of others demonstrates sincerity in asking forgiveness from God."[156]

The forgiveness Jesus Christ called for is precious. In the Lord's Prayer the gravity of the trespass that God forgives is great. Sin alienates people from the heavenly Father. Forgiveness opens up the way of reconciliation. Therefore, the forgiveness of sin for which we plead is incalculably precious.

Jesus told a parable to teach that the one who has been forgiven the most loves the most (Luke 7:41–50). God's children who think they have not sinned grievously do not truly understand forgiveness. They have never struggled with debilitating guilt before our holy God. They may think of themselves more highly than they ought. As people who feel they need his mercy the least, they have never been amazed by the heavenly Father's love.

Apology and Forgiveness

Forgiveness is widely misunderstood and abused. An apology does not always engender forgiveness. Some maintain that an apology is saying the right thing after doing the wrong thing. But a true apology is heart-felt and genuine. An apology, as I understand it, is an implied appeal for forgiveness. The offender is eager to make things right.

We often hear of people demanding an apology. Unfortunately, many seem to have no intention of granting forgiveness if an apology is given. On one occasion I made an apology and asked forgiveness of the church I was pastoring. If an apology had not been requested, it would not have occurred to me to apologize.

This was the matter that occasioned my apology: Liz and I were driving back to the Midwest after visiting our son and his family in Reno, Nevada. Instead of taking the major interstate route through Nevada we decided to take a highway less traveled. Hwy 50 in Nevada is called the Loneliest Highway in America. For the most part it is straight, flat, and safe. I decided to put the car up to its maximum limit before the electronic governor prevented further acceleration. That was about twice the posted speed limit. I did it for only a few minutes, slowing down when I came upon a solitary car poking along at a mere 90 miles per hour. On my first Sunday back in the pulpit I unwisely mentioned the experience in some brief comments about our time in the West. A few days later I received a letter from a congregant who was deeply offended that I would joke about breaking the law. The rebuke was gentle and valid. An apology to the church was expected. But first I told some friends about it. They were amused, saying it had elevated my "cool" quotient among the younger folk in the church. Nevertheless, I had done wrong. The individual pointed out a sin in me that required repentance. I sent the person a note admitting my fault. I confessed it and gave a sincere apology to the congregation the next Sunday morning. Unfortunately, my relationship with the individual remained distant. Neither of us reached out to the other. For that I must assume the blame.

Someone who demands an apology usually has no intention of granting genuine forgiveness or repairing a relationship. An apology grudgingly granted in response to a demand is not a true apology. It is a forced confession. Then the one who gets the apology is the winner and the one who gives it is the loser. The loser does not consider himself reconciled with the person to whom he apologized. Instead, the resentment is stronger and the rift between them deeper because the apology was coerced. There is no kindling of warmth in the relationship. The winner may remain as cold as a cast iron commode on the shady side of an iceberg.

Genuine forgiveness is not even in the same galaxy as an apology reluctantly granted.

Authentic Forgiveness

I have learned crucial lessons from friends who can scarcely believe that God would forgive them. They consider themselves to be least deserving. The wonder of divine forgiveness stirs their souls to passionate worship. Those who have the keenest sense of God's mercy have the most to teach us. They may lack theological sophistication, but they have grasped an essential truth of Christian faith. Their personal stories make the awe of God's forgiveness come alive.

In contrast, I groan over those who have been socialized into the Christian faith. Since childhood they have heard the familiar words of God's forgiveness of sinners. Outwardly they go through the motions that give them the appearance of devout children of God, but inwardly they are not what they appear to be. Glossy restaurant menus illustrate menu options with beautiful pictures. But the meal delivered to your table may be a huge disappointment. You realize that the photographer is better than the cook.[157] I wonder what they would do if you took your plate of food and the menu into the kitchen, and asked, "Why isn't my food as good as the food in this picture?" Some Christians are like those food items—impressive to look at, but they leave a sour taste in your mouth.

I suspect that some who have grown up in the church have not truly repented of their sins or placed their faith in Jesus Christ for the forgiveness of their sins. They are God's children in name only. They adhere to the conventions of their religion, but are actually far from God the Father. They are goats among the sheep. There is no evidence of the fruit of the Spirit in their lives. They demonstrate no gratitude for

God's grace, they do not pray, they cannot worship God from the heart. They do not delight in God's forgiveness.

Many years ago one of my spiritual mentors told me about an incident earlier in his life. He had been an associate pastor to a well-known preacher-author at one of the most famous churches in America. One night after a rancorous meeting of the church board the senior pastor returned to his study. As my mentor walked by in the hallway he called out to him. With tears he asked, "Can you give me a reason why I should believe that any of those men know our Father?" Situations like that are unfortunately common. The mean-spirited abuse of godly pastors leads many to jettison their pastoral calling. Church splits as a result of nasty power struggles occur every day. After more than forty years as a pastor I have concluded that the nicest and the nastiest people on earth can both be found in churches.

But there is nothing that can take away the beauty of God's grace. I have seen it over and over in the church. A young man was rescued by God's mercy from severe addictions that had landed him homeless on the streets. As a newborn child of God, his love for God and for God's children was beautiful. He was an accomplished musician— a saxophonist. About a year after God restored him, the Lord in mercy reached out and saved a single mother who had lost all to a life of sin. She too was a fine saxophonist. In her joy of being a child of the Father she longed to share in the worship music at church. The young man had two saxophones, an old beat-up one and his favorite beautiful instrument. As he was praying he sensed a spiritual prompting to give a saxophone to this woman. He was prepared to give her the old one. But God's Spirit checked him; he was to give her his best instrument while he played the old one. I'm sure he had tears of joy at seeing her with the worship team using her new instrument to praise God.

He understood God's forgiveness. God gave his best to rescue him from hopelessness. He, in turn, gave his best. That's what God's forgiveness does in those who desperately need it and receive it with gratitude.

The forgiveness that we grant to others is of inestimable worth. If you deny forgiveness to someone, you cannot be neutral toward that person. It's a fallacy to say, "I neither love nor hate him. I'm completely neutral." Our human constitution does not allow us to remain neutral. To refuse to forgive is to create or maintain active enmity. It is tantamount to considering that person your enemy.

People Change

Another reason why forgiveness is good and right is simply because people change. None of us is exactly the same as what we were a week ago, a year ago, or a decade ago. We change for the better or for the worse, even if the change is minuscule. God's children are expected to grow in grace and knowledge of the Lord Jesus Christ. The New Testament letters to the churches are replete with appeals to believers to move on, to put off the old sinful nature and to put on the new nature renewed in Christ. Paul urged the Roman Christians not to be conformed to this world, but to be transformed by the renewing of their minds (Romans 12:2). Transformation means a major change. Change is a condition of maturing. When a child of God matures spiritually he acknowledges his sins and asks to be forgiven. To refuse to forgive is to be in jeopardy of forfeiting God's forgiveness (Matthew 6:15). People who once caused us harm may since have been changed by God's grace. How tragic it is if the offended one continues to harbor bitterness, and remains unchanged! John Stott said, "God forgives only the penitent and . . . one of the chief evidences of penitence is a forgiving spirit."[158]

Remember that the word "forgive" in the Lord's Prayer is heavily freighted with the concept of dismissing and removing. When our Father in heaven looks at us, he does not see the sin he forgave as still attached to us. When we forgive a person, we thereafter consider the offense completely dismissed. It has been removed from the person; it is no longer a factor in our relationship. It should never be brought up again—to the one who sinned or to anyone else.

How can we be certain that we are taking the words of our Lord to heart, that we have forgiven others and that our Father has forgiven us? (Matthew 6:11, 12) A. W. Pink proposed a question that we should ask ourselves: "Do I sincerely rejoice when I hear of any calamity befalling one who has wronged me? If so, I certainly have not forgiven him."[159]

Think for a few moments about the people who have wronged you, and whom you claim to have forgiven. If the name of one of those people comes up in conversation, do you tell others what that person did? Do you share the details of the offense? Do you speak ill of someone you claim, in the presence of your Father in heaven, to have forgiven? How would you feel if this were done against you? You had done wrong to someone and then sincerely sought forgiveness. The person granted you forgiveness, but later you learned that the so-called forgiver had been going about sharing the details of your offense and turning people against you. Would you consider yourself forgiven?

Is that the kind of forgiveness we expect from God—a forgiveness of which we are never completely confident; a forgiveness that may be revoked on a whim? Never! David said about God's forgiveness: "as far as the east is from the west, so far has he removed our transgressions from us" (Psalm 103:12).

Questions for Discussion and Personal Application

1. How do the two words "forgive" and "debts" help you appreciate the full meaning of "forgive us our debts?

2. There are six petitions in the Lord's Prayer. What can we learn from their sequence?

3. As an adult, have you ever been coerced to ask for forgiveness? How did you feel?

4. What does Scripture teach about a person who claims to be a child of God but flaunts an ungodly lifestyle?

5. God's children are those who have received Jesus and believed in his name (John 1:12). They repented and believed for the forgiveness of their sins (Acts 2:38; 10:43). Why, then, does Jesus instruct God's children to pray, "Forgive us our sins"?

6. Explain the role of the first humans in providing the means of access for sin into the world.

7. How did the devil gain legitimacy in God's perfect creation?

8. Do you pray for forgiveness of sin each day, or only when you are keenly aware that you've committed a sin?

9. When you survey the surrounding secular culture, what evidence do you find that biblical standards are being marginalized in order to accommodate majority opinion?

10. How do the Apostle Paul, the prophets Micah and Jeremiah, and the psalmist David extol God's amazing forgiveness?

11. How must you pray so that you will have the confidence that the heavenly Father hears and forgives you?

12. Give some examples of how God's children speak of wicked, ungodly people as their enemies.

13. How do church people frequently become the devil's accomplices in destroying churches?

14. When do you think it may be appropriate not to "turn the other cheek" to someone who has deliberately harmed you?

15. What are some differences between justice and forgiveness?

16. How would you lovingly correct a person who says to somebody, "I will never forgive you for what you have done"?

17. Have you ever felt that you reached the limit of your ability to forgive? What did you do about it?

18. What is an indicator that our forgiveness is genuine?

19. Thielicke said the words "forgive" and "forget" should never be mentioned in the same sentence. Why is that?

20. Why must we forgive people who do not confess that they have done wrong or do not ask to be forgiven?

21. How have you dealt with bitterness in your heart and a reluctance to forgive?

22. Of the various themes in the Lord's Prayer, why did Jesus select forgiveness for additional instruction (Matthew 6:14–15)?

23. Why are you amazed at your heavenly Father's forgiveness of you?

24. Why is an apology that is demanded ineffective in gaining forgiveness?

25. What is frequently a negative characteristic of people who have been raised in the Christian religion from infancy?

26. What is the most heart-warming account of human forgiveness that you have ever heard or seen?

27. Why is it foolish to hold a grudge against someone for an offense committed years or decades ago?

28. If you have forgiven someone who wronged you, have you refrained from sharing the details of the offense with others?

11. LEAD US NOT INTO TEMPTATION, BUT DELIVER US FROM THE EVIL ONE

If in this darksome wild I stray,
Be thou my Light, be thou my Way;
No foes, no violence, I fear,
No fraud, while thou, my God, art near.
Nicolaus Ludwig and Graf von Zinzendorf[160]

Test or Temptation?

In both Matthew's and Luke's accounts of the Lord's Prayer, the Greek word for "temptation" in "lead us not into temptation," is *peirasmon*. This word can mean either testing or temptation. Since it may have either meaning, should we not understand it as a request to our Father to spare us a test? After all, Scripture insists that God does not tempt anyone to evil.

> Blessed is the man who perseveres under trial, because when he has stood the test, he will receive the crown of life that God has promised to those who love him. When tempted, no one should say, "God is tempting me." For God cannot be tempted by evil, nor does he tempt anyone, but each one is tempted when, by his own evil desire, he is dragged away and enticed (James 1:12–14).

The word "trial" in verse 12 above is a form of the verb translated "tempt" in the same paragraph. James used the same root term to show us that a trial may have a worthy purpose in our heavenly Father's dealings with his children.

321

But it is contrary to God's nature to entice anyone to evil. Do not confuse trials or tests under God's hand with temptation that leads to evil. Temptation to sin does not come from God.

It is fruitless to debate whether Jesus meant "lead us not into temptation" or "lead us not into a test." Either way, Jesus instructs God's children to pray to be spared testing and temptation. Robert Gundry observed,

> *peirasmon* can connote either enticement to sin or testing of faith. But it would be a mistake to distinguish the connotations sharply; for every enticement to sin tests faith, and every test of faith holds an enticement to sin.[161]

What, exactly, is the difference between temptation and a test? Temptation's purpose is to destroy, to cause failure, or a fall. Testing's purpose is to strengthen or refine, to bring success or victory. Temptation is malevolent in intent; testing is benevolent. By praying, "lead us not into temptation" we do not ask God to quit leading us to evil temptations. The idea that we should ask our heavenly Father not to tempt his children to evil is ridiculous. It is akin to asking the president of the Indianapolis Motor Speedway not to put speed bumps on the racetrack. Our Father does not place anything in the path of his wayfaring children that will cause them to fall or to fail. Our Father wants his children to be victorious. His actions on our behalf are for our success.

We are the ones responsible for many or most of the traps that ensnare us. It is said that most people who flee from temptation leave a forwarding address. Nineteenth-century hymn writer and theologian F. W. Faber said:

He who dallies with temptation . . is never safe. People say that such and such a man had a sudden fall, but no fall is sudden. In every instance, the crisis of the moment is decided only by the tenor of the life; nor, since the world began, has any man been dragged over into the domain of evil, who had not strayed carelessly, or gazed curiously, or lingered guiltily, beside its edge.[162]

More often than not we dig the pit into which we fall. Sir Robert Watson Watt was a pioneer in the development of radar. Years afterward, while driving in Canada, the highway patrol caught him in a radar trap. Watt wrote about the experience:

Pity Sir Robert Watson Watt,
strange target of his radar plot,
and this, with others I could mention,
a victim of his own invention.[163]

"It is what it is" is a popular contemporary maxim. This truism is a sort-of watchword for those who benignly acquiesce to something they consider unchangeable. "It is what it is" means there is nothing you can do about it, so do not waste your time and efforts on something futile. Sadly, this saying falls readily from the lips of some of God's children. They do not call out to our Father for guidance when facing a challenging prospect or for deliverance when trapped in a tight spot. They find a sorry solace in telling themselves, "it is what it is." The Lord's Prayer banishes such a notion from the worldview of the heavenly Father's children. Jesus tells his followers to ask their heavenly Father for his intervention.

The Scriptures report many instances of God testing people. Moses prepared the Israelites for unusual tests by the Lord their God:

> If a prophet, or one who foretells by dreams, appears among you and announces to you a miraculous sign or wonder, and if the sign or wonder spoken of takes place, and the prophet says, "Let us follow other gods" (gods you have not known) "and let us worship them," you must not listen to the words of that prophet or dreamer. The Lord your God is testing you to find out whether you love him with all your heart and with all your soul. It is the Lord your God you must follow, and him you must serve. Keep his commands and obey him; serve him and hold fast to him. That prophet or dreamer must be put to death because he preached rebellion against the Lord your God, who brought you out of Egypt and redeemed you from the land of slavery. He has tried to turn you from the way the Lord your God commanded you to follow. You must purge the evil from among you (Deuteronomy 13:1–5).

In the above scenario, the false prophet's sign or wonder was real. That prophet then told the people to turn from the Lord to follow other gods. It was an example of a miraculous sign that contradicted a clear command of the Lord their God. Moses said it was a test that came from the Lord. Its purpose was to underscore the timeless principle that nothing is to supersede God's word, no matter how compelling the opposing evidence. Any temptation to turn from the Lord God to follow other gods challenged the Lord God's command to his people to have no other gods before him, to love him with all their heart and all their soul, and to hold fast to him.

Reasonable people acknowledge something to be true if it is corroborated by empirical proof. But the evidence may be part of a test, as in the example cited above by Moses. An immature child of God would undoubtedly be confused by such a test. This in itself is a crucial reason to pray "lead us not into temptation—or a test—but deliver us from the evil one."

Divine Help

James tells us to face our trials with joy (James 1:2). We all encounter hardships and challenges. All God's people will experience trouble in this world (John 16:33). The writer in Hebrews says this about Jesus: "Because he himself suffered when he was tempted, he is able to help those who are being tempted" (Hebrews 2:18).

Our heavenly Father involves himself in both our temptations and our tests. Paul told the Corinthian Christians that all their temptations are of the kind people everywhere encounter. Then he assured them that God is faithful and will not leave them to be tempted beyond the level of their endurance (1 Corinthians 10:13). Our Father will not allow his children to face temptations from the evil one that they are not equipped to overcome. This assures God's children that they can be victorious in the myriad temptations common to daily life. God has given his Holy Spirit to be a companion to help his children on their trek through enemy territory.

God imposed an extreme test on Abraham. God told him to sacrifice his son on Mount Moriah (Genesis 22:1–18). It was a test of Abraham's devotion to God. Our heavenly Father may choose to lead any of his children into an extreme test that may tempt us to turn away from our divine Guide. That is the nature of the temptation in the Lord's Prayer. We may scurry to try to find a way out of the dark valley into which our Father takes us. We plead with him to spare us the severe tests.

G. A. Young wrote a song about God leading his children into difficult tests:

In shady green pastures so rich and so sweet,
God leads his dear children along;
Where the water's cool flow bathes the weary one's feet,
God leads his dear children along.

The third stanza and refrain address the testing:

Though sorrows befall us and evils oppose,
God leads his dear children along;
Through grace we can conquer, defeat all our foes.
God leads his dear children along.

Refrain
Some through the waters, some through the flood,
Some through the fire, but all through the blood;
Some through great sorrow, but God gives a song,
In the night season and all the day long.[164]

Divine Intention

Does the evil one have permission to tempt the Father's children? God's children are not impervious to afflictions perpetrated by the evil one, but never apart from our Father's purpose. Not his permission; his intention. To hold that God may permit what he does not intend for his children distorts our understanding of God's sovereign purposes. Ambiguity is not a divine attribute.

The psalmist David frequently referred to God as his stronghold. A stronghold is a place of safety. In his psalm regarding the treachery of Doeg the Edomite, David wrote,

> The righteous will see and fear; they will laugh at him, saying, "Here is the man who did not make God his stronghold but trusted in his great wealth and grew strong by destroying others!" But I . . . trust in God's unfailing love for ever and ever (Psalm 52:6–8).

Does praying, "lead us not into temptation" obviate divine testing? If our Father spares someone temptation, does it mean the individual has attained to a spiritual stature that cannot be bettered by enduring a difficult trial? Would testing be superfluous for such an individual? There is scant biblical support for such a notion.

God's children who please him by their upright conduct also have to deal with extreme tests according to God's will. Job was upright and blameless. He feared God and shunned evil. But God initiated the merciless testing of Job perpetrated by Satan (Job 1:8–12).

Jesus Christ, the sinless One, was subjected to temptation. The Spirit led him into the desert to be tempted by the devil (Matthew 4:1). The devil tested Jesus' commitment to be who he was supposed to be and do what he had come into the world to do. Jesus' instruction to pray "lead us not into temptation" implies that our Father may choose to expose his children to powerful temptations as tests of our devotion. As his children we ask our Father to spare us temptation.

Proof of Devotion

Does our heavenly Father need to test us in order to find out if we are truly devoted to him? Being all-knowing, surely God does not need to await the outcome of our tests to discover our sincerity. The test, therefore, is for our benefit, even though God is depicted as seeking the truth (Genesis 22:12). I like to watch track meets. When interviewed after a particular contest a victorious athlete often says, "I needed to prove to myself that I could do it." Similarly, the tests God's children face are so that through a difficult ordeal we may prove to ourselves the genuineness of our devotion to God

Peter wrote, "Do not be surprised at the painful trial you are suffering, as though something strange were happening to you" (1 Peter 4:12). Inevitably every child of God faces trials and temptations. Jesus told his disciples to watch and pray so that they would not enter into temptation (Matthew 26:41; Luke 22:40). William Barclay observed that "temptation comes sometimes not from our weakest point but from our strongest point . . . Nothing gives temptation its chance like over-confidence."[165]

The way to face temptation is to acknowledge our need of the help God gives to those who humble themselves in prayer. James admonished God's children, "Humble yourselves before the Lord, and he will lift you up" (James 4:10). David prayed, "Search me, O God, and know my heart; test me and know my anxious thoughts. See if there is any offensive way in me, and lead me in the way everlasting" (Psalm 139:23–24). Peter likewise advised, "Humble yourselves, therefore, under God's mighty hand, that he may lift you up in due time" (1 Peter 5:6).

Temptation Spawned by Victory

We tend to give ourselves credit for spiritual victories. We ask God our Father for strength to be victorious over a strong habit or addiction or a powerful temptation. By his strength we win the victory and are exhilarated by the success. This itself is a temptation, unseen but potent. The temptations we overcome tend to spawn new temptations. By God's strength we stand firm in facing the initial temptation, but then an unseen attack of the evil one may ambush us.

'Lead us not,' is literally, "bring us not" (*me eisenegkes*). It buttresses our understanding that the Lord's Prayer is for pilgrims who look to the Lord for guidance. As we travel through enemy territory, the dangers are greater than we can withstand in our own strength or by our own wisdom. The psalmist David uses the metaphor of God as our shepherd who protects his flock from dangers too great for them to withstand. He says,

> . . . he restores my soul. . . . Even though I walk through the valley of the shadow of death, I will fear no evil, for you are with me; your rod and your staff, they comfort me (Psalm 23:3–4).

Vigilance

Prudent itinerants traversing enemy territory are vigilant for ambushes, traps, and pitfalls. As our Father guides his children homeward we ask him to bypass those places where the dangers lurk menacingly. In this vein Thielicke wrote:

> The petition "lead us not into temptation" really does show us that life is dangerous, that it is something that can trip us up and ruin us, a place where we can stake everything on the wrong card.

> The dangerousness of life lies precisely in the fact that the dangers lurk in unexpected places and that

the wildest wolves that lie in wait for us always wear the most harmless-looking sheep's clothing, that they may even hide themselves behind the faces of the persons we most love.

Jesus teaches his own to pray, "Let nothing become a temptation to us," and thus makes it clear that *everything* can become a temptation, indeed, that life itself is but one long peril and temptation.[166]

A strong warning applies here. If we deliberately choose the pathway of evil, we should not expect our Father to hear and answer our prayer. We cannot pursue the sinful allurements of the devil's domain and at the same time ask our Father to protect us from their destructive effects. A man who defiantly violates a sacred marriage vow and seeks intimacy in the embrace of another should not expect God to answer his prayer that his family not suffer any deleterious effects of his infidelity.

The Two Appeals

This final petition in the Lord's Prayer incorporates two appeals: one for guidance, the other for deliverance. Both are appeals for our Father's protection of his children. A person following a guide may ask, "Please don't lead me down a dangerous path, but if I am waylaid, please rescue me."

In this final supplication in the Lord's Prayer we acknowledge our dependence upon our heavenly Father to safeguard our spiritual welfare. The apostle Peter points to Lot, Abraham's relative, as an example of God's deliverance: "The Lord knows how to rescue godly men from trials" (2 Peter 2:9). Lot was an example of God's righteous people living as aliens in a degenerate culture.

Because we understand ourselves to be in the same kind of situation, we pray, "Deliver us from evil."

We all want to be safe. We take precautions each day to feel secure. You can spend a small fortune on a security system to protect your family and your property. Fear motivates people to minimize their vulnerability. What they fear most is death. But nothing can forestall the inevitability of death. George Bernard Shaw said, "Death is the ultimate statistic. One out of one will die."[167] Security for earthly life and for eternal life is found only in God our Father (Psalm 91:14–15; John 3:16). If we love God with all our heart and soul and mind and strength, we trust him to keep us safe. Jude wrote, "To those who have been called, who are loved by God the Father and kept by Jesus Christ" (Jude 1). Our heavenly Father can protect us from the rash of fears that may seize our souls. If we put our trust in our heavenly Father's guidance the vicissitudes of political, social, or financial conditions cannot tyrannize us.

On the pilgrimage to our Father's home it is foolish to release our grip from his hand. But stubborn pride pulls us away from our Father's protection. Then we cry out to be rescued from the clutches of predators along the way. Jesus instructed us to ask our heavenly Father to lead us safely home. We are not naïve gadabouts, slipping and stumbling as we trudge along (Philippians 3:20). One of Fanny Crosby's hymns gives comforting assurance:

All the way my Savor leads me;
what have I to ask beside?
Can I doubt his tender mercy,
Who through life has been my guide?

All the way my Savior leads me,
Cheers each winding path I tread,

Gives me grace for every trial,
Feeds me with the living Bread.
Though my weary steps may falter,
And my soul athirst may be,
Gushing from the Rock before me,
Lo! A spring of joy I see.[168]

The words of Jesus in the final petition of the Lord's Prayer imply that if we fail to pray to our Father we will fall prey to the evil one. Our heavenly Father can protect his children from the deceptive allurements in a world under the control of the evil one. Unfortunately, sometimes we keep a longing eye on the temptation we pray not to be led into. But God's children who pray the Lord's Prayer sincerely each day recalibrate their lives to conform to the Father's will.

The devil, the evil one, is an ever-present threat to every child of God. But Luther's great hymn, *A Mighty Fortress is Our God* expresses our assurance,

The Prince of Darkness grim,
We tremble not for him;
His rage we can endure,
For lo! his doom is sure,
One little word shall fell him.[169]

Jesus Christ is the pioneer in whose steps God's children follow through this inhospitable world. Imagine this life as a field through which you must pass on your way to the place prepared for you in our Father's house. There is a narrow pathway through the field. As a child of the Father you step along that pathway. Suddenly a gigantic, ferocious beast lunges at you. It can tear you to shreds. You could not survive its attack. But the huge animal stops in mid leap and falls to the ground. You see that a chain around its neck restrains it. That beast is the evil one. Jesus Christ has gone through the field of this life as our pioneer. He confronted, defeated, and restrained our enemy. If we follow the path our Savior trod we will arrive safely at our Father's home. If we turn aside from the path of our Pioneer that is laid out for us in God's Word, we are at great risk of being mauled by the roaring lion (1 Peter 5:8–9). The way may be hard, but our heavenly Father guarantees that his children will arrive home safely. Using a different metaphor, "The Lord has not promised smooth sailing, but he has promised safe landing."[170]

The Evil One

The last clause in the prayer has two optional renderings, "deliver us from evil," or "deliver us from the evil one." Both are valid renderings of the New Testament Greek text. The Apostle John employs a similar statement, "We know that we are children of God, and that the whole world is under the control of (lit., 'lies in') evil—or the evil one" (1 John 5:19).

The evil we contend with is not an impersonal force. It is better to understand Jesus' words in the Lord's Prayer to mean, "deliver us from the evil one." This view is consistent with a biblical theology of evil in the world. John Stott proposed that "evil" here is best understood as "evil one," as in Matthew 13:19, where the evil one snatches away the message of the kingdom that is sown in a person's heart. He explained, "In other words, it is the devil who is in view, who tempts God's people to sin, and from whom we need to be 'rescued' [rusai]." He paraphrases the request in this way: "Do not allow us so to be led into temptation that it overwhelms us, but rescue us from the evil one."[171]

A commentary on this petition in the *Catechism of the Catholic Church* adds: "The last petition [in the prayer] to our Father is also included in Jesus' prayer, 'I am not asking you to take them out of the world, but I ask you to protect them from the evil one'" (John 17:15).[172] Jesus includes this declaration in his prayer, "They are not of the world, even as I am not of it" (John 17:16). By the will of the Father we are sojourners in this corrupt world, but we do not belong to it any more than Christ belongs to it.

The devil prowls where we are making our pilgrimage (1 Peter 5:8). But God's children have been rescued from the authority (*exousia*) of the ruler of the dark domain and transferred into the kingdom of God's Son (Colossians 1:13). In the prophet Daniel's vision a splendid spiritual being that looked like a man had been sent in response to Daniel's prayer. He told of being delayed for twenty-one days because "the prince of the Persian kingdom resisted me." The devil had assigned one of his evil minions to exercise control over the Persian kingdom. Daniel was exiled in Persia. (Daniel 10:12–13) Daniel prayed to God; God heard his prayer and sent help to him.

We maintain our vigilance of the evil one's schemes because he is not a toothless predator. His lies and temptations to draw the Father's children away from the path set for us can cause severe spiritual harm. Pete Hammond of InterVarsity Christian Fellowship expressed his concern that the church today is producing children of God "with a bunny rabbit faith who go into a roaring lion world."[173] Each new day we need protection from the evil one's aggressions.

We are not apathetic as we utter this prayer. We do not "pass the ball" to God, expecting him to run through the opposition and win the game for us. We are responsible to make every effort to resist the evil we ask him to deliver us from. God our Father guards us as we forge ahead. The psalmist instructed, "Let those who love the Lord hate evil, for he guards the lives of his faithful ones and delivers them from the hand of the wicked" (Psalm 97:10). Latin Church father Ambrose, Bishop of Milan, in the fourth century wrote:

> The Lord who has taken away your sin and pardoned your faults also protects you and keeps you from the wiles of our adversary the devil, so that the enemy, who is accustomed to leading into sin, may not surprise you. One who entrusts himself to God does not dread the devil. "If God is for us, who is against us?" (Romans 8:31)[174]

Thielicke said the temptations to which we are exposed as the children of the heavenly Father are similar in kind to those the evil tempter used to accost Jesus.[175] The one we appeal to for deliverance from the evil one has already defeated the evil one.

When God chooses so to test his children, it has a worthy purpose. God knows exactly the kind of test that will strengthen our resolve. A faithful husband who loves his wife dearly should readily repel the immoral advances of a colleague at work who attempts to entice him to violate his marriage vows. He resolutely dismisses the solicitations of a prostitute when he is alone on a business trip away from home. If a temptation is by our Father's permission, it is also his intention that his child should face it.

Does the prayer "deliver us from the evil one" imply that the devil is holding God's children hostage? We cannot reconcile such a view with the declaration that those who belong to God have been rescued from the kingdom of darkness (Colossians 1:13). Deliverance does not necessarily mean the evil one has (or had) possession. James gives God's children the assurance that if they resist the devil he will flee from them (James 4:7). The Apostle Paul warned the Father's children to put on the armor of God because we are in a spiritual battle (Ephesians 6:10–18). Cardinal Bergoglio (Pope Francis) wrote, "Man's life on earth is warfare." He said, "And in my personal experience, I feel him [the Devil] every time that I am tempted to do something that is not what God wants for me. I believe that the Devil exists."[176]

Synopsis

The bedrock truth of our faith declares that we are the children of God through repentance of sin and faith in the Savior Jesus Christ. But as residents in a corrupt world, we have an enemy, the devil, who is hell-bent on deceiving and waylaying God's children. Satan deceived the first humans. They were not under his control on the occasion of the deception, but they were vulnerable to his lies. In their pristine environment they had not previously encountered deception. Today this enemy of God and of God's children still employs the strategy of deception. But the heavenly Father's children should not become the gullible victims of Satan's lies. The Apostle Paul wrote, "For we are not unaware of his schemes" (2 Corinthians 2:11). Our enemy is still adept at ambushing God's children by deceit; but he will never possess us. We belong to our Father in heaven.

Many people hastily pray the Lord's Prayer after a moral failure, or if they are in a desperate plight. They have no interest in changing their values or their lifestyle. They just want God to fix their problem and to do it quickly. They misunderstand this final petition in the Lord's Prayer. It is, in effect, a request that God's children will not become corrupted, but will be who they should be. An earthly father may appeal to his son who is away from home, "always remember who you are." As children of our Father in heaven we must not forget who we are as sojourners away from home. For this reason we pray each day, "lead us not into temptation, but deliver us from the evil one." If we become careless and allow ourselves to be led astray through the deceit of the evil one, we will not be who the children of the Father are supposed to be.

This is not a prayer to pray with a casual attitude, ". . . until I sin again." The Father's children pray it with sincerity and humility. D. A. Carson's remark is most fitting here:

> Thus the Lord's model prayer ends with a petition that, while implicitly recognizing our own helplessness before the Devil whom Jesus alone could vanquish (Matthew 4:1–11), delights to trust the heavenly Father for deliverance from the Devil's strength and wiles.[177]

Questions for Discussion and Personal Application

1. Describe the differences between temptation and testing. What is the nature and purpose of each?

2. How can you distinguish between temptation from the devil and temptation that comes from your own desires?

3. What is the ultimate standard for determining if something is according to God's will, or if it is an evil temptation?

4. Tell of an extreme trial you suffered, but you sensed in your spirit it was from your heavenly Father and he was watching over you.

5. What kind of temptation did Job have to deal with (Job 1:8–12)? Do you think godly people today may face the same kind of test?

6. William Barclay warned that over-confidence makes us vulnerable to temptation. What is our protection? See James 4:10; 1 Peter 5:6.

7. What is our motivation to pray this final petition in the Lord's Prayer?

8. Explain the nature of the evil from which we ask to be delivered in the Lord's Prayer.

9. What is our responsibility as we ask our heavenly Father to deliver us from the evil one?

10. What strategy does our enemy, the evil one, use on us that he used with the first couple in the garden? How have you dealt with it?

12. JOURNEY'S END

If we could see beyond today as God can see,
If all the clouds should roll away,
The shadows flee;
O'er present griefs we would not fret,
Each sorrow we would soon forget,
For many joys are waiting yet
For you and me.
If we could know beyond today
As God doth know,
Why dearest treasures pass away,
And tears must flow.
We'd know that darkness leads to light,
And dreary days will soon grow bright;
Some day life's wrong will be made right,
Faith tells us so.
If we could see, if we could know,
We often say,
But God in love a veil doth throw
Across our way
We cannot see what lies before,
And so we cling to Him the more,
He leads us till this life is o'er;
Trust and obey.

Norman Clayton[178]

Most translations of the Lord's Prayer in Matthew's Gospel conclude with the plea, "And lead us not into temptation, but deliver us from the evil one." Some later manuscripts add "for yours is the kingdom and the power and the glory forever. Amen." This appendix is familiar to most of us. It is part of the musical rendition of the Lord's Prayer as well as many church liturgies. When I pray this prayer, I often include this addendum. Repetition since my boyhood has made it my custom.

The few words in this epilogue, whatever their origin, are distilled from the greater text of Scripture. God's kingdom, power, and glory are indispensable components of our heavenly Father's holy name. They are a fitting conclusion because this sentence declares in effect, "May you be exalted; may the truth of who you are in all your glory and majesty as God be eternally exalted above everything you have created." The theology of the epilogue is strong, but the manuscript evidence for it is weak; hence it does not appear in the current versions of the Bible. D. Martyn Lloyd-Jones commented:

> We do not know for certain whether Christ did actually utter it at this point or not; but whether he did or not, it is very appropriate. What can one say after facing such a prayer, and such words? There must be a kind of final thanksgiving, there must be some kind of doxology."[179]

The Apostle Paul remarked in a letter to Timothy, "Now to the King eternal, immortal, invisible, the only God, be honor and glory forever and ever" (1 Timothy 1:17) This parallels the grand appendix to the Lord's Prayer.

Jesus Christ gave this great prayer to the heavenly Father's children on earth. Its greatest value is in framing the right perspective on God, on his earthly children, on his kingdom, on his will, and on this fallen world that is under the control of an evil usurper. We may pray confidently that our Father will deliver us from the evil one, because our Father in heaven has the kingdom and the power and the glory forever. As the Sovereign Lord of the entire universe he has all authority everywhere. He is the omnipotent Lord and he has all the power to do whatever he wills. No force can impede him in the accomplishment of his purposes. How crucial it is, then, for the children of the heavenly Father to stay close to him through a dangerous world on their pilgrimage to their heavenly home.

We may view the epilogue to the Lord's Prayer as a series of transit petitions for our pilgrimage:

First, the Father's children should not be held captive by evil, because we belong to God's kingdom. To be held captive in the dark domain of evil would be a shocking anomaly for the children of God's household.

Second, all the power belongs to our Father. Those who belong to God our Father in heaven do not need to capitulate to the authority of any contrary force.

Third, the glory belongs to our Father in heaven. God's children must, therefore, not indulge evil. If the children of God become enmeshed in evil, it is an assault against our Father's glory.

The heavenly Father's children care about God's kingdom coming. They care about people of all nations being rescued from the dominion of darkness and being brought into the Kingdom of God's Son. Therefore we do well to offer this prayer to our heavenly Father daily, reverently, and deliberately. AMEN.

ENDNOTES

CHAPTER 1 THE PRIORITY OF PRAYER

1. Lloyd-Jones, D. Martyn. 1971. *Studies in the Sermon on the Mount, Volume Two.* Grand Rapids: Eerdmans, 46.
2. Bunyan, John. 1999, Quoted in *Prayer.* Carlisle, PA: Banner of Truth, 23.
3. Stott, John R. W. 1972. Course on *The Sermon on the Mount*, Trinity Evangelical Divinity School.
4. Milne, A. A. 1924. Vespers. In *When We Were Very Young.* London: Methuen & Co.
5. *Time Magazine* article. June 24, 2001.
6. Bunyan, John. 1873. *Grace Abounding to the Chief of Sinners.* London: Blackie and Son, 278.
7. MacDonald, George. 1985. *The Curate's Awakening.* Michael R. Phillips. Ed. Bloomington, MN: Bethany House, 176.
8. Stott.

CHAPTER 2 THE CHALLENGE OF THE LORD'S PRAYER

9. Lloyd-Jones, 49.
10. Urich, Robert. Television interview, June 1997.
11. Koestler, Arthur. 1967. *The Ghost in the Machine.* New York: Macmillan.
12. Note: The original quote is "I shot an arrow into the air. It fell to the earth, I knew not where" by Henry Wadsworth Longfellow. The statement in the text is my own.
13. Stott, John R. W. 1978. *Christian Counter-Culture: The Message of the Sermon on the Mount.* Downers Grove, IL: Inter-Varsity Press, 145.
14. Lloyd-Jones, 48.
15. Ibid, 49.

16. Eclov, Lee. 2012. *Pastoral Graces: Reflections on the Care of Souls.* Chicago: Moody Publishers, Kindle e-book.
17. O'Sullivan, Msgr. J. Bumper sticker quote taken from *It's His Fan Club.*
18. Bounds, E. M. (n.d.) *Power through Prayer.* Chicago: Moody Press, Acorn Booklets, 89.
19. Aquinas, Thomas. 1995. Quoted in *Catechism of the Catholic Church.* New York: Image Book/Doubleday, 727.
20. Hodge, Charles. 1962. *Systematic Theology, Volume Three.* Grand Rapids: Eerdmans, 692.

CHAPTER 3 THE DIVINE RENDEZVOUS

21. Orben, Robert. *Current Comedy.*
22. Balmer, Randall. 2001. *Growing Pains.* Grand Rapids: Brazos Press, 24.
23. Gaither, Gloria, & Greene, Buddy. 1994. I Don't Belong (Sojourner's Song). On *Sojourner's Song* [Album]. www.buddygreene.com/lyrics.html#hthruj
24. Bergoglio, Jorge Mario, & Skorka, Abraham. 2013. Chapter 2: On the Devil. In *On Heaven and Earth.* Random House Publishers, Kindle e-book.
25. Robinson, Robert. 1758. Come, Thou Fount of Every Blessing. (Public Domain)
26. Wesley, Charles. 1886. A Stranger in the World Below, published in *A Collection of Hymns for Public, Social, and Domestic Worship.* Nashville, TN: Southern Methodist Publishing House, 512. (Public Domain)
27. Reeves, Jim. 1962. This World Is Not My Home. On *We Thank Thee* [album].
28. Havner, Vance. 1986. *The Vance Havner Quote Book.* Dennis J. Hester, compiler. Grand Rapids: Baker Book House, 48.

29. MacDonald, George. 1985. *The Vicar's Daughter.* Dan Hamilton, Ed. Wheaton, IL: Scripture Press, Publications, 143.

30. *The Valley of Vision: A Collection of Puritan Prayers and Devotions.* Arthur Bennett, Ed. 1975. The Banner of Truth Trust, 136.

31. Mayer, Louis B. (1884-1957) Quoted in *Permalink.* www.lifequoteslib.com/authors/louis_b_mayer.html

32. Newton, John. 1779. Amazing Grace. Olney Hymns. (Public Domain)

33. Lewis, C. S. *Mere Christianity.* London, England: Collins Publishing/Fontana Books, 116.

34. Drummond, Henry. (n.d.) *The Greatest Thing in the World.* Cleveland, Ohio: World Bible Publishers, 80.

35. Watts, Isaac. 1784. I Sing the Almighty Power of God. (Public Domain)

36. In this way they mute the divine image in people. They lavish their deepest affection on pets that have become their idols. To a tame canine or feline creature they grant residency in the place in their psyche that belongs exclusively to God. That is an outrageous affront to our Father in heaven who made people alone in his image and likeness.

This distortion of human nature, albeit socially "respectable," is evident even among many who call God their heavenly Father. The adoration of a pet is tantamount to the worship that is due God alone. The Bible does not accord pets and other animals such a place of honor. Instead, we read what God said through David:

"I will instruct you and teach you in the way you should go; I will counsel you and watch over you. Do not be like the horse or the mule, which have no understanding, but must be controlled by bit and bridle or they will not come to you" (Psalm 32:8–9).

Asaph used a similar metaphor to describe his personal struggle: "When my heart was grieved and my spirit embittered, I was senseless and ignorant; I was a brute beast before you" (Psalm 73:21–22). Sadly, some people become increasingly like animals, controlled by cravings and without moral standards.

Many want assurance that their pets will join them in heaven. But the Bible is silent on the question of pets in heaven. There is insufficient basis to establish a biblical doctrine of the eternal state of all the animals on earth. The only implied affirmation of pets in Scripture is in the parable that the prophet Nathan told King David in 2 Samuel 12.

This is what happened: David had an affair with Bathsheba, the wife of Uriah the Hittite, who was with David's army fighting the Ammonites at Rabbah. Bathsheba became pregnant. David summoned Uriah home to be with his wife. He schemed to get Uriah to be intimate with his wife and so assume the child to be born would be his. But Uriah did not go home to enjoy his wife's company. He could not do so with good conscience while his comrades were away at war. So David sent him back to the battle and instructed General Joab to place Uriah in the heat of the battle, and then withdraw from him so that he would be killed. It was tantamount to murder.

When the Lord sent the prophet Nathan to confront David, Nathan told a story of a poor man whose family pet lamb was taken by a rich man, slaughtered and prepared as a meal for a guest. Nathan described the pet as a little ewe lamb the poor man had bought. He said, "He raised it and it grew up with him and his children. It shared his food, drank from his cup and even slept in his arms. It was like a daughter to him." (2 Samuel 12:3)

On hearing the story, David became extremely angry. I infer from David's reaction that he recognized the beloved role of a pet in the family. He said, "the man who did this deserves to die." Nathan said to David, "You are the man!"

God had established a hierarchy in his creation. He gave to mankind the mandate to rule over all the creatures. He said to the man and the woman, "Rule over the fish of the sea and the birds of the air and every other creature that moves on the ground" (Genesis 1:28). Animals must remain animals, whether they are wild, domesticated, or pets.

37. Gretzky, Wayne. *Brainy Quotes.* www.brainyquote. com/quotes/wayne_gretzky_383282
38. *All in the Family.* 1972. The Election Story [Season 2]. New York: CBS.
39. Bounds, 89.
40. Wells, David. 1992. Prayer: Rebellion against the Status Quo. In *Perspectives on the World Christian Movement.* Ralph Winter & Steven Hawthorne, Eds. Pasadena, CA: William Carey Library, 84.

CHAPTER 4 OUR FATHER

41. Pascal, Blaise. *Pensées.* Begun in 1654; incomplete at Pascal's death in 1662. This quotation is commonly revised and rendered as "There is a God-shaped vacuum inside each of us." www.gutenberg.org/files/18269/18269-h/18269-h.htm
42. Hamer, Dean. 2004. *The God Gene.* New York: Doubleday, 4.
43. Ibid., 6, 13.

44. Thielicke, Helmut. 1965. *The Prayer that Spans the World* [Compiled and Published as *Das Gebet das die Welt umspannt,* 1953]. Cambridge: James Clark & Company Ltd., 20.

45. MacDonald, George. 1986. *The Lady's Confession.* Michael R. Phillips, Ed. Bloomington, MN: Bethany House, 98.

46. Stott, *Christian Counter-Culture,* 146.

47. Oatman, Johnson, Jr. Holy, Holy, Is What the Angels Sing. (Public Domain) https://hymnary.org/text/there_is_singing_up_in_heaven

48. Johnson, Paul. June 1985. Readers Digest.

49. Thielicke, 24.

50. Barclay, William. 1975. *The Gospel of Matthew, Vol.1.* Revised Edition. Philadelphia: The Westminster Press, 204.

51. Tasker, R. V. G. 1968. *Tyndale Bible Commentaries, Vol. 1 Matthew.* Grand Rapids: Eerdmans Publishing Company, 81.

52. Hendriksen, William. 1973. *New Testament Commentary: Matthew.* Grand Rapids: Baker Book House, 363.

53. Carson, D. A. 1984. *Matthew: Expositor's Bible Commentary.* Frank E. Gabelein, General Ed. Grand Rapids: The Zondervan Corporation, 187.

54. Barclay, 201.

55. Morgan, Reuben, & Ingram, Jason. 2010. Forever Reign. On *A Beautiful Exchange* [album]. Hillsong Music.

56. Barclay, 198

57. Hendriksen, 326.

58. Thielicke, 37.

59. Oh, Be Careful Little Eyes. Child Bible Songs: Lyrics from children's Bible songs taught in church, Bible class, and Vacation Bible School (VBS). Author and date unknown. http://childbiblesongs.com/song-12-be-careful-little-eyes.shtml

60. Lehman, F. M. 1917. The Love of God. *Hymns of Faith* #286. (Public Domain)

61. Shea, George Beverly. 1955. Wonder of It All. *Rejoice Hymns* #116. Greenville, SC: Majesty Music.
62. Thielicke, 93.
63. Lewis, C. S. 1940; reprint 2001. *The Problem of Pain.* San Francisco: Harper, 150–51.
64. D'Souza, Dinesh. 2007. *What's so Great about Christianity?* Washington, DC: Regnery Publishing Inc., 178.
65. Thielicke, 21.
66. Heber, Reginald. 1826. Holy, Holy, Holy, Lord God Almighty. (Public Domain)
67. Carson, 169.
68. Bergoglio, & Skorka, Chapter 7.

CHAPTER 5 IN HEAVEN

69. Doddridge, Philip. Our God Ascends His Lofty Throne. (Public Domain) https://hymnary.org/text/ our_god_ascends_his_lofty_throne
70. *Catechism of the Catholic Church.* 1995. New York: Image Book/Doubleday, 736.
71. D'Souza, 301.
72. I Met Jesus at the Crossroads. *Salvation Songs for Children, No. 4.* 1951. R. P. Overholtzer, Ed. Pacific Palisades, CA: International Child Evangelism, 195.
73. Stanphill, Ira. 1949. Mansion Over the Hilltop. Warner/Chappell Music, 410.
74. Smith, Wilbur. 1968. *The Biblical Doctrine of Heaven.* Chicago: Moody Press, 50.
75. Grudem, Wayne. 1994. *Systematic Theology.* Grand Rapids: Zondervan Publishing House, 1159.
76. Ibid., 1162.
77. Spurgeon, Charles Haddon. Quoted in *Developing Christian Character Study Guide* by R. C. Sproul, 67.

78. Studd, C. T. Only One Life. https://joshuavandermerwe. wordpress.com/2014/01/23/only-one-life-a-poem-by-c-t-studd

CHAPTER 6 HALLOWED BE YOUR NAME

79. Furler, Peter, & Taylor, Steve. ©2003. He Reigns. Brentwood, TN: Ariose Music. https://home.snu.edu/~hculbert/hereigns.htm
80. Irish Hymn. 8th–10th Century. Be Thou My Vision. Translated by Mary E. Byrne and versified by Eleanor H. Hull. https://hymnary.org/hymn/WOV/776
81. Hendriksen, 328.
82. MacDonald, George. 1987. *The Laird's Inheritance*. Michael R. Phillips, Ed. Bloomington, MN: Bethany House, 136.
83. Pink, Arthur W. 1983. *An Exposition of the Sermon on the Mount*. Grand Rapids: Baker Book House, 162.
84. Ibid.
85. Lloyd-Jones, 59.
86. Charnock, Stephen. 1815. *The Works of Rev. Stephen Charnock, Vol II*. London: Paternoster Row, 496.
87. Grudem, 157–58.
88. Redman, Matt. ©2011. Ten Thousand Reasons (Bless the Lord). www.youtube.com/watch?v=XtwIT8JjddM
89. Pink, 162.
90. Brown, Brenton, & Baloche, Paul. ©2006. Hosanna (Praise is Rising). (*Everlasting God,* 2006) www.youtube.com/watch?v=hlEKQN7ydGY
91. Chalmers, Thomas, D.D. 1908. "The Expulsive Power of a New Affection" in *The World's Great Sermons, IV*. Grenville Kleiser, Compiler. New York: Funk & Wagnalls Company, 76.
92. Augustine. 2008. *Confessions of St. Augustine of Hippo. Book 1*, Chapter 1, Penguin Classics.

CHAPTER 7 YOUR KINGDOM COME

93. Anonymous. 1598. Come, Thou Almighty King. (Public Domain) https://hymnary.org/text/come_thou_almighty_king_help_us_thy

94. Ladd, George Eldon. 1974. *A Theology of the New Testament.* Grand Rapids: William B. Eerdmans Publishing Company, 111.

95. Carson, 170.

96. Osborne, Grant R. 2002. *Baker Exegetical Commentary on the New Testament: Revelation.* Grand Rapids: Baker Academic, 66–67.

97. Freud, Sigmund. 1963. *Psychoanalysis and Faith: The Letters of Sigmund Freud and Oskar Pfister.* Heinrich Meng and Ernst L. Freud, eds. Eric Mosbacher, translator. New York: Basic Books.

98. Stott, *Christian Counter-Culture,* 147.

99. Thielicke, 108.

100. Wholey, Dennis. American television host and producer. https://www.quotes.net/quote/18958

101. Thielicke, 70.

CHAPTER 8 YOUR WILL BE DONE ON EARTH AS IT IS IN HEAVEN

102. Lewis, C. S. 1945. *The Great Divorce.* London: The Centenary Press, 90.

103. Lloyd-Jones, 65.

104. Klink, Edward. W. III. Sermon at Hope Church, Roscoe, Illinois, July, 2014.

105. Carson, 170.

106. Law, Robert. 1909. *Commentary on 1 John: The Tests of Life.* Edinburgh: T & T Clark, 304.

107. Murray, Andrew. 2005. *Absolute Surrender.* Peabody, Massachusetts: Hendrickson Publishers, 67ff.

108. Barclay, 199.

109. D'Souza, 64.

110. Also reported in New York Times, July 22, 1986. www.nytimes.com/1986/07/23/world/tutu-denounces-reagan.html

111. In a letter from 19th century British politician Lord Acton to Cardinal Wiseman in 1862.

112. Henry, Patrick. In a speech made on March 23, 1775 in St. John's Church in Richmond, Virginia.

113. Hendriksen, 331.

114. Barclay, 212.

115. Thielicke, 70.

CHAPTER 9 GIVE US TODAY OUR DAILY BREAD

116. Merrick, James. 1886. *Far as Creations Bounds Extend.* In *A Collection of Hymns for Public, Social, and Domestic Worship.* Nashville, TN: Southern Methodist Publishing House, No. 70, p.57.

117. Murray, Andrew. 1912. *The Prayer Life.* Chicago: Moody Press, 21.

118. Maher, Matt. ©2013. Lord, I Need You. In *All the People Said Amen* [Album].

119. Bennis, Warren, & Nanus, Burt. 1985. *Leaders: The Strategies for Taking Charge.* New York: Harper & Row, cover lines.

120. Peterson, Eugene H. 2002. *The Bible in Contemporary Language.* Colorado Springs: Navpress, 1754.

121. Hendriksen, 333.

122. Stott, Quoted in *Christian Counter-Culture,* 149.
123. Franklin, Benjamin. "The Whistle: Parable to Madame Brillon." 1779. In *The Oxford Book of American Essays.* Brander Matthews, Ed. New York: Oxford University Press, published 1914.
124. Reapsome, Jim. December 1992. "Suleyman's Magic Underwear." *Pulse Magazine.*
125. Milligan, Spike. British humorist and actor.
126. Spurgeon. *Ask and Have.* Sermon by C. H. Spurgeon, October 1, 1882 at Metropolitan Tabernacle, Newington. *Metropolitan Temple Pulpit,* Vol. 28. Sermon #1682.
127. Foerster, Werner. 1964. *Theological Dictionary of the New Testament, Vol. II,* translated and edited by Geoffrey W. Bromiley. Grand Rapids: Eerdmans, 592–93.
128. Ibid., 597.
129. Ibid., 597, 599.
130. Schwartz, Stephen. 1971. Day by Day. From *Godspell: A Musical Based upon the Gospel According to St. Matthew.*
131. Berg, Carolina Sandell. 1865. Day By Day (Blot en Dag). Translated by Andrew L. Skoog. (Public Domain)
132. Gundry, Robert H. 1982. *Matthew, a Commentary on His Literary and Theological Art.* Grand Rapids: Wm. B. Eerdmans, 107.

CHAPTER 10 FORGIVE US OUR SINS AS WE ALSO FORGIVE THOSE WHO SIN AGAINST US

133. Lapide, Pinchas. Heard in an interview by John Ankerberg on *The John Ankerberg TV show.*(Date unknown)
134. Tasker, R. V. G. 1961. *Tyndale Bible Commentary: The Gospel According to Matthew.* Grand Rapids: Wm. B. Eerdmans, 73.

135. Ferrell, Willard D. April 1999. "Quotable Quotes," *Readers Digest.*
136. Orben.
137. Shakespeare, William. *The Tragedy of King Lear.* Act III, Scene 2.
138. Hare, Rev. Malcolm. 1970. *Keswick Address.*
139. Grudem, 740.
140. MacDonald, George. 2015. *The Princess and the Goblin.* LULU Press, Kindle edition.
141. Guinness, Os. 2015. *Fool's Talk: Recovering the Art of Christian Persuasion.* Downers Grove, IL: InterVarsity Press.
142. Hendriksen, 334, 317.
143. Luther, Martin. 1915. *The Works of Luther, Vol. I.* Adolph Spaeth, L. D. Reed, Henry Eyster Jacobs, et.al. Trans. & Eds. Philadelphia: A. J. Holman Company, 29.
144. Hall, Doug. 1985 Cartoon.
145. Manning, Brennan. 2009. *The Furious Longing of God.* David C. Cook, Kindle Edition.
146. Berg.
147. *Catechism of the Catholic Church,* 749.
148. Pink, 167.
149. Dana, H. E., & Mantey, Julius R. 1927. *A Manual Grammar of the Greek New Testament.* New York: The MacMillan Company, 193.
150. Hendriksen, 334–35.
151. Pink, 169.
152. Thielicke, 110.
153. Ibid.
154. Ibid., 113.
155. Law, William. 1762. "A Serious Call to a Devout and Holy Life." In *The Works of the Reverend William Law, M.A. Volume IV.* London: Printed for J. Richardson, 228.
156. Gundry, 109.

157. Hammond, Pete. Staff with InterVarsity Christian Fellowship. In an address in Rockford, IL.
158. Stott, *Christian Counter-Culture,* 149.
159. Pink, 171.

CHAPTER 11 LEAD US NOT INTO TEMPTATION BUT DELIVER US FROM THE EVIL ONE

160. Ludwig, Nicolaus, & von Zinzendorf, Graf. 1721. O Thou, to Whose All-Searching Sight. John Wesley, Trans. (Public Domain)
161. Gundry, 109.
162. Faber, F. W. Nineteenth century hymn writer and theologian, quoted in "On Your Mark," by George O. Wood in *Pentecostal Evangel,* December 28, 2014.
163. Robert Watson-Watt, Poem: *Rough Justice.* https://watsonwatt.wordpress.com/2013/04/08/rough-justice-poem-by-watson-watt/
164. Young, G. A. 1903. God Leads Us Along. (Public Domain)
165. Barclay, 230.
166. Thielicke, 119, 122, 125.
167. Shaw, George Bernard. Quoted by Cliffe Knechtle, In *Give Me an Answer.* 1986. Downers Grove, IL: InterVarsity Press, 159.
168. Crosby, Fanny J. 1875. All the Way My Savior Leads Me. (Public Domain)
169. Luther, Martin. 1529. A Mighty Fortress Is Our God. (Public Domain)
170. http://thedailyprayerblog.blogspot.com/2011/09/ smooth-sailing.html
171. Stott, *Christian Counter-Culture,* 150.
172. *Catechism of the Catholic Church,* 752.
173. Hammond.
174. *Catechism of the Catholic Church,* 753.

175. Thielicke, 131–35.
176. Bergoglio, & Skorka, Chapter 2.
177. Carson, 174.

CHAPTER 12 JOURNEY'S END

178. Clayton, Norman J. 1943. If We Could See Beyond Today. In *Word of Life Melodies #1*.
179. Lloyd-Jones, 77.

SCRIPTURE REFERENCES

359

362

THE AUTHOR

John Crocker was born in South Africa to English parents. When he was a teenager his family moved to Canada. John came to the United States for his college and graduate education. John holds the Master of Divinity and Doctor of Ministry degrees from Trinity Evangelical Divinity School (Trinity International University).

John served as a pastor for thirty-three years in three churches in Indiana, California, and Illinois. He then served an additional seven churches as interim pastor in the Midwestern United States for over eight years.

He met and married Elizabeth (Liz) in suburban Chicago. They have one child, John Desmond Jr. He and his wife Molly live in Rhode Island. They have twin children, Wrigley Michael and Lucy Elizabeth.

John and Liz make their home in Indianapolis, Indiana.

This book is available from Amazon.com.

This book is also available in the Kindle format from the Amazon Kindle Store.

Made in the USA
Columbia, SC
22 December 2019